· MARY HILL ·

GOLD

THE CALIFORNIA STORY

University of California Press   Berkeley   Los Angeles   London

UNIVERSITY OF CALIFORNIA PRESS
Berkeley and Los Angeles, California

UNIVERSITY OF CALIFORNIA PRESS, LTD.
London, England

Library of Congress Cataloging-in-Publication Data

Hill, Mary, 1923– .
    Gold : the California story / Mary Hill.
            p.   cm.
    Includes bibliographical references and index.
    ISBN 978-0-520-23680-6 (pbk. : alk. paper)
        1. California—Gold discoveries.   2. California—
History—1846–1850.   I. Title.
    F865.H535   1999
    979.4'04—DC21   99-19408
                                                        CIP

Manufactured in the United States of America

15   14   13   12   11   10   09   08
    12   11   10   9   8   7   6   5   4   3

The paper used in this publication meets the minimum requirements of
ANSI/NISO Z39.48-1992 (R 1997) (*Permanence of Paper*). ∞

To my dearly beloved, long-gone mother,
who valued goodness above gold

Contents

PLATES *follow page 148*

Acknowledgments

I thank no one for typing the manuscript of this book. I did it myself. It's about all I did by myself. A host of people, living and dead, helped me, directly or indirectly, and I am most grateful to them.

I thank the hundreds of authors of articles and books, historical and scientific, that I consulted in the preparation of *Gold: The California Story*. Without them, there would be no book. Some I have known personally; some were gone long before I was born. I have not cited them here because the list is too long. I have provided a list of references to give the reader more information on the subject of gold, and particularly gold in California. Through these references, much of my work can be traced back to its source material.

Many of my friends and colleagues have kept a weather eye out for news clippings and scientific articles about gold. John B. Hamilton, Elisabeth L. Egenhoff, and the late Lucy Birdsall were particularly assiduous in keeping me up to date on gold in California. The late Marin County historian Helen Van Cleave Park told me tales of hidden gold in California. Geologist Mort D. Turner shared his gold files—scientific and popular—with me. Many other people who knew of my interest sent me notes and clippings on gold, among them Susan Moyer, Edmund F. Kiessling (who helped in other ways as well), Irene Miller, Dorothy Hall, and Bette Myerson. Who can do without librarians? Jacquelyn Freeberg came out of her retirement from the U.S. Geological Survey to chase down technical articles I could not locate here in New Mexico. Librarians at San Francisco State University and the Oliver La Farge branch of the Santa Fe Public Library obtained articles and books by interlibrary loan—a great service to scholarship. I wish I could list the numerous libraries who so generously sent their books for my use. Lisa Ann Libby, of the Huntington Library, did excellent detective work in ferreting out a source I could not find.

Of the specialists who saw the manuscript of this book, I am especially grateful to my friend historian Ruth Sutter, who read the manuscript, kept me from many errors, and gave me new insights into history. Her help was magnanimous and great. My gratitude also goes in a considerable measure to geologists Don Garlick and Paul Bateman, who took a great interest in the manuscript, not only correcting my errors, but also contributing material of their own—I thank them for this. I owe much in many ways to my old friend and colleague the geologist and editor Elisabeth Egenhoff, who compiled *The Elephant as They Saw It,* one of the best books on the early history of gold mining in California. Her enthusiasm and advice cheered and helped me. Other geologists, too, gave me advice on the manuscript, among them Thomas Rogers. The late geologist William B. Clark contributed much to this book. I wish I could tell him so. Samuel Estris, of the Gold Institute, graciously gave me help with information on gold itself. Darrell R. Wanner, of Placerita Canyon Nature Center, supplied information on Don Francisco López.

My friend Rafaelita Bachicha told me, over dinner and by letter, of her experiences as foreperson of the jury that convicted Ed Barbara, giving a personal touch to the story I would not have had. I thank her.

Three numismatists kindly helped me understand gold coinage, particularly early California gold coins. These were Michael and Karen Marie Locke, specialists in California fractional gold coins, and Donald H. Kagin, author of a valuable work on private gold coinage in the United States.

Many people and institutions assisted me with the illustrations. I used illustrations Adrienne Morgan and Alex Eng had previously drawn for me, and I thank them again. Doris Marsh and Bill Nelson contributed new drawings. The U.S. Geological Survey; the U.S. Bureau of the Mint; Wells Fargo Bank Historical Services (through Robert J. Chandler); the Museum of the City of New York (through Wendy Rogers); the California Division of Mines and Geology; the Mariners' Museum, Newport News, Virginia (through John Pemberton and Mike Davis); the National Maritime Museum Association in San Francisco (through Bill Kouiman); the California Historical Society (through Emily Wolff); the Bancroft Library (through Richard Ogar); the Huntington Library (through Lisa Ann Libby); the Smithsonian Institution (through David Shayt, David Burgevin, Dane Penland, and in particular, Gwen Neild of *Smithsonian Magazine,* who helped me find my way to the source of photographs, even though it was not her responsibility); the Homestake Mining Company (through Michael A. Steeves); the National Air and Space Agency (NASA); the Los Alamos National Laboratory (through Fred Rick); the Lawrence Livermore National Laboratory (through Craig Savoye); the Mirage Hotel, Las Vegas (through Robyn Campbell-Ouchida); Handy and Harmon; Levi Strauss (through Kay McDonough); and White's Electronics (through Melissa

Wise) all helped me with illustrations. Dover Publications, the University of Oklahoma Press, and Stanford University Press kindly let me use material that, although in the public domain, was excellently reproduced in their books. Ellen Harding, of the California State Library, gave me a great deal of help with illustrations I was unable to get elsewhere; Sheryl Waller of the Calaveras County Historical Society went out of her way to help me locate a portrait of Black Bart.

The sources of all illustrations are given at the back of the book.

Some people can do without editors. I cannot. I sometimes get so involved with the tale I'm telling that I don't notice I've made a limping sentence, garbled my material, or run on too long. My friends Ute Haker and Cecil Dawkins helped me improve the text. Arthur C. Smith, the general editor of the California Natural History Guides series, kept me moving with the project. It is always a pleasure to work with him. Doris Kretschmer, sponsoring editor at the University of California Press, worked with me endlessly and patiently to bring this book to fruition. Rose Vekony, Sheila Berg, Dave Peattie, and Nola Burger helped make it the book you see.

To all of these, much thanks.

CHAPTER ONE

The Gold That Changed a Nation

This is the saga of California gold—where it comes from, where it goes. Here is the story of those who sought it, how they lived and mined it. The tale is not finished, because California's gold rush is still going on, along the streams where thousands of present-day gold hunters dig and dive for gold, in the huge mines where trucks as large as houses carry rock containing invisible gold to a place where a lump of gold the size of a fingernail will be recovered from one truckload. And the tale continues in the legacy of legend: of bandits, real or merely fabled, of gold mines lost and found, of buried treasure, of gold-laden ships lying at the bottom of the sea.

In 1848–1849 California hosted the first world-class gold rush, luring would-be miners from all over the globe. Americans came by sea or land. For those who came by land it was a revelation. For the first time ordinary Americans, not just wild trappers and intrepid explorers, began to realize how wide the continent was, and that from sea to shining sea it was all theirs. And California gold was theirs, too. Those in the nation's capital greeted the gold with joy. Quickly, California, unlike other regions of the West, became a state without ever being a territory.

Some Americans, seeing the mines teeming with men who spoke languages they could not understand, tried to keep the foreigners out. This led to violence, which was directed not only against those who had just arrived from foreign lands but also and more profoundly against the Native Americans who had lived there for thousands of years and the Spanish-speaking residents (Californios) who had received grants of land from Spain and Mexico. Bigotry set its mark on California and has yet to be totally erased.

In the great California gold rush the American dream was iterated: anyone, no matter his family, his education, or his station, could attain the good life. Although many gold rushers banded together to get to California, once they arrived it was—

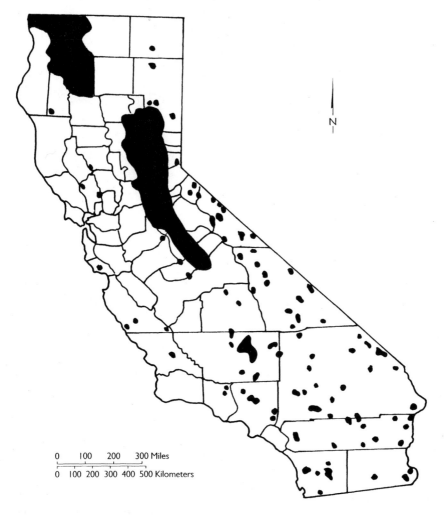

MAP 1. California's gold country. It has been said that nowhere in California can one lift a spadeful of earth that will not contain gold. Perhaps so, but in many places the amount of gold would be infinitesimal. Shown here are areas where gold has been found in large enough quantities to make it worth mining.

especially in the early days—by individual efforts that they succeeded or failed. In the process of their search for gold, the miners learned a bit about geology and about gold's habits, where it came from on the mountainside, how it got into the rivers, and how and where it lodged until they, with their pans and rockers and sluices, tore it loose from its hiding place and sent it to the markets of the world. A few miners in the early days got rich, but many who made rich strikes gambled or drank them away. Many of those who started their fortunes in the gold rush did so in commerce, mining the miners rather than the gold.

As the easy pickings began to run out—California gold, the miners found, was not inexhaustible as advertised—miners banded together for efficiency and turned from pocket knife and pan to machines. Soon mining was chiefly in the hands of companies that could afford expensive machinery to go deep in the Earth, or that built huge dredges to sift through the riverbeds or tear up dry land gravel beds to take gold from fossil rivers.

One mechanical method used streams of water forced out of a nozzle, much like a garden hose but with enormously greater force. This method, called hydraulicking, tore apart mountains of gravel, taking out millions of dollars worth of gold but washing the remains toward the lowlands, thereby silting up rivers and harbors, farms and orchards below. Farmers fought the mines to save their lands. For decades the battle went on, in the courts and the legislature as well as in the mines and fields, pitting miner against farmer in the world's first great environmental conflict settled by law.

California experienced another gold rush in the Great Depression, when thousands of desperate people turned to mining in hopes of finding gold earlier miners had overlooked. After World War II, when scuba (self-contained underwater breathing apparatus) gear was invented, underwater mining—again by individuals—became a popular hobby. But gold was only $35 a troy ounce—a good price in the depression but a pittance after postwar inflation.

When the U.S. government finally gave up deciding the price of gold for its citizens and let the marketplace take over, an altogether new gold rush, a corporate gold rush, began. New mines producing invisible gold from ore of very low grade opened up; old mines long known to California miners to still have gold again became profitable. Thanks to these new mines and revitalized old ones, California once more became a leader in the nation's gold production. Big business had taken over the gold rush, but not without environmental conflicts.

Most of California's gold went to make coins or to be held as bullion reserves—in other words, to make money. In the mid-nineteenth century, much of the money went, as gold often does, to fuel a war—this time, the Civil War. Now that gold coins have been replaced by paper and plastic in commerce, much of California's gold has gone to other uses. But gold's usefulness does not account for its mystique. For millennia gold has been held in high regard by so-called civilized people in every inhabited continent. In much of the world gold was the key to a better life. It was the mirror of human dreams, its luster casting a golden glow over a hoped-for splendid future.

Why should California be so favored with gold? Where did the gold come from? It came ultimately from deep within the Earth. How this happens is nature's story, as fascinating as the human story of gold.

CHAPTER TWO

Whodunit?

When Sam Brannan cried "Gold! Gold!" at the corner of San Francisco's Portsmouth Square in 1848, he deliberately started the great California gold rush. He was advertising James Marshall's discovery of a small nugget of gold at Sutter's Mill. But Marshall's nugget was not the first gold discovered in California, nor did it trigger the first gold rush.

American gold was the talk of Europe in the sixteenth century. Shiploads of gold bars and gold sculptures of incredibly detailed animals and plants, of gold llamas with their babies, of gold jaguars with jasper eyes, of gold butterflies so light they floated on air, as well as magnificent pieces of jewelry from the goldsmiths of the Inca and Aztec empires were sent to Charles V, then Holy Roman Emperor and ruler of Spain. But Europe did not get a chance to admire the splendid work; all of it was tossed into the melting pot to use for war.

Not content with gold wrested from the natives of Latin America, the Spanish and Portuguese conquistadors, together with a few German conquistadors and English interlopers, including Sir Walter Raleigh, spent the rest of the sixteenth century searching for the elusive golden man—"El Dorado." The legend of El Dorado began with a rite of the Chibcha tribe in what is now Colombia. Each year its members covered their chief with a layer of gold dust. He washed it off by plunging into Lake Guatavitá. Although the Chibcha had ceased practicing the rite years before the Spanish came, the idea of it, of a golden man, grew into a golden temple and then into a city of solid gold.

Europeans never found a golden temple or a golden city, and when they found Lake Guatavitá they did not realize at first that they had reached the end of their quest. When they finally identified Guatavitá as the lake of the gilded man, they tried to probe its depths, with very little success. Through the years many others have tried to rob the lake of its golden riches, but no one has succeeded. The lake's mud was so sticky when wet and hard when dry it held the gold in a grasp mining techniques could not surmount. Today the Colombian government forbids further effort.

Rumors of seven golden cities, not just one, spurred another expedition, led by Francisco Vásquez de Coronado, to the region north of Mexico where the golden cities were supposed to stand on high mesas, gleaming in the sun. When Coronado's group reached a mesa in what is now New Mexico on July 7, 1540, they found golden brown adobe villages but no gold. Coronado pressed on, going as far as what is now Kansas in search of Quivira, another legendary land of gold, but again no gold.

One branch of Coronado's expedition went west as far as California. They had been preceded the year before by a seagoing party under the leadership of Francisco Ulloa, who had hoped to find a river that would carry them back to the east. They got as far as today's Santa Barbara, then made their way inland where they found a native village. The villagers welcomed them, but the Spanish got dysentery from the water. All but the three men who had stayed with the ship eventually died. One of those who had remained on board, Pablo Salvador Hernández, came ashore to find Ulloa dying. Ulloa urged him to bury the gold they had been carrying—the fortunes of the party, intended as their nest egg in the new land. That gold has never been found—or at least, no one has admitted it. So the first Spanish expedition to reach California left gold instead of finding it.

A naval branch of Coronado's 1540 expedition sailed off to explore the Sea of Cortez that the three survivors of Ulloa's party told of. Perhaps, the naval group thought, they could find the seven golden cities in the land of the Gran Khan (China). Surely China could not be far away. Hernando de Alarcón, who led this group, planned to rendezvous with Coronado if only he could find a route that would lead him back to Coronado.

When Alarcón's party, in two small ships, arrived at the Sea of Cortez, Alarcón elected to go up the mighty river—the Colorado—in spite of the fearful fifteen-foot tidal bore, the first white people to do so. Coronado's group, meanwhile, had been ranging far and wide through the Southwest and had stumbled on the Grand Canyon, becoming the first Europeans to see the great chasm. Now, Coronado, also on the Colorado at the Grand Canyon, could only glimpse the river a mile below. After two tries, Alarcón managed to get as far as the site of today's Yuma, Arizona, where he erected a large cross with a message on it for Coronado.

Alarcón was gone so long Melchior Díaz of Coronado's party took some men to look for him on foot. The West is vast, yet Díaz found the very spot where Alarcón had left letters. The letters told Díaz that Alarcón was returning to Mexico, so Díaz felt free to continue on his own. He spent several days exploring Baja California, once passing a steaming lava flow. When the expedition's greyhound started chasing and scattering their sheep, Díaz threw a lance at it, missed, fell on the lance himself, and died. The leaderless party returned to Mexico. Once again, the Spanish missed California gold.

But the Spanish did find gold in the New World, as well as silver in great abundance. For more than three centuries towering Spanish galleons laden with silver and gold plied the waters from the New World to Spain, often losing treasure-carrying ships along the way.

Non-Spanish explorers, however, found California gold well before the nineteenth century. Francis Drake, an English privateer, set out in 1577 to capture gold and silver from the Spanish in the New World. He left England with five ships: one his hundred-ton flagship he then called the *Pelican*, three smaller ships, and a storeship. He intended to enter the Pacific and surprise the Spanish on the western side of Latin America.

At the Strait of Magellan, near Cape Horn at the tip of South America, where horrendous storms batter ships and land alike, Drake destroyed the storeship and one other so there would be no turning back. Here he rechristened his own ship the *Golden Hind*, perhaps hoping that she would have the speed of a hind and bring home gold. He knew it could take months to get around the Horn; the Spanish average was six to seven weeks. Ferdinand Magellan, the first on record to push through the strait, had had a lucky run: thirty-seven days. Drake was even luckier. True to her new name, the *Golden Hind* made it in sixteen days. But when he got to Pacific waters, the *Golden Hind* was alone. One of his ships had sunk; the other, separated from Drake, had searched and, not finding him, had gone back to England.

Drake and his crew sailed on. They captured several Spanish ships, laden with gold and silver, so much that they had to jettison forty-five tons of silver to be light enough to continue. Drake determined to search for the Northwest Passage, a route that mariners and geographers of the day believed would link the Pacific and Atlantic across the north as the route around the Cape of Good Hope in Africa did in the south.

Drake knew also that Spanish Manila galleons regularly made the passage from the west coast of North America to the Orient, taking silver to the East and bringing back luxury goods from the Orient to the Americas. So the little *Golden Hind,* too, followed along the California coast. The ship stopped in California long enough to "discover" and claim the land for Queen Elizabeth I.

Exactly where Drake landed is still debated. A small scallop in the Point Reyes National Seashore, Marin County, is known as Drake's Bay or Drake's Estero. Many believe this was his anchorage, as it neatly fits the description in Drake's chaplain's account of the landing site. While the ship was at anchor, Drake had a brass plate

FIGURE 1. A European artist's conception of how the Miwok tribe welcomed Francis Drake and his party to California in 1579, assuming that they did land in Marin County. Drawn after Drake's return to England by Theodor de Bry, Frankfort, in 1589.

made to commemorate the occasion, and to ensure his Queen's claim to the land. It was "a plate of brasse, fast nailed to a great and firme post; whereon is engrauen her graces name, and the day and yeare of our arriuall there, and of the free giuing up, of the prouince and kingdome, both by the king and people, into her maiesties hands: together with her highnesse picture, and armes in a piece of sixpence currant English monie, shewing it selfe by a hole made of purpose through the plate: vnderneath was likewise engrauen the name of our generall &c."

A plate answering this description was found not far from Drake's Bay, near what is now Larkspur Landing for the Marin County Ferry on the shore of San Francisco Bay. It is on display in the Bancroft Library, University of California, Berkeley. Historians debated for years whether the plate is truly the one fashioned by Drake and have come to the conclusion that it is not, that it is a very elaborate forgery. If that is true, it leaves an even more intriguing mystery: who devised such a carefully and cleverly done hoax, why did they not make sure it was found by someone who would recognize its possibilities—or did they?—and at whom was the hoax aimed?

Other possible landing places are Bodega Bay, San Francisco Bay, and even Santa Barbara. Five old cannons were unearthed in a storm in the 1980s near Santa

Barbara, giving rise to speculations that they might have belonged to the *Golden Hind*.

Wherever Drake landed, legend says that he buried silver bars there to lighten his load. Some treasure hunters maintain that the old chart of Drake's landing site, drawn a few years after his return to England by the Dutch cartographer Hondius, is actually a treasure map telling where Drake buried several tons of silver bars. Newspaper accounts in 1985 said a page of Drake's diary, dated June 25, 1579, had mysteriously appeared in the hands of a sailor. This page said that Drake and his company buried the treasure on a "low but sparsely wooded hill half way between the sea and a large inland body of water." This could refer to Tomales Bay, Drake's Bay, or Bolinas Lagoon, if, indeed, Drake landed in Marin County at all.

Drake left behind other treasures as well, not to be recovered for three centuries, but he may have been aware of their potential. "There is," wrote Richard Hakluyt at the turn of the seventeeth century in his account of Drake's around-the-world voyage, "no part of earth here [in California] to be taken up, wherein there is not some probable show of gold or silver." Hakluyt does not say how he or Drake knew this.

If Hakluyt means that Drake and his party actually saw California gold, then they were the first Europeans to do so. By sailing the *Golden Hind* westward across the Pacific Ocean and thence to England, Drake and his crew became the second group to circumnavigate the globe. The English now officially claimed California, but they did nothing about it or the gold. California was too far away (no one knew the width of the North American continent) to be easily colonized, gold or no. In any event, it was the long-sought Northwest Passage, not California, that interested both the English and the Spanish.

Spanish explorations near the end of the sixteenth century seemed to show that Baja, or Lower, California (the peninsula) and Alta, or Upper, California (now the U.S. state) were one big island. Beyond the island of California lay the elusive Northwest Passage, the linking strait. The Spanish did not care about England's claim to California, but they did want a port of call for their Orient-bound Manila galleons. In 1599, while a land party from the Manila galleon *San Agustín* was off exploring, the ship was wrecked off Point Reyes. The late archaeologist Robert Heizer found more than one hundred fragments of Ming china in excavations of Miwok Indian sites along the Marin peninsula. His finds and the story of the sinking of the *San Agustín* prompted the marine archaeologist Robert Marx to search for the ship in the 1980s.

A mapping and salvage party sent by the Spanish in 1602 recovered little of the cargo of the *San Agustín*, but they did establish a colony at San Diego. Now that they had a foothold in California, and the Russians and English were beginning to show interest in it, the Spanish decided to incorporate California firmly into the Spanish empire. Father Eusebio Kino and Isidro Atondo y Antillón led a colonization project to California in the 1680s. Although this project failed, Kino continued to explore over the next few years and learned that California definitely was not an island and that San Diego could be reached by land as well as sea.

A land route meant missions could be established and colonies founded, so they chose a Franciscan monk, Padre Junípero Serra, who had a record of successful mission work in Mexico, to Christianize California. Serra worked his way from south to north, picking good spots for settlement along the route. The first established was Mission San Diego de Alcala, founded in 1769; the last, Mission San Francisco de Solano at what is now Sonoma, was founded in 1821. Serra did not live to see them all brought into being; he died after founding San Buenaventura in 1782, when the work was only a quarter finished. Altogether there were thirty-two missions and numerous *asistencias* (supporting structures), but they did not last long. Mexico won its independence from Spain in 1821, and the secularization of the missions was soon completed—that is, their vast landholdings taken from them, making the land available to individuals. After independence Mexican governors gave at least six hundred grants for *ranchos* in the new territory, including, but not limited to, mission lands. The ranchos ranged in size from 4,500 acres to more than 100,000.

Gen. Mariano Vallejo, the Spanish official in charge of northern California when it came into American hands, held a large tract of land north of San Francisco Bay. The Peralta family was granted a huge rancho that extended from San Jose to East Bay, including what are now Oakland and Berkeley. Johann Augustus Sutter, a German-born Swiss, became a naturalized Mexican citizen so he, too, could have a piece of California. His holdings, some 230 square miles, larger than anyone in Europe except crowned heads could imagine, were centered around what is now Sacramento, and the great California gold rush was to center around him.

While the building of the missions and the redistribution of land were taking place, the Spanish did find gold. Throughout their tenure in California the Spanish had intimations of gold and sometimes acquired gold itself. As early as 1510 the story was current that an "island called California" was peopled by a nation of women, called Amazons, who had arms and armor of solid gold. The Amazons kept griffins as pets, which ate any unlucky men who happened by. Stories as wild as this started gold "rushes" and launched expeditions, but they were not the spur to the great California rush. The Amazon story was the invention of an adventure fiction writer, Garci Ordoñez de Montalvo, who based it on medieval European legend as well as Columbus's tale of a land of women warriors. Montalvo set his tale not in South America, where the legend originated (hence the word *Amazon*), but on "an island called California." The only metal on the island, he said, was gold.

As early as 1775 Spanish miners worked gold mines in the Potholes district, in the southeastern corner of the state, now in Imperial County. Where water was scarce, in the desert away from the Colorado River, the miners tossed the gold-bearing dirt in the air and caught it in a blanket, trusting the wind to blow away lighter particles and leave gold. The mines were worked throughout the 1800s, with as many as five hundred Mexican and Indian miners busily increasing the airborne dust. Other miners worked on the Colorado River, where water was available, rolling gravel around in their wooden *bateas* (gold pans) to get the gold.

In the early days of the mines near the Colorado River, the miners were working under the direction of the padres at Mission San Pedro y San Pablo de Bicuner, established by Franciscan priests in 1780. A few years later the Indians rebelled, destroying the mission and killing the priests. It is rumored that the accumulated gold was either buried or tossed into the river.

Legend says many other California missions operated gold mines using native labor. Mission San Gabriel, Arcángel; Mission San Juan de Capistrano; Mission Santa Bárbara, Virgen y Mártir; and Mission San Buenaventura all operated secret— and now lost—gold mines. Three missions together worked a mine in the Ben Lomond Mountains of Santa Cruz County, and Mission de San Fernando, Rey de España, shipped "quantities" (it is said) of gold from another mine. Most of the mines were probably first found by Indians, as time after time legend says the padres were shown the mine, or the Indians brought gold to them. So the Indians discovered and worked the mines but shared little in the benefits. Gold was said to have been mined at Black Mountain in San Diego County in the 1820s, and other Mexican mines in the far south may date to the 1840s.

An unlikely story was told by George C. Yount, who came to California in 1826. Twenty-nine years later Yount recalled that the trapper Jedediah Strong Smith had discovered gold at Mono Lake in 1825 and along the San Joaquin River in 1829. Yount said that Smith and his men each took $75,000 worth of gold back to Missouri, intending to bring back mining equipment, but Smith was killed before he could return.

This has the ring of a typical "lost mine" story (see chapter 12), most of which have a grain of truth but very little substance. Historians have traced Jed Smith's route very carefully, almost meal by meal, and find no evidence that he ever passed by Mono Lake. Since Yount was an elderly man when he told this story, perhaps he had confused Jed Smith with another trapper, Tom (PegLeg) Smith, who left the legend of the Lost PegLeg Smith mine. The Lost PegLeg Smith mine is supposed to have been found and lost in 1829 by PegLeg Smith, who may have been following the route Jedediah Smith took in 1826 across the desert to the California coast.

The old mission at San Jose was even the site of a working gold refinery. Here is

FIGURE 2. Dry washing, a Mexican method of collecting gold when water was scarce. Judging by the background of this drawing, the site is somewhere in southeastern California.

what Juan José Pico, the civil administrator of the missions in the nineteenth century, said:

> Padre Martinez . . . gave . . . to me, [and three young friends] about 20 ounces of gold [each], not coined, but in little balls of an ounce. . . . That gold . . . I believe had been collected at the point of San José near the mission. There were then, when we were little boys, about 12 Spaniards working in the square of the mission; I believe they were refining silver and gold because the Padre had many flasks of mercury and

instruments and materials for refining those metals. I know many times we wanted to go in to see what they were doing, and they never permitted us. They allowed only some Indian alcaldes [officials] to enter under [threat of] severe punishment if they divulged any secret.

(Pico speaks here of "ounces." He probably means "troy ounces," as that has been the standard measurement for gold and silver for centuries. A troy ounce is slightly heavier than an avoirdupois ounce. Only 12 ounces make up a troy pound. Officially, a troy ounce weighs 480 grains, or 31.1 grams. The word *troy* refers not to Troy of ancient Greek history but to a French trade fair held at Troyes, France, in the Middle Ages. Here gold and silver were bought and sold, and to make certain that everyone was using the same weights and measures, the "troy ounce" was set. In the late twentieth century the metric gram weight is used to measure gold, but the metals market still quotes gold in troy ounces, so I have followed that practice here. Avoirdupois measurement is never used for precious metals, so in this book, "troy ounces," "ounces," and "ounces troy" all mean the same thing.)

Two geologists, James Dwight Dana, who stopped along the coast in 1841, and Eugene Duflot de Mofras, who visited California in 1842, both mentioned gold or possible gold mines in California. As far as science was concerned, gold was official.

As early as 1840 Yount himself found gold on Catalina Island and tried to mine it. Then in 1841, according to another California pioneer, Gen. John Bidwell, who had led a party to California that year, a Canadian fur trapper, Jean Baptiste Ruelle, who had worked in New Mexico mines, discovered gold near Mission San Fernando. "His discovery of gold in California caused no astonishment or excitement whatever," Bidwell wrote.

Bidwell missed being credited as the discoverer of California gold by a hair's breadth. M. C. Nye, who had been a member of Bidwell's overland immigrant party, said,

Bidwell discovered the first gold in California, but he did not know it. We were traveling across a stream, after crossing the mountains, and Bidwell stopped to drink; we did not wait for him, as he was always lagging behind, looking at the rocks and flowers and bushes, and getting specimens. We called him the schoolmaster. Looking in the water, he saw some strange pebbles, and put some of them in his bulletpouch to show to the boys. He looked across the stream and saw Indians coming, and ran to join his companions, losing his hat and pouch in his flight, and forgetting for several days about the pebbles, which he described as yellow and not hard, and he thought they were some kind of metal.

Bidwell worked for Sutter for several years, which is when he met Ruelle, another of Sutter's employees.

Baptiste Ruelle [Bidwell wrote] had been in Sutter's employ for several months, when one day he came to Sutter, showed him a few small particles of gold, and said that he had found them on the American River, and he wanted to go far into the mountains on that stream to prospect for gold. For this purpose he desired two mules loaded with provisions, and he selected two . . . Indian boys whom he wanted to go into the mountains with him, saying he would have no others. Of course he did not get the outfit. Sutter and I talked about it and queried, what does he want with so much provision—the American River being only a mile and the mountains only twenty miles distant? And why does he want those two Indians? Our conclusion was that he really wanted the outfit so that he could . . . go to Oregon and remain.

Ruelle's locality proved to be a short distance from Coloma, now credited as "the" place where gold was discovered. To his dying day, Ruelle protested that he was the first to find gold in California.

In 1844 Pablo Gutiérrez, a Mexican laborer on Sutter's Hock Farm in the Sacramento Valley, where Bidwell was manager, took Bidwell to where he had found gold on the Bear River. He showed Bidwell the spot, but when he could not fish out a nugget, Bidwell asked him how he would get the gold. Gutiérrez replied that he would need a batea. Here is Bidwell's account:

He talked so much about the "batea" that I concluded it must be a complicated machine. . . . I did not know that a batea is nothing more nor less than a wooden bowl which the Mexicans use for washing gold. I said, "Pablo, where can you get it?" He said, "Down in Mexico." I said, "I will help pay your expenses if you will go down and get one," which he promised to do. I said, "Pablo, say nothing to anybody else about this gold discovery, and we will get the batea and find the gold."

As time passed I was afraid to let him go to Mexico, lest when he got among his relatives he might be induced to stay and not come back, so I made a suggestion to him. I said, "Pablo, let us save our earnings and get on board a vessel and go around to Boston, and there get the batea. I can interpret for you, and the Yankees are very ingenious and can make anything." The idea pleased him, and he promised to go as soon as we could save enough money to pay our expenses. He was to keep it a secret, and I believe he faithfully kept his promise. It would have taken us a year or two to get enough money to go. . . . But . . . our plans were interrupted. [A revolt of native chiefs threatened, and Gutierrez was sent to carry dispatches to the Governor. He returned] and was sent again to tell the Governor that we were on the march to join him in Monterey. This time he was taken prisoner and hanged to a tree, somewhere near the present town of Gilroy. That, of course, put an end to our gold discovery; otherwise, Pablo Gutierrez might have been [credited] as the discoverer.

Poor Pablo. Had Bidwell questioned him more closely as to just what a batea was, history might have been different. On three other occasions before 1848 Bidwell tried to mine gold, but with little success.

FIGURE 3. "Antonio Mendoza, the Mexican gold washer in California, first discoverer of the large gold trackt—taken from life, 1842." Drawing by G. M. Waseurtz of Sandels. Here Sandels—he was called by the aristocratic portion of his name—gives us another gold "discoverer."

The year Bidwell arrived in California, 1841, Don Francisco López, a well-to-do rancher, discovered placer gold forty-five miles west of Los Angeles. His discovery started a small rush to the goldfields, which were in the drainage of the Santa Clara River. It did not seem like a small rush at the time; some six thousand people flocked to the mines, most coming from Sonora, Mexico. Sonorans were experienced miners and particularly adept at mining gold. They were able, as the historian Hubert Howe Bancroft said, "by merely looking at the ground, to tell whether or not it contained gold, and would scrape the surface with a scoop or spoon made of bullock's horn." From this comes the expression, "By the great Horn Spoon," popular at the time of the '49er gold rush. Later López made another strike, in nearby San Feliciano Canyon. It is possible that the López discovery and Ruelle's first discovery are of the same gold field, found twice.

The two drawings above were made by G. M. Waseurtz of Sandels, a European who visited the gold mines near Los Angeles in the early 1840s. Figure 3 is his draw-

FIGURE 4. "Gold fishing on the coast of California Bay." Drawing by G. M. Waseurtz of Sandels. "California Bay" may be the San Pedro Bay locality, discovered in 1840, shown on map 3 as number 14.

ing of a Mexican miner of the time, Antonio Mendoza, using a batea to gather gold. He also tells us Mendoza was the first discoverer of the "large gold trakt," adding yet another name to our list of claimants to the title of the first to discover gold. Figure 4 depicts miners working the cliffs at "California Bay"—likely San Pedro Bay. Probably he intended to show the miners rappelling down to a gold-bearing layer to pick out sand and gravel to wash.

Don (the Spanish equivalent of the English title "Sir") Francisco was a Californio, a Spanish-speaking native of California, and a member of a prominent Spanish (Mexican) family. By the 1840s the Californios, unlike their hard-bitten conquistador ancestors, had developed gracious living into an art. They had very little money, as the nearest mint was in Mexico. They didn't need it—if you were to travel through Californio country, you could stay at the ranchos and be feted and entertained at each stop. The ranchos grew fruit, vegetables, and meat, so food in bountiful California was not a problem. The *patrón* of the rancho sold hides to passing ships, such as the one Richard Henry Dana served on that gave him grist for his book *Two Years Before the Mast*. Some of the ranchos, according to Thomas O.

Larkin, the American consul in California in the 1840s, had gold and silver mines, as well as excavations for coal, slate, and bitumen. Luxury items, imported from Mexico, Europe, or the Far East, were brought by the ships.

Because the officers and crew of trading ships were almost the only outsiders Californios saw, the ships provided another service to rancho *patrones*. It was not easy to find marriage partners of suitable social status for all of their daughters. They chose sailing ship captains as well as the few American-born merchants. Jacob Leese, a rancher and merchant who acquired several grants of land from Mexico and who built a redwood frame house in San Francisco (then called Yerba Buena) in 1836—the second house in San Francisco—married General Vallejo's daughter at a sumptuous wedding that left the guests reeling for days. In this case, however, it was the daughter's choice of husband, not her father's. Americans were conquering California by marriage before they took it by arms.

The Reverend Walter Colton, who was living in Monterey in the 1840s, wrote of the Californios: "There are no people that I have ever been among who enjoy life so thoroughly. . . . Their hospitality knows no bounds; they are always glad to see you, come when you may; take a pleasure in entertaining you while you remain; and only regret that your business calls you away." Another early settler said, "If happiness, in the full sense of the word, was ever enjoyed by mankind, it was by the old settlers and inhabitants who were here before [Marshall's] discovery of gold." (Colton does not mention that although slavery was prohibited by the Mexican government, peonage was not. This Eden was made possible for the upper classes by the labors of poorly paid Spanish peons and Indians.)

Unlike many of his contemporaries, Don Francisco had studied history, literature, and languages, at the university in Mexico City. He also took courses in mining at the Colegio de Minería and often spent his spare time in California prospecting. Here is the account of his discovery of California gold by one of his relatives, Doña Francesca López de Belderrain, given in explicit and colorful detail:

> The first important discovery of gold in California of which there is definite record took place in the month of March, 1842, in one of the canyons of the San Francisquito Rancho, later called Placerito [*sic*] Canyon, about forty miles northwest of the city of Los Angeles. One fine morning in the Spring of 1842, when making one of his periodical visits to his niece's ranch, Don Francisco Lopez made preparations for an all day outing in the mountains. Garbed in his hunting attire, Don Francisco stood ready to start on his trip on that eventful day, which would immortalize his name. He wore a wide-brimmed hat, a silk handkerchief around his neck, and gauntlet gloves; chaparreras made out of bear skins, a pistol and hunting knife in their scabbards on a strong leather belt. His horse was a fine sorrel. The saddle was of brown leather, with large tapaderas covering the stirrups; a Mexican bridle, a rope made of horse hair of different colors, wound around the horse's neck, a rifle across

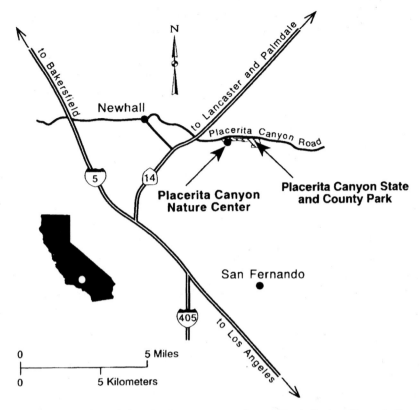

MAP 2. Location of Placerita Canyon Nature Center, Newhall, site of López's discovery of gold in 1842.

the pommel of the saddle and canteen with water hanging from the bow of the saddle. It was the Lenten season and the country was luxuriant with verdure. As he was bidding good bye to his wife at the San Francisquito ranch house, she asked him to bring her some wild onions which grew in abundance in the canyons. After inspecting the stock and taking a hard stroll up and down the mountains, he felt rather fatigued, and, as the hour of noon had arrived, he selected a shady tree under which to rest and have lunch. Recently [this was written in 1930] the tree has been acclaimed the oldest in Southern California. It is an oak, said to be 500 years old. He alighted from his horse, and his servant spread a sarape or Mexican blanket on the ground, unsaddled his master's horse and placed the saddle on one end of the sarape, that it might serve as a head rest. The boy then made the coffee and served the lunch. After a lengthy siesta, Don Francisco awoke and suddenly remembered his wife's request. Taking the knife from his belt he went to the slope near by and began to dig up some of the wild onions. Noticing some yellow particles clinging to the roots, he examined them wonderingly. He shook the earth from the roots, set them down and started to dig again with vigour. Upon examining the earth closely, he suddenly started to his feet and shouted, "Gold! I have found it at last! Gold! Gold!"

There followed a grand fiesta, and the news and some gold samples were sent to the governor in Mexico City. The mines were worked for nearly four years, although the yield was small. Eighteen and three-quarters ounces of this gold was sent to the U.S. Mint in Philadelphia, but neither it nor the small rush it occasioned made much of an impression on the world or on history. William Heath Davis estimated in 1889 that from $80,000 to $100,000 worth of gold (when gold was officially valued at $20 an ounce) came from these placers. Today Placerita Canyon near San Fernando is marked as the site of the first commercial discovery of gold in California.

Juan B. Alvarado, governor of California from 1836 to 1842, even used California gold for his wedding rings in 1831, and later had earrings with an ounce of gold in quills made for his wife and a ring made for his daughter. Because a Russian jailed in Monterey in 1814 had gold on him and would not reveal its source, Alvarado thought the Russians, too, knew of California gold. The Spanish Californios even knew of gold in the Sierra but did not search for it, as the Indians were dangerously hostile.

The Spanish never advertised the gold—it was a secret they kept to themselves. As Padre Mercado of Mission Santa Clara told Davis, if the gold were made public, many might immigrate, and this "would be dangerous; [the immigrants] would pour in by thousands and overrun the country; Protestants would swarm here, and the Catholic religion would be endangered, the work of the Missions would be interfered with, and as the Californians had no means of defense, no navy nor army, the Americans would soon obtain supreme control; they would undoubtedly at some time come in force."

There were others who claimed to have been the original discoverers of gold in California. Among them was Capt. Charles Bennett, whose tombstone in Salem, Oregon, reads:

CAPTAIN CHARLES BENNETT
WAS THE DISCOVERER OF
GOLD IN CALIFORNIA
AND FELL IN
DEFENSE OF HIS COUNTRY
AT WALLA WALLA

Bennett was certainly in the gold country; he even worked for Sutter, and may well have found gold at Sutter's Mill.

Map 3 shows early mines and discoveries. There may have been more; some of these may not be correct. Those marked "find" (in quotation marks) indicate doubt. Nevertheless, the map shows that the early mines, worked in the 1700s and early 1800s by the Spanish, were in southeastern California. Those worked by Mexicans (after independence from Spain) were along the southwestern part of the state, from

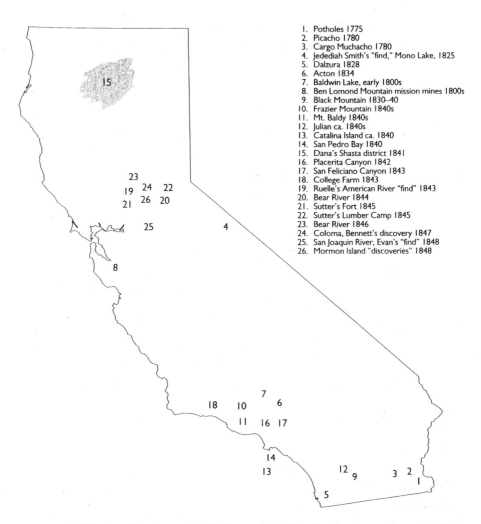

1. Potholes 1775
2. Picacho 1780
3. Cargo Muchacho 1780
4. Jedediah Smith's "find," Mono Lake, 1825
5. Dalzura 1828
6. Acton 1834
7. Baldwin Lake, early 1800s
8. Ben Lomond Mountain mission mines 1800s
9. Black Mountain 1830–40
10. Frazier Mountain 1840s
11. Mt. Baldy 1840s
12. Julian ca. 1840s
13. Catalina Island ca. 1840
14. San Pedro Bay 1840
15. Dana's Shasta district 1841
16. Placerita Canyon 1842
17. San Feliciano Canyon 1843
18. College Farm 1843
19. Ruelle's American River "find" 1843
20. Bear River 1844
21. Sutter's Fort 1845
22. Sutter's Lumber Camp 1845
23. Bear River 1846
24. Coloma, Bennett's discovery 1847
25. San Joaquin River, Evan's "find" 1848
26. Mormon Island "discoveries" 1848

MAP 3. California gold mines and gold discoveries before the discovery at Sutter's Mill. The group in extreme southeastern California was worked by the Spanish; those in the Los Angeles area and number 8, near Santa Cruz, were worked in Mexican times; those near Sacramento were found just before Americans took over California. Locality 15 shows what James Dwight Dana considered to be a potential gold district in the Shasta area.

San Diego as far north as the area around Los Angeles, except for Ben Lomond north in the Santa Cruz Mountains, which was worked by the mission padres. American (more properly, "Anglo," as the United States did not yet own California) finds were near Sacramento.

One American exception to this generalization is the alleged discovery by the trapper Jedediah Smith, first near Mono Lake and later on the San Joaquin River (only the find at Mono Lake is shown on the map). His finds—if this account is true—were early and dangerous, as the Mexican government did not look kindly on strangers in their territory. Number 15 on the map merely indicates that James Dwight Dana, on an exploring trip, thought the Shasta area would contain gold deposits. He was right.

All of these "discoveries" were well before the "official" discovery of gold in 1848 that started the great California gold rush. Gold can be found in many places in California, so it is likely most of the reported finds are correct. Who was the "real" discoverer? Throughout most of the early narratives one fact stands out: the natives already knew. Without doubt, the "original" discoverer of California gold was an anonymous Native American of long ago.

CHAPTER THREE

Cry Gold!

By the middle of the nineteenth century Johann Augustus Sutter had a large down payment on his dreams. He had been born in Germany in 1803, moved to Switzerland, then emigrated to the United States in 1834, leaving his wife and family, as well as large debts and a warrant for his arrest, behind. Once in the new world, Sutter invented a new personal history, including a military education, the rank of captain in the elite Swiss Guard, and service in two major campaigns. (He did actually volunteer for the reserve corps but saw no such service.) Sutter had a charisma that charmed women into his bed and money from the pockets of men.

Sutter immediately moved westward, long before Horace Greeley suggested it as a direction to go. He tried his hand as a trader on the Santa Fe Trail. He used his silver tongue to talk some Germans into letting him sell the goods they had brought to rich Mexicans, then decamped with the money, stopping long enough at Westport, Missouri, to build a hotel using Native American labor and to charm young Shawnee women. He never revealed the source of his funds for the hotel, but those who knew him suspected him of selling illegal whiskey to the Indians. Even such illicit activities did not yield enough money to pay his debts, so once again he sneaked out of town, ending up in Hawaii. And once again he used his charisma to obtain a common-law Hawaiian wife and to talk a company in Honolulu into giving him $3,008.68 to finance a California adventure, taking with him several Hawaiian men and his wife. It took ten years and much pushing for him to pay them back.

In California he became a naturalized Mexican citizen (California was then part of Mexico) and persuaded the Mexican government to grant him almost 150,000 acres near what is now Sacramento. By the end of 1847 he had Indian laborers to work his rancho, a few European-trained vintners for his grapes, Mexican vaqueros to tend his herds, and a group of Mormon craftsmen for construction work. These last were members of a Mormon battalion that had fought for the United States in the Mexican War and were on their way to join Brigham Young in Utah. When Young sent word that the promised land wasn't quite ready yet—food was scarce—and they should stay where they were for the winter, Sutter hired them.

Sutter was nervous about what might happen now that the United States was about to acquire California. The Mexican-American War, which had taken the U.S. Marines to the halls of Montezuma, had resulted in the loss of Mexican holdings in what are now New Mexico, Arizona, and California—although the treaty ceding this territory to the United States was not yet official. But Sutter, like his friend General Vallejo, the Mexican military commander of northern California, believed that an American government on the spot was probably preferable to an absentee, centrist Mexican one. Vallejo was well educated and cultured (he even composed music) and was the outstanding Californio in 1849. A career soldier, he had been put in charge of the secularization of Mission San Francisco de Solano (the Sonoma mission) and assigned the project of founding the town of Sonoma to demonstrate a military presence to the Russians, who were showing interest in California. For this he was granted large tracts of land, some of which, including his *casa grande* (mansion), are now part of the state park system. Vallejo was much respected by Americans and would be one of the forty-eight members of California's constitutional convention, convened in late 1849.

Sutter built an imposing structure, which everyone called Sutter's Fort, on high ground above the Sacramento River, now within the modern city of Sacramento. It was a fort in the sense that it could be defended, like other nongovernment forts on the American frontier—Bent's Fort, near Pueblo, Colorado, for example. Sutter's was nearly square and had adobe walls eighteen feet high and two and a half feet thick—enough that arrows and bullets could not penetrate it. It was like a medieval town, containing within it granaries and stores, rooms for lodging, even a hospital. One odd enterprise within it about the time of the gold rush was a restaurant run by a member of the ill-fated Donner party—the only member of the party who was suspected of not waiting until his next human meal had departed this life naturally before preparing it.

It was to the fort that the survivors of the Donner party came to recover from their ordeal. Sutter, a gracious, kindly man, welcomed them and cared for them, as he did other travelers and settlers. All passing by were assured of a California welcome from Sutter: he fed them and housed them, helping in any way he could. They would, after all, be settlers and customers in his burgeoning empire.

Except for the specialized labor of the craftsmen, vintners, and wranglers, Sutter's ranch was built on Native American labor—essentially slave labor. Slavery had been outlawed in Mexico but not yet in the United States. The Indians who

FIGURE 5. Sutter's Fort as it appeared in 1848.

worked at the fort all slept in one big room with a bare floor and no sanitary facilities. Sutter could never have operated his empire without them, and most worked under duress. Sutter did not call them slaves, but he acted as if he owned them. Once, when an Indian threatened rebellion, Sutter executed him and hung his head on the gate of the fort.

When his Hawaiian wife, Manaiki, who had borne him several children, grew too old to suit him, he gave her to one of the Hawaiian men to marry. He had no further use for her, as he had acquired numerous "personal servants"—Indian women and his favorites, young girls. He even gave two of them to his friends for their pleasure.

Sutter was a striking figure. Although he was not very tall, he was erect and soldierly, with piercing blue eyes and neat side whiskers. Here in California he was the closest thing to a major corporation. He owed a great deal of money—what corporation doesn't?—but he was always confident that he would soon be able to pay. He had dreams of empire. He had even founded a town he called New Helvetia (New Switzerland) about a mile from the fort, and he expected it to grow rapidly as settlers came to California. If his empire was to become a reality, he could no longer run out on his debts, but many he never managed to pay.

By 1848 the fort itself had deteriorated. Sutter needed lumber for repairs, and he saw lumber as a good commodity to sell to the new immigrants, who were arriving more and more frequently. Good timber was in short supply in the Sacramento Valley, so Sutter, in partnership with a New Jersey–born carpenter, James Marshall, planned a new sawmill in lovely Coloma Valley in the Sierra Nevada foothills.

Marshall and the crew of Mormons built a frame for the sawmill on the banks of the American River and by January 1848 had installed machinery and a flutter wheel for power. They dug a 150-yard ditch to channel water from the river to the mill. One afternoon in late January Marshall checked the downstream end of the ditch to see if it was deep enough. He saw glitter in the sand, picked it out, and realized he had found gold. He promptly told his Mormon laborers, who could scarcely believe it. One of them, Henry Bigler, noted in his diary, "This day [January 24] some kind of mettle was found in the tail race that looks like goald."

The next morning Marshall looked again and found a nugget the size of a pea. Was it pyrite—fool's gold? He checked by hammering it. Pyrite, he knew, was brittle and would break; gold was malleable and would not. Sure enough, the pea flattened .without breaking. Again he showed his skeptical men what he had found. One by one, they, too, began to believe it was gold. Among them, they picked up a vial full. The only woman in the camp, Jennie Wimmer, tossed a piece into a kettle of soap she was making. If it was not gold, she reasoned, it would corrode. Despite the high alkalinity of the soap, it came out untarnished.

Only Marshall's camp knew about the find. (Later, rumor had it that the Mormons had been mining gold from the river long before Marshall saw it, but Brigham Young said the story was "a mistake.") The nearest white man was twenty miles away. They could drop their tools and gather gold—never mind the sawmill. They could get it all, or at least have a long head start on anyone else. But they did not. Marshall promised them that if they finished the mill, he would give them time to prospect later. For now it was to be a secret. They all agreed.

On January 27 Marshall rode off to Sutter's Fort to show Sutter the gold. Together Sutter and Marshall consulted an encyclopedia and made further tests. They hammered the gold pebbles. They were malleable, as gold is. They piled silver on one side of a set of scales and Marshall's gold on the other until the scales were balanced. Lowering the scales into a pail of water (thereby making a crude Jolly balance), they saw the gold sink to the bottom. It did, indeed, have a greater specific gravity. Other facts, too, seemed to check out. It was gold. They agreed to continue to keep the gold a secret. If the men at Sutter's other mill—a grist mill—were told, they would quit in a body, as would the laborers at the fort—all except, perhaps, the Indians.

At this point Sutter tried to ensure his legal claim to the land the sawmill was on by obtaining a lease from the Colomas, the local tribe. Sutter sent the lease to the military authorities in the capital at Monterey, along with a bottle of gold. En route his emissary stopped off in Benicia and couldn't help bragging, passing the gold around as proof. At Monterey the authorities scoffed at Sutter's "lease." Indians couldn't grant leases!

FIGURE 6. Sutter's sawmill, where James Marshall recovered the tiny nugget of gold that set off the gold rush of '48 and '49.

Even Sutter himself could not keep the secret. His overseer at the fort thought he "acted queerly," and before a week was out Sutter was writing to his good friend Vallejo that he had a "mina de oro" that was "extraordinaria rica." And meanwhile, up at the sawmill a teamster, Jacob Wittner, heard about the gold from the Wimmer children and carried the news back to the fort.

The news was out. The Mormons, true to their promise, kept working at the mill. On March 11 they completed it and were free to prospect. Soon they were making as much in a week as an eastern laborer could in a year.

Still no one from San Francisco rushed to the goldfields. "All sham," said teenaged Edward Kemble, editor of the *California Star*. "Can't be," others said. It remained for Samuel Brannan, leader of the Mormons in California and Kemble's boss, to convince the town.

By 1848 San Francisco had actually become a town. In 1835, when Richard Henry Dana passed by, there was one lonely tent near the harbor. It belonged to the Richardson family. An Englishman, Capt. William A. Richardson (for whom

Richardson Bay is named), had been granted a piece of land that included Yerba Buena Cove in exchange for teaching navigation and carpentry to young Mexicans. As a master mariner, Richardson particularly liked the harbor. It was his plan to found a port town around Yerba Buena Cove. The Mexican governor agreed, and Richardson became San Francisco's first harbor master. Later, under Vallejo's direction, he became captain of the Port and Bay of San Francisco.

By 1836 Richardson was ready to build his dream house, La Casa Grande, a large adobe structure on what is now Dupont Street. That same year Jacob Leese built his redwood house, which he used as both home and office, at what would be the intersection of Grant and Clay streets. Leese's house doubled the number of houses in town.

By 1846 ships were a common sight in San Francisco Bay. On July 8 of that year, the U.S. ship *Portsmouth* anchored at what is now the corner of Clay and Leidesdorff streets to take Yerba Buena for the Americans, and a shipload of sailors were loose in San Francisco. Three weeks later, on July 31, the *Brooklyn* arrived, bringing 238 Mormons (70 men, 68 women, and 100 children) led by Sam Brannan. The Mormons bustled about while they waited for word to come that they could go on to Utah. Some of the Mormon men went off to work for Sutter; others found work nearby. Richardson lent them La Casa Grande for their religious services.

The Mormons swelled the San Francisco population, and soon the town began to look like one. So when Brannan shouted "Gold!" at the corner of the plaza, several hundred Americans could have heard him, as well as Californios who might have dropped by on their way to their homes near the now-crumbling mission.

Brannan was the canny businessman Sutter was not, but both had dreams of glory. Like Sutter, Brannan was openhanded and generous, even while watching for chances to make a fortune. He cut a fine figure in San Francisco. Young, deep chested, black haired, and vigorous, he wore an impeccable frock coat much of the time and walked as if he were truly going somewhere. And he did. Through business and land speculation, Brannan would become the state's first millionaire. It was hard to believe that not many years earlier the dapper Brannan had been tarred and feathered in Ohio for preaching his Mormon doctrine.

Like Sutter, Brannan, too, had left a wife behind. With Brigham Young's knowledge and permission—Mormons allowed themselves multiple wives—he had wed his second wife without telling her of the first, who had remained in the East along with their child. Years later a costly divorce, spurred by this duplicity and demon alcohol, was to be Brannan's downfall. But in 1848 he was one of the most important nonmilitary men in San Francisco. As deputy for Brigham Young, he made a trip to visit the Mormon miners and to collect tithes. The gold was real, he found. Taking a bottle of it (the workmen's tithes), he made his plans. He opened a store on

Mormon Island, where the group from the sawmill was mining, and another at Coloma. Then he went back to Sutter's Fort, where he found nearly everybody had gone prospecting, to talk with Sutter about constructing a warehouse at the Sacramento River Landing. A short time later he would build a hotel in Sacramento for travelers.

Brannan believed in advertising. When he felt he had his mercantile empire in order, he deliberately started the gold rush. Standing at the corner of what is now Portsmouth Square in San Francisco on May 12, he waved the bottle of gold with one hand, his hat with the other. "Gold!" he cried. "Gold from the American River!" It worked. By May 29 virtually the entire male population of the town had decamped for the goldfields. Soldiers left their posts, and sailors deserted their ships, leaving behind a forest of masts and slowly rotting hulls.

When the people in Monterey became convinced, they left in a body. Whole families picked up to go to the mines. The Reverend Mr. Walter Colton, then *alcalde* (chief magistrate) in Monterey, wrote, "The blacksmith dropped his hammer, the carpenter his plane, the mason his trowel, the farmer his sickle, the baker his loaf, and the taster his bottle. All were off for the mines, some on horses, some on carts, and some on crutches, and one went in a litter. An American woman who had recently established a boarding-house here pulled up stakes and was off before her lodgers had even time to pay their bills." Only one old man held out, saying it was "a Yankee invention got up to reconcile the people to the change of flag [Mexican to American]." Three seamen, Colton said, "ran from the *Warren*, forfeiting their four years' pay; and a whole platoon of soldiers from the fort left only their colors behind."

As Brannan and Sutter were making plans at Sutter's Fort, a military courier was saddling up in Los Angeles to carry the news and a bit of gold to Washington, D.C. A man more famous in his time than Sutter or Brannan or even Brigham Young, he was Christopher "Kit" Carson. Riding with a small group of men, he made his way to Santa Fe, where the paper noted his arrival but said he had "nothing of importance to report." No doubt he stopped in Taos, where his wife and family lived. Then on to Missouri, where he boarded a steamboat. He arrived in Washington on August 2, after a three-month trip.

Carson carried letters about the gold and a copy of the *California Star*, which Brannan as publisher and Kemble, his editor, had prepared. In it was a piece about the natural resources of California, including paragraphs about the gold finds. Brannan sent the paper also to eastern newspapers, some of which printed an abbreviated version of the story. The St. Louis and St. Joseph papers omitted mention of the gold, and the Washington, D.C., *Daily Union* followed suit. It was not until August 19 that any eastern newspaper took notice. The New York *Herald* published a story based on information from a member of the New York Volunteers who had been in California during the Mexican-American War. No doubt the newspapers thought it was "puff" or "humbug." In those days newspapers delighted in practical jokes—tall tales they tried to foist on gullible readers.

Even so, the information on gold was so buried in the wealth of detail about copper, quicksilver, asphaltum, and other mineral resources that "gold" did not impress the reader. It was not until after Col. Richard Mason, the U.S. military commander and acting American governor in California, in company with young Lt. William Tecumseh Sherman (later of Civil War fame), made an official tour of the mines that Americans not actually in California would believe it. On July 2 Mason's company stopped at Sutter's Fort, where, in contrast to deserted San Francisco, men were bustling about, bragging about their gold and buying supplies for another foray into the mines. Sutter butchered a steer and several sheep for a true Independence Day celebration and feted his guests royally at the table, not stinting on his finest champagne.

The next day the hung-over group toured Mormon Island in the Sacramento River, where the Mormons who had been working for Marshall were digging gold. About two hundred men were at work, knee-deep in the icy water. From there the party moved on to Coloma, where Marshall pointed out the momentous spot where he had first seen gold. Mason's entourage encountered another official group as well—four Frenchmen, led by the French consul, who were there for the same reason as Mason, to report back to their government.

Mason intended to continue his tour to the Feather, Bear, and Yuba rivers but was called back to Monterey for an important reason: the Treaty of Guadalupe Hidalgo, officially ending the war between the United States and Mexico, had not yet been ratified. California still did not legally belong to the United States. Even though he did not get to visit all the mines, his report was glowing:

> [At the Mormon diggings] the hill sides were thickly strewn with canvass tents and brush arbors. A store was erected, and several boarding shanties in operation. The day was intensely hot, yet about two hundred men were at work in the full glare of the sun, washing for gold, some with tin pans, some with close-woven Indian baskets, but the greater part had a rude machine known as a cradle. . . . The gold in [the Mormon diggings] is in fine bright scales, of which I [have] sent several specimens.
>
> Mr. Marshall guided me up the mountain, on the opposite or north bank of the South Fork [of the American River], where in the beds of small streams, or ravines, now dry, a great deal of the coarse gold has been found. I there saw several parties at work, all of whom were doing very well. . . .
>
> [On Weber's Creek] I found a great many people and Indians; some engaged in the bed of the stream, and others in the small side valleys that put into it. These latter were exceedingly rich, and two ounces were considered an ordinary yield for a day's work. A small gutter, not more than a hundred yards long by four feet wide and

two or three feet deep, was pointed out to me as the one where two men . . . a short time before obtained in seven days $17,000 worth of gold. . . .

Another small ravine . . . [had yielded] $12,000 worth of gold. Hundreds of similar ravines, to all appearances, are as yet untouched. . . . An agent of Commodore Stockton had been at work about three weeks . . . and showed me . . . over $2,000 worth of gold; and Mr. Lyman [who had worked below Sutter's sawmill, reported] that his share was at the rate of fifty dollars a day; but hearing that others were doing better at Weber's place, [he and his party] had removed there. . . .

[Mr. Dye of Monterey said that his party] worked seven weeks and two days . . . and that their gross product was 273 pounds of gold. . . . A soldier [returning from furlough had] made a sum of money [in a week] greater than he receives in pay, clothes, and rations during a whole enlistment of five years.

Colonel Mason calculated the value of gold at $16 an ounce. He pointed out that men could now earn more in one day in the mines as laborers than a soldier's pay amounted to in a month. No officer, he said, could now live in California on his pay at the inflated prices gold had brought. Soldiers were deserting right and left, not just to be day laborers, but to make their own "pile" in the mines. "No capital is required to obtain this gold," he wrote, "but pick, shovel, and tin pan with which to wash the gravel; and many frequently pick gold out of the crevices of rock with their butcher knives in pieces from one to six ounces."

Mason sent a tea caddy full of gold along with his letter. He entrusted these items to U.S. Army Lt. Lucien Loesser. Bearing the official news, Loesser left on August 30, opting for a sea voyage, except for a foot crossing of the Isthmus of Panama. A second courier, sent two weeks later by Colonel Mason, with duplicate copies of the letters in case Loesser did not get through, crossed Mexico and arrived in Washington on November 22.

On July 27 another messenger, U.S. Navy Lt. Edward Fitzgerald (Ned) Beale, had also set out for Washington, bearing a small sample of gold and the navy's report intended for Secretary of State James Buchanan and Secretary of the Navy James Mason. Beale's trip took him by sea to San Blas, then on horseback across the 400-mile, bandit-ridden Sierra Madre Occidental to Mexico City. He rode alone, disguised as a Mexican, and made this leg of his journey in eight days. From Mexico City he and a Mexican guide raced on horseback to Vera Cruz, a 275-mile leg they covered in forty-eight hours. There he caught a warship to Mobile, Alabama. At several places along the way he was approached by what he took to be bandits but eluded them all. He had an audience with President James K. Polk on September 18, but the president didn't seem to believe him, despite the gold samples he had brought.

Loesser did not arrive in New Orleans until November 23. He was still some distance from Washington, but he had the tea caddy full of gold, including Marshall's nugget.

FIGURE 7. Pick, pan, and shovel said to be Marshall's own. Whether these were Marshall's or not, implements like this were the chief tools of early miners.

So the news got to Washington in stages. Kit Carson arrived with letters and Brannan's *California Star* article on August 2. Beale, with his remarkable hell-for-leather spirit, arrived on September 16, only forty-nine days after he had left La Paz, his trip being more than a month faster than Kit Carson's. Mason's second courier arrived on November 22, two weeks before Loesser.

Now even President Polk began to believe. In his message to Congress on December 5 he told the nation of the great discovery. When Lieutenant Loesser finally arrived on December 7, President Polk put the gold, tea caddy and all, on display at the War Office. All doubt ceased, and once the eastern newspapers were convinced, they lost common sense. The *Literary American* of New York quoted the San Francisco alcalde as saying, "The streams are paved with gold—the mountains swell in their golden girdle—it sparkles in the sands of the valley—it glitters in the coronets of the cliffs."

California's gold was about to be harvested.

AFTER THE RUSH

For most of those who rushed to California when they heard the news of gold, it was to be the greatest adventure of their lives, whether they found any gold or not. For those already in California, the gold was a mixed blessing. Here is what happened to four of the leading figures in the California of 1848 and 1849.

JOHANN AUGUSTUS SUTTER
(1803–1880)

Sutter dreamed of empire in 1839 when he was granted 230 square miles of land near what is now Sacramento by the Mexican government. Born in Germany, he had moved to Switzerland, and then emigrated to the United States in 1834 and to California in 1839. He built Sutter's Fort, an imposing trading center for trappers, settlers, and merchants, on his land; near it he established the colony of Nueva Helvetia (New Switzerland).

When the hordes of forty-niners came, Sutter's dreams turned into nightmare. The title to his land grants cost so much to defend in court—the case went as high as the Supreme Court—that it took most of his money. Alcohol and mismanagement depleted the rest. Squatters tore up his property; gold rushers rustled his cattle. He held on to his Hock (*hoch*, German for "high") Farm, farther north in the Sacramento Valley, until creditors took it. He got it back, and an irate creditor set fire to it. He petitioned the government for assistance, claiming he had contributed materially to the development of California—certainly true, but nothing came of it. His family, who had remained in Switzerland most of the time he was in the United States, joined him in California; then all moved to Pennsylvania. To the end, he was charming and courteous, but poor. He died in Washington, D.C., in 1880.

Sutter's "fort," now part of the state park system, gives a glimpse of the California of long ago.

JAMES WILSON MARSHALL
(1810 – 1885)

Marshall arrived in California in 1845, in time to start the gold rush, and settled at Sutter's Fort. He was one of the Americans who declared themselves independent of Mexico during what has been called the Bear Flag Revolt in 1846. The small band of revolutionaries, encouraged by Capt. John Charles Frémont, captured Gen. Mariano Vallejo as well as the town of Sonoma, where they ran up over the plaza a flag of their own design bearing the image of a grizzly bear facing a red star and proclaimed the new California Republic. The republic lasted less than a month before U.S. troops occupied California.

Marshall and Sutter joined in building and operating a sawmill on the American River, where Marshall discovered gold. In spite of this success, which has reverberated through history, he was never good at finding gold again, although he was hired for his magic touch, which failed him.

He grew bitter through the years and trusted no one who came to California after 1848. The state legislature gave him a pension of $200 a month in 1872 but rescinded it when they heard he spent most of it on liquor. He died penniless. But Marshall was not forgotten. Five years after refusing his last request for help, the legislature voted $9,000 to erect a monument to him at Coloma, and his small nugget went to the Smithsonian Institution.

SAMUEL BRANNAN
(1819 – 1889)

The saddest end of all the leading figures was Sam Brannan's, advertiser of the gold find. Dapper, engaging, friendly, he became the state's first millionaire through his business efforts. He acquired large holdings in San Francisco and Sacramento, including a bank that issued his own paper money. He helped found the first English-language school (before the gold rush) and was generous to charities. His was the first newspaper, the California *Star*.

He enjoyed being a "good fellow" and took up drinking with the "boys." He gave up being a Mormon, never joined Brigham Young in Utah, never forwarded the tithes he had collected from the gold-mining Mormons. He even cheated his friend, Sutter. His wife, who had accompanied him to California in 1846, did not realize he was already married and had left his first wife and child behind. He said he had the church's permission (Mormons allowed themselves multiple wives), but he was certainly a backslidden Mormon by the time his second wife found out. The divorce settlement cost him most of his fortune.

Drink finally claimed him. When he died in 1889, his body was held in a San Diego vault for sixteen months until his nephew removed it and buried him.

JOHN BIDWELL
(1819 – 1900)

Of all the forty-eighters who mined gold, perhaps John Bidwell came out the best. General Bidwell (he was a general in the California militia) had led the first overland party of settlers to California, arriving in 1841. He, like Marshall, worked for Sutter, but not for long. He may have missed being recognized as the first discoverer of California's gold (see chapter 2), but he did find the first gold on the Feather River—a very rich bar that would bear his name: Bidwell's Bar. Bidwell did not mine long, but he found a lot of gold and used it to buy land to farm. He developed an agricultural showplace of 20,000 acres, enclosed in 60 miles of board fence, kept a crew of 100 men to take care of 2,500 acres in wheat, 700 in barley, and nearly 700 more in oats; 1,500 head of cattle, 3,000 sheep, 300 horses; and 300 acres of orchard planted with pomegranates, figs, English walnuts, cherries, peaches, apricots, almonds, and apples. His experimental orchard included 1,800 acres of every species and variety that would grow in the region.

Always a public servant, he was a state senator, a delegate to the Democratic Convention, and a member of Congress. He was a candidate for governor in 1890 on the Prohibition ticket and was nominated for president on the same ticket but chose not to run.

In 1860 he founded the town of Chico on his ranch. In 1889 he helped found what is now Chico State University, donating the land for it. Bidwell's home is now part of the California state park system. After his death (he died while cutting down a tree), his widow donated 1,900 acres for lovely Bidwell Park in his memory.

Bidwell had his priorities right. He had found California's true worth—the land. In his diary for 1892, on file at the California State Library, he made a brief note saying he'd been asked to run for president. On another leaf, in large capital letters taking up the whole page: "FIRST RIPE STRAWBERRY!"

CHAPTER FOUR

Rushing to Cash In

Even Sam Brannan was not prepared for the results his words would bring. Events moved so fast no one could keep close track of them. The world rushed in to California, and time rushed by, giving little chance to pause for reflection.

By the end of May 1848 people already in California had taken out a fortune in gold. In June people in Hawaii heard of the strike, and ships sailed at once for California. In August word got to Oregon, and by early fall gossip passed down to Mexico and the rest of Latin America. The "rush" of '48 was small, but it was a portent of things to come.

When people on the eastern seaboard became convinced about California gold—some even saw Colonel Mason's gold at the War Department—they were ready to believe anything, and many of them set right out for California. They went home, took their life savings if they had any or borrowed if they didn't, pawned what they could, and hurried down to the waterfront to get space on a ship heading west. The year before they would have had difficulty borrowing money at all. The United States was a poor country in the 1840s; people were working for low wages, and frugality was the watchword. But now California beckoned and purse strings loosened. Relatives, neighbors, even banks lent money for the California adventure.

Besides his fare, each passenger carried with him money as a grubstake. An early handbook advised capital of about $750, which was not enough, according to most emigrants. The proper amount was about $1,000, but many had only $600, most of it in gold coins.

Once they got money for their trip, the argonauts, as they were called, after the crew of Jason's ship *Argo,* who set out to find and rob the Golden Fleece, bought themselves what merchants told them was a proper California outfit. It consisted of a red or blue woolen shirt, homespun flannel underwear, a wide-brimmed felt hat, a knee-length coat, high boots, baggy jeans, trunks, and waterproof rubber bags for gear. One young man took 17 pairs of underwear, 12 new flannel shirts, 18 new checked shirts, 5 white muslin shirts, 7 coats, and 5 waistcoats, most of which he ended up giving or throwing away. Some who expected to strike it rich and live the life of luxury even took evening clothes.

Everyone went well armed. A revolver at the belt, a small pistol in the vest pocket, heavy bowie knives, even walking sticks with concealed swords and blackjacks for hip pockets were recommended. Some took all this and added a rifle or shotgun. They expected to use this arsenal to protect their claims when they got to California. If they went by land, the guns would help find meat for the table and kill Indians. They paraded around town, dressed in all their glory, to the envy of their family and neighbors, who stayed behind to carry the daily burdens.

An alternative to sea or land travel was offered by Rufus Porter, founder of the then new journal *Scientific American.* He advertised three-day balloon flights powered by steam engines from eastern states to California at a cost of $50 per person, wine included. It would be a comfortable trip, he said, sailing over the mountains to the astonishment of staring grizzly bears. He calculated that his eight-hundred-foot-long Aerial Locomotive, as he called it, would travel as fast as one hundred miles per hour, but he forgot to factor in air resistance. His ship did not go, as he failed to scrape up enough takers. Then bad weather set in and vandals wrecked his aircraft and destroyed his hopes.

But men from Boston, New York, Nantucket, all along the coast, part of a seafaring tradition, thought only of the sea. In 1849 virtually all uncommitted ships on the East Coast, including many that had not been considered safe for many years and had been abandoned as useless, their hulls rotted out, were fitted up for California. More than seventy of New England's whaling fleet were turned into passenger ships, although the whaling stench remained. All too many of the old ships became "floating coffins" that ceased floating on the stormy seas or in the ice-bound Antarctic and disappeared.

In mid-January 1849, in the very early days of the gold rush, Horace Greeley's newspaper, the New York *Tribune,* which tried to keep some track of the rush, admitted that there was a "wide diversity of opinion" as to how many people had left the East for California. More than 10,000, the *Tribune* guessed, and placed the number of persons who had already sailed at 2,212. So great was the fever that by January, a fifth of the voting population of Plymouth, Massachusetts, had left for the goldfields.

Those who came by ship could go around the tip of South America, either around Cape Horn next to Antarctica—the longer route—or, like Drake, through the more dangerous Strait of Magellan. It was a 13,000- to 15,000-mile passage

FIGURE 8. Mr. Golightly on his way to California, 1849. Although he is not on Rufus Porter's Aerial Locomotive, he has a fast way to the Golden State. Below him are ships bound for California the slow way. On his back is a Patent Gold Washing Machine as well as tobacco and other goods for sale. Mr. Golightly is saying, "I wish Jemima could see me now, goin through the Firmament like a streak of greased lightnin on a telegraphic wire. I guess she'd feel sorter vexed that she didn't pack up her fixins and go long—When I get to Californy I'll let others do the diggins while I do the swappins."

(depending on how you went) fraught with boredom, insect-ridden food and foul water, disease, extremes of weather—from the heat of the tropics to the icy cold of Antarctica—and the ever-present possibility of shipwreck. South and Central American cities were treated to constant streams of brash, arrogant, swaggering young Americans, ready to find their fortune by sheer braggadocio. They criticized everything unusual or foreign to them and caused trouble wherever they stopped. The local populace viewed this horde with alarm and cupidity, sequestering their daughters and charging high and sometimes extortionate prices for food and lodging.

Many of the ships sailing from the eastern United States for California in 1849 carried joint stock companies especially organized for the trip. During that year 102

FIGURE 9. The steamer *Hartford* as she leaves New York for California in February 1849.

such companies sailed from Massachusetts alone, each consisting of from 5 to 180 members, for a total of 4,200. Many companies tried to incorporate the magic word "California" in their names. The companies pooled their resources, chartered or bought a ship, elected officers, and voted rules of conduct. On all ships hopes were high. Members of the Hartford Union Mining and Trading Company ruled that members would deposit the gold they found in the company's strongbox on the ship every day. (They had no idea how far it was from the mines to the port of San Francisco.) If they were to find so many tons that it would overburden the ship, part would be left behind, under guard.

Even if they found no gold, the joint stock company members counted on making a great profit on the goods they took to sell to the newly rich but deprived Californians. Swords, ladies' hats (although there were almost no women in San Francisco or the mines), fur-lined overcoats, robes, mittens, and bolts of cloth were a few of the choices. Honey, dried apples, varnish, and furniture were others. The bark *San Francisco*, reported Oscar Lewis in *Sea Routes to the Gold Fields*, loaded up with 63,000 feet of lumber, 10,000 bricks, and 8 prefabricated houses. Some ships brought items that did not survive the voyage: barrels of wine that went to vinegar,

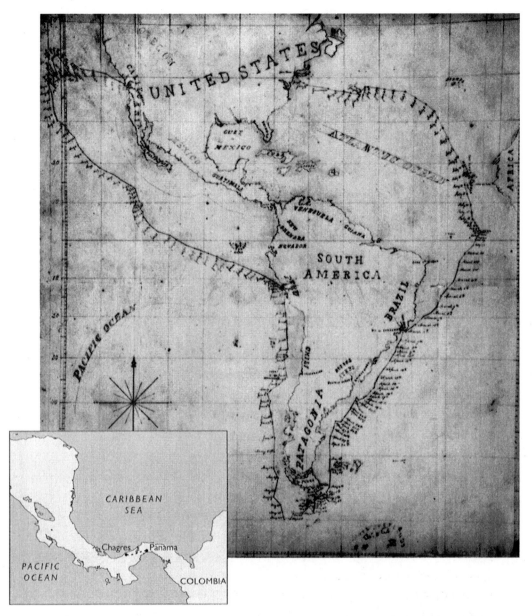

MAP 4. Sea routes to the goldfields. Some passengers took ships going around the tip of South America (the Horn), which carried them into Antarctic waters. The ship's captain could choose to go all the way past the tip of South America or sail up the Strait of Magellan. Other passengers sailed only as far as Central America (inset map), where they took canoes partway and then walked across the isthmus.

Shown here is the route of the *Apollo,* which left New York on January 16, 1849, and arrived in San Francisco on September 18, 1849. This map was hand drawn by a passenger on board. This is a reduction of what he originally drew. What appear here to be tiny "tick" marks are notes giving the date and location of each point. The final resting place of the *Apollo* is shown on page 59.

meat that rotted, fruit juice that fermented and exploded, candles that melted in the heat. No one could tell what would sell and what wouldn't. One enterprising young French journalist set up his own outdoor market when he got to San Francisco. The two items that sold best were toothpicks and French watches. The toothpicks he sold in packs of twelve for fifty cents; the watches, for which he had paid nine francs each, went for $3 to $6, depending on size. He told his customers they came from the Royal French Watch Company and would keep perfect time for five years. In actual fact, he confessed, "some ran for 10 minutes, some for a quarter of an hour, others for half an hour, and a few even for a whole day; but to make up for this it cannot be denied that many would not run at all."

Rich and poor, somebodies and nobodies made the trip. The *Pacific* brought young Mark Hopkins, later to be one of the "Big Four" builders of the transcontinental railroad. The bark *Orb* carried only twenty-two passengers, mostly from leading Boston families, including Charles Francis Adams, Jr., grandson of one president, great-grandson of another. In spite of the high cost of the passage— $1,000—the *Orb* was overloaded, neither fast nor comfortable, and took nearly seven months to arrive in San Francisco.

The *Edward Everett*, almost as expensive as the *Orb*, left Boston on January 13, 1849, with one hundred fifty men, including eight sea captains, four doctors, a clergyman, a mineralogist, a geologist, merchants, farmers, artisans, manufacturers, and students. The ship's equipment included lightning rods and even cannons to fend off pirates. The hold was stuffed with what the passengers considered vital: wagons, spades, picks, wheelbarrows, bricks, a steam-powered launch, four steam engines, and lumber for two houses.

The cheapest fare on record—$200—was paid by the sixty members of the Cochituate Company who sailed in late 1849 on the schooner *Civiliana*.

After the first weeks of seasickness, most passengers found poor food and boredom their major problems. They sublimated the former by complaining loudly, and the latter by keeping diaries that make interesting reading today. And there were other antidotes to boredom. Musicians among the *Edward Everett*'s passengers formed a band, and would-be reporters published a newspaper. The mineralogist and geologist gave informative weekly lectures. The doctors manned a small dispensary, and even a police force was appointed. When this fine ship reached San Francisco, she, like hundreds of others, was sold, as no crew could be found to take her back. She brought only $11,000, far less than her value.

On the *Edward Everett*, as on many California-bound ships, practical jokes were the order of the day. Word was passed around as they prepared to round the Horn that whoever wanted to escape the feared trip could debark at Patagonia and walk across to Valparaiso, braving cannibals and ferocious wild beasts. About twenty vol-

OH, CALIFORNIA!

Tune: "Oh, Susannah"

I came from Salem City,
With my washbowl on my knee,
I'm going to California,
The gold dust for to see.
It rained all night the day I left,
The weather it was dry,
The sun so hot I froze to death
Oh, brothers don't you cry!

Chorus:
Oh, California,
That's the land for me!
I'm bound for San Francisco
With my banjo on my knee.

I jumped aboard the 'Liza ship
And traveled on the sea,
And every time I thought of home
I wished it wasn't me!
The vessel reared like any horse
That had of oats a wealth
I found it wouldn't throw me, so
I thought I'd throw myself!

I soon shall be in Frisco,
And there I'll look around,
And when I see the gold lumps there,
I'll pick them off the ground.
I'll scrape the mountains clean, my boys,
I'll drain the rivers dry
A pocketful of rocks bring home—
So brothers don't you cry!

unteered and were drilled every morning to put them in good physical shape and instill proper discipline. Apparently no one bothered to check the ship's charts to note that it was more than eight hundred miles from Patagonia to Valparaiso as the crow flies. After following a "drill sergeant" through rigorous exercises for some days, they got the joke.

On another ship passengers spent their time pilfering the galley. When the cook set out a hot mince pie to cool and found it gone, he'd had enough. He baked a special pie laced with jalap, a quick-acting purgative. The thievery stopped.

On the *James W. Paige,* passengers started a rumor that pirates were about to attack. One night they threw barrels overboard to simulate the pirate ship, then shouted that the ship was being boarded. The intended butt of the joke, who had confessed his deathly fear of pirates, to his credit snatched up a pump handle and raced to where the fictitious pirates were supposed to be clambering on board, bent on selling his life dearly.

On most ships all the men sang—even those who couldn't. The greatest favorite was a new popular song by Stephen Foster, "Oh, Susannah!" With its humorous verses, it easily lent itself to parody and became the theme song of the California argonauts.

The voyage around the end of South America was what the argonauts remembered best. Although the route through the Strait of Magellan was shorter in miles, it could be longer in time. It took thirty-six days for the *Sea Eagle* to make the 150-mile trip up the strait to Port Famine, a Chilean penal colony and the only anchorage in the strait. Whether they went this way or around the tip, the ship and all in it were constantly wet or frozen. Scarcely any passenger could keep his meals down. Many ships did not leave the East Coast until the spring of 1849 and did not reach the Horn until the dead of the Antarctic winter. Still, most passengers voted to go around the Horn. There they encountered constant wind (from the wrong direction), subzero temperatures—sometimes as low as –60°F—and nights sixteen hours long. To make a mile of progress required twenty miles of sailing, and that progress might be erased in a few minutes of heavy gale.

All the ships did not make it, and for some, no one ever knew what had become of ship or passengers. Those that did make it proceeded up the South American coast, where the weather grew warmer and warmer until it was so hot the passengers slept on deck and could not imagine ever having been cold.

Some ships made very fast passages. The handsome clipper ships were the fastest. The clipper *Flying Cloud* made the passage in 89 days in 1851. The longest trip was 300 days in a paddle-wheel steamer. Most who made it at all took at least 115 days to get from Boston or New York to San Francisco.

One of the sights 'round-the-Horn travelers welcomed as a break in their otherwise generally monotonous routine (storms excepted) was a glimpse of Juan Fernández, a group of three islands off the coast of Chile. The argonauts knew well Daniel Defoe's book *Robinson Crusoe*, one of the few classics they all had read. Many felt they knew Robinson personally and were eager to point out where and how he lived. Few of them remembered that "Robinson Crusoe" was not his name, that the real person Defoe took as a model was one Alexander Selkirk, who later regretted leaving his island.

Something of the difficulties of the 'round-the-Horn trip can be gleaned from the adventures of Captain and Mrs. D. B. Bates of Kingston, Massachusetts. They left Baltimore on July 27, 1850, on board Captain Bates's ship, the *Nonantum*. It was a small ship, carrying only six passengers, fifty tons of freight, and coal. Off the Falkland Islands it caught fire. The crew and passengers barely made it to shore. For a month they languished on the islands until a passing ship, the *Humayoon* from Dundee, agreed to take them and a goat they had acquired in the Falklands on board. This small Scottish ship lasted only as far as Tierra del Fuego, where it caught fire and burned. Their wait was shorter this time, as the first vessel passing by, a coaler named the *Fanchon*, took the Bateses and goat on board. By this time the goat and a small carpet were all the Bateses had.

By Christmas the ship had worked its way up to a point near the Galápagos Islands, but Christmas festivities were disturbed by the smell of burning coal. The captain made for the coast of Peru. This time Mrs. Bates, having been shipwrecked twice before on the journey, elected to wear men's clothing in order to be better protected from unknown danger and exposure. She chose black pants, a green hunting coat, a black satin vest, and a purple velvet smoking cap. In this striking garb she landed, with her husband and the goat, on the coast. The *Fanchon* burned to the waterline.

The Bateses were two months in Valparaíso before a passing ship would take them toward the Golden Gate, and then only at the sacrifice of the pet goat, which the captain of the vessel *Republic* required they give the cook for food, even though he also charged them $1,200. Finally, ten months after leaving Massachusetts, the unsinkable couple arrived in San Francisco.

Ships from Europe could go around the Horn, too, and most did; but they could also sail east and cross the Pacific to join ships from Australia and the Orient. No one will ever know how many people set out for the goldfields, either from the United States or from foreign lands, or how many actually arrived. France sent 35 ships and more than 2,000 people to California early in the gold rush and held a lottery in 1850 to send 5,000 more. Each ticket cost one franc (roughly twenty cents). The tickets sold rapidly all over Europe. Frenchmen who won the lottery and traveled to California arrived too late to win the early mined gold, and many had to be helped home by the French consulate.

Australia and New Zealand together contributed at least 7,000 to 8,000 people to the rush—a large percentage of the population of the two territories. Shipload after shipload left to go to California, including some convicts and ex-convicts Americans called Sydney Ducks. A few convicts were hardened criminals, but others, sentenced to "transportation" (i.e., out of England) were guilty only of petty crimes. The Ducks were to gain an unsavory reputation in San Francisco, deserved or not, but the other Australians, petty criminals and immigrants alike, either blended into California life or sailed back to Australia. One who sailed back after finding little gold was Edward Hargraves, who thought the geology in Australia looked similar to what he'd seen in California. He went out prospecting with the help of a young boy and opened up Australia's fabulous gold box. Ships from the South Pacific found a danger not reported by those going around the Horn: pirates. The danger was not great. Only one or two ships were taken by pirates, and one of them was taken by a group of Australian ex-convicts who stole the ship right out of an Australian port.

Some American and European argonauts went to the Pacific from Atlantic ports another way, by a route that cut thousands of miles and many weeks off their trip. They took a ship from New York to Panama or to Nicaragua. In Panama, a land route began at Chagres, on the Caribbean side of the Isthmus of Panama. There the

FIGURE 10. Forty-niners who chose to go through Central America, a shortcut that saved time but was perilous and hazardous to health, traveled along the Chagres River in native canoes called bungas.

argonauts boarded a small steamboat for a seventeen-mile trip up the Chagres River. Then they switched to small, flat-bottomed native boats called *bungas*. The land bordering the Chagres was lush and tropical; bright-colored birds flitted through the trees, monkeys leaped from limb to limb, flowers overhung the river, crocodiles waited in it, and "nekid negroes," who quickly learned to sing "Oh, Susannah!" plied the bungas. When navigable water ran out at the village of Gorgona, the travelers walked or boarded mule trains with native drivers to take them onward to Panama City on the Pacific.

The trip by mule was only four or five days long, but it was petrifying. The rain forest was so thick on either side of the narrow trail that the argonauts could see no more than ten feet into it and the undergrowth so dense they could scarcely breathe. In places the trail had been eroded so deeply that the normal hillside was thirty feet above the mule's head and so narrow a loaded animal could scarcely squeeze along it. One traveler counted forty dead mules and horses along the route in 1849. Many gold seekers made this mule crossing while plodding ankle deep in mud in a hot

FIGURE 11. Bungas could go only some of the way. California-bound travelers took mules and walked across a part of the Isthmus of Panama.

tropical downpour, unable to see the trail beneath their feet through the clouds of mosquitoes.

Each passenger had to have his own equipment, including blankets and food. He—now and then she—would sleep either in the dripping open or in mosquito- and flea-infested bamboo huts. They were under constant threat of malaria, dysen- tery, cholera, and Panama fever.

Among those who took the Central American cutoff was twenty-four-year-old Jessie Benton Frémont, wife of John Charles Frémont, called the "Pathfinder." She braved Panama in 1849, while her husband's exploring party was snowbound in the San Juan Mountains of Colorado, struggling to survive without resorting to eating one another. Besides Mrs. Frémont, Irene McCready, soon to be one of San Francisco's earliest madams, and numerous would-be politicians made the crossing. One wag said that at one point there were 600 lawyers waiting impatiently in Panama, of whom 400 expected to be California congressmen. Seventeen, he said, were already stumping for governor, and 21 for U.S. senator.

The cost of the sixty-mile crossing was about $100, plus meals and "lodging." In 1855 the Panama railroad began operation, and the length of the trip was reduced to three hours, the cost to $25.

When the forty-niners arrived at Panama City they found crowds of gold seekers lined up waiting for ships to take them to California. During the wait many came down with what the argonauts called "tropical fever." They blamed it on whiskey and fruit, not realizing the source was polluted water. Some died, far from home. One party, after having been drenched by rain for sixty hours without respite, came down with fever; all but one died.

Despite shipwreck and disaster, most argonauts got to California. The San Francisco Custom House logged 15,597 immigrants arriving in San Francisco via Cape Horn in 1849, and 6,489 managed the trip across the isthmus.

The sight that greeted the newcomers at San Francisco was like none any had seen in other ports of the world. To be sure, the land was beautiful: flower-bedecked hills, shining clear water, a few sandy beaches, a bay of lovely shape took the new-comers' breath away. But closer up the view was startling. A tent city flapped on a nearby hillside, and a forest of masts filled the natural harbor—the masts of many abandoned ships, far more impressive than the small city itself. "Shipping in such numbers it was absolutely impossible to enumerate them," wrote one forty-niner. "They looked to us as if they were piled up one on top of the other." These were, of course, the ships of those who had gotten there earlier, abandoned by their crews in haste to get to the goldfields. By July 1849 the forty-niners could see more than 200 stranded ships, among them Chinese junks, lateen-rigged Mediterranean sailing ships, and others that had once flown the flags of many nations. A year later there were 526 abandoned ships visible, and some had already sunk or been converted to other uses.

By 1852 the ships were beyond repair. "These ships," wrote a newcomer, "had a very old, ruinous, antiquated appearance, and at first sight, gave me an impression, that this new-born city had been inhabited for ages and was now going to ruin. Most of them have their lower masts standing, supported by a few ropes and chains. . . . [Some] have been converted to storeships. . . . [Some] had doors cut into their sides, with short flights of steps from the water. Some were run aground near the shore, and wharves and streets were built around them, where, with houses erected on them they could scarcely be distinguished from the surrounding stores." One ship had become a bank, another a church, and one a prison.

The ships all came to San Francisco rather than Monterey, California's capital, because from San Francisco would-be miners could board ships and boats that would take them up the Sacramento River as far as Sutter's Fort. This saved many miles of walking or riding on horseback and was more comfortable except for the clouds of mosquitoes that lurked near the riverbanks.

Argonauts from North and South America could come by land if they wished, and most did, particularly if they did not hail from a seafaring tradition. Those from the United States who came by land generally chose a Missouri town as staging point. Independence, St. Louis, and St. Joseph got most of the traffic, although Council Bluffs, Iowa, was another gateway. If the miners had not already formed into companies much like those who came by ship, they did so in these towns. In Missouri or Iowa they could purchase oxen, mules, wagons, and supplies—perhaps hire guides—to take them to the golden land. Even so, not everyone chose to be a member of a wagon train. One Scotsman pushed a wheelbarrow containing his gear to California; another walked all the way from Maine with his bulldog at his feet and his knapsack on his back.

The covered wagons chosen by most forty-niners were small and light, about ten feet long by four feet wide. They were pulled by oxen or mules. A team of three yoke of oxen (a total of six animals) could pull more than a ton of food and other supplies. The wagons had neither brakes nor springs. If necessary, the wagon beds could be caulked and used as rafts. The top was canvas, stretched over hickory bows. Most wagons started out painted in gaudy colors—red, white, and blue being favorites. Some had names: "Gold Hunter" and "Wild Yankee," for example. By the time the travelers reached California—if they did—the paint and name had long ago worn off.

Men on horseback rode alongside the wagon train to herd the thirty or more extra cattle planned as replacements for the yoked oxen as well as food for the trip. The wagons had little room for seats, so most forty-niners walked to California in the dust kicked up by the train. Because everyone was deathly afraid of Indians, the trains were oversupplied with weapons. Before the journey was over, more people were accidentally killed or wounded by wagon train guns than were killed or wounded by arrows.

Several land routes led across the United States (see map 5). Some wagon trains worked their way west to the Santa Fe Trail, which began at St. Joseph, Missouri, and ended at Santa Fe, New Mexico. From there they had a choice of several routes to California. Others chose the Mormon Trail, blazed just a few years before by Brigham Young and his followers, fleeing from persecution in eastern states. That trail went to Salt Lake City, then on to Los Angeles, because the Mormon Battalion had been recruited to serve the United States in California during the Mexican-American War. Nearly paralleling the Mormon Trail part of the way was the slightly older Oregon Trail, which bypassed Salt Lake City and went north to Fort

MAP 5. The United States as of 1846. Settlers headed for California then were pushing into Mexican territory. President James K. Polk, through diplomacy and war, acquired a vast territory in the west for the United States (west of the gray line). He succeeded in consolidating the nation but died before realizing the magnitude of his accomplishment. The routes marked were those available to forty-niners, if they did not mind braving Indian and Mexican wrath as well as deserts. Several of these routes are now designated National Historic Trails: the Anza, the Mormon, the Oregon, and the Santa Fe.

Forty-niners and settlers who did not stay with established trails sometimes met disaster. The Hastings Cutoff — now the Donner Pass, near Interstate 80 — led an immigrant party of 1846 into serious trouble. They were stranded in the mountains during a very severe winter, and many died. Some were able to survive by eating the dead bodies of their comrades. Another forty-niner party nearly died of thirst and starvation when they took an ill-advised cutoff through Death Valley.

Vancouver in Oregon Territory. To get to California, travelers branched off the Oregon Trail and took another route over the Sierra Nevada, often the California Trail, which led to Sutter's Fort. One variant, used by few, was to take a ship to Refugio, Texas, then travel the Sonora Trail through Mexico to San Diego.

The two-thousand-mile trip from St. Joseph or Independence along the Oregon-California road was popular with the argonauts. During much of the journey, travelers could see wagon trains ahead of and behind them, like elephants in a circus parade. But travelers had to choose the right time to leave. Too soon, and the grass had not grown enough to support the animals. Too late, and it would all be eaten. According to one count made at Fort Kearney (now in Nebraska), 2,754 wagons, averaging four to five people per wagon, had passed by May 21, 1849. Seventy-six of the travelers were women. At Fort Laramie, Wyoming, the register listed 32,000

FIGURE 12. Horses being driven into a corral formed by wagons, to keep them from straying or being stolen. Horses did not pull the wagons; they were ridden alongside. Generally oxen pulled the wagons, as they were sturdier, cheaper, and less desired by Indians and could be eaten in an emergency. Mules, chosen by some immigrants, were more expensive but faster, which sometimes meant the difference between life and death for the travelers. This print is from the 1860s, but the equipment the forty-niners used was nearly the same.

men, women, and children by June 16. By late August the total was 42,000. One guess is that 26,000 to 30,000 people took the Oregon-California road in 1849.

All travelers faced three major dangers: desert, hostile Indians, and disease, particularly cholera. No matter which way the forty-niners went, there were deserts ahead. The Sonoran Desert in Mexico daunted the Mexico travelers; the Mojave and Colorado deserts had to be faced by those on the southern routes. The Oregon and Mormon trails passed through the dreaded salt deserts of what is now Utah. Deserts the travelers had never heard of, like the Black Rock Desert of Nevada and Death Valley of southern California, brought ruin or death to some.

One group of forty-niners who called themselves the Jayhawkers got to Salt Lake too late in the winter of 1849 to attempt to cross the Sierra Nevada. They decided to take the Mormon Trail, cut down to Los Angeles, and then go north again. But some impatient, gold-hungry young men decided to take a shortcut over the mountains. They were given a map they never understood and within a few days were hopelessly lost deep in the California desert. They went this way and that, looking for a way over the mountains, but found none. They ate their cattle, and when they killed one, they used the bloody hide to wrap their own feet, now virtually shoeless, and the feet of the animals that were still alive. They baked in the sun by day and shivered in the cold by night. Once they came upon a marker they hoped would be a trail sign, but it merely marked the grave of a comrade they had buried the day before. They had been going in circles. They were always hungry. Their tongues turned black and became so swollen they could neither speak nor swallow. A providential snowstorm, which melted at once, saved their lives.

As the cattle died, they picked the carcasses, sucked the marrow bones, even chewed the hides. For three months they roamed the desert. At last, mere skeletons, they looked over into a valley with rich green grass where fat cattle grazed. They shot one, and when the kindly Spanish Californio owner found them clawing like wild beasts at the uncooked flesh, he took them to his hacienda to recuperate.

As the forty-niner migration continued, the road from Missouri to California became known as "the trail of the moldering ox." Tens of thousands of the patient, surefooted, plodding creatures left from Missouri. Thousands died of thirst, of bad water, of starvation, of being eaten, and of Indian arrows. No one stopped to bury the animals—the forty-niners were too greedy for gold—and the stench of the rotting corpses hung heavy in the air. Eventually the flesh decomposed or was eaten by wild animals and the skeleton bleached in the hot sun. Rows of white bones, punctuated now and then by crosses on the graves of luckless forty-niners, marked the trail.

Wagon trains that had started jubilantly wound into California decimated, exhausted, hungry, and often destitute. As the animals died and the trail got more difficult, they were obliged to leave food and possessions behind. Some forty-niners, eager to get all the gold for themselves, poisoned the flour and food they had to leave, and even burned the grass behind them so there would be no food for animals. Others, aware that their abandoned possessions might save someone else's life, stored them carefully. Wagons, too, had to be left when there was no beast alive to pull them, and cherished, heavy possessions—even pianos—were unceremoniously dumped by the trail.

Eastern Americans were less fearful of the deserts than of Indians, chiefly because they had no idea of the dangers of the desert. Early travelers had little trouble with Indians—Indians even saved the lives of some forty-niners—but by the time arrogant, bigoted young male America made its way across the continent, the Indians had lost patience. The youthful forty-niners were eager to shoot at anything

SWEET BETSY FROM PIKE

Oh, don't you remember sweet Betsy from Pike,
Who crossed the big mountains with her lover Ike,
With two yoke of oxen, a big yellow dog,
A tall Shanghai rooster and one spotted hog.

The Shanghai ran off, and their cattle all died;
That morning the last piece of bacon was fried.
Poor Ike was discouraged, and Betsy got mad
The dog drooped his tail and looked wonder-
    fully sad.

They soon reached the desert, where Betsy gave out.
And down in the sand she lay rolling about;
While Ike, half distracted, looked on with surprise,
Saying, "Betsy, get up, you'll get sand in your eyes."

They suddenly stopped on a very high hill,
With wonder looked down upon old Placerville;
Ike sighed when he said, and he cast his eyes down,
"Sweet Betsy, my darling, we've got to Hangtown."

Long Ike and sweet Betsy attended a dance;
Ike wore a pair of his Pike County pants;
Sweet Betsy was covered with ribbons and rings;
Says Ike, "You're an angel, but where are your
    wings?"

---

that moved, and wagon masters and scouts had a hard time keeping them under control. From the time of the gold rush until the end of the century it was to be "White versus Red." Both sides suffered from a lack of discrimination of guilt. Americans might shoot an Indian trying to steal a forty-niner horse—a brave deed by Indian standards, a hanging offense by white standards. The Indians, in retaliation, attacked not that wagon train, which may have gone on by, but the next. This provoked retaliation by the next wagon train to see the carnage, and so on. The particularity of guilt was ignored, and soon all whites saw any and all Indians as enemies, and vice versa.

The total number of people who died by Indian attack was fairly small, despite Hollywood propaganda. More Indians were killed by whites than whites by Indians. Disease was the main killer. Cholera was the most feared as it swept through North America in 1849 and devastated whole wagon trains and ships. Many were the pitiful grave markers left along the trail where fathers, mothers, and children died of the virulent disease.

The party led by John Woodhouse Audubon, son of the naturalist John James Audubon, was nearly eliminated by cholera on the southern route through Texas and Mexico. Audubon survived and went on to California, not so much for gold as to study the wildlife. He took many specimens and made countless sketches, all of which were lost when he sent them back East on the ill-fated steamship *Central America* in 1857 (see chapter 11).

FIGURE 13. An immigrant party on the way to California. Wagons have broken, animals have died.

Cholera had moved up the Mississippi River from New Orleans to St. Louis, a major rendezvous for the gold miners, then to the other outfitting towns. One argonaut wrote home that he saw at least four fresh graves each day for the first 170 miles of wagon travel. Bayard Taylor, a journalist covering the gold rush, later estimated the total of deaths by cholera among forty-niners on the various trails at four thousand.

The long trail just wore some travelers out, particularly when they got to the waterless deserts, where older people, children, and tired, thirsty animals in particular succumbed.

When they arrived in California—those who did—whether they came by ship to San Francisco or overland to Sutter's Fort, the forty-niners were shocked to find thousands there before them and prices sky-high. One could live a week in the East for what it took to live a day in San Francisco or the mines. A full meal in San Francisco cost at least $3—three times what an ordinary laborer earned for a day's work back East. Whiskey went for $40 a quart. It was cheaper to go on the wagon, but even water sold for $1 a pail. Regular hotel rooms, with some privacy, cost as much as $250 a week. Rooming houses offered wooden planks against the wall for $8 a night. It was BYOB—bring your own bedding (although rooming houses did furnish fleas)—and share the room with as many strangers as could be packed in. A few amenities were included: one lodging establishment provided a tied-down toothbrush and comb for communal use.

Despite this attempt at cleanliness, San Francisco was filthy, flimsy, and crowded. Few permanent buildings lined the streets. Tents serving as stores, gambling halls, or dwelling places flapped in the strong winds. When the winter rains came, the streets turned to mud. Dogs and—it was said—even drunks drowned in the mire, and horses sometimes sank so deep they could not be pulled out and were shot. One jokester posted a sign at a major intersection: "This street is not passable, not even jackassable." To try to provide some footing in the mud, San Franciscans threw all manner of unwanted or unsold, often smelly, goods into the mud—rotten food, dead animals, even a shipload of cookstoves. San Francisco's civic enterprise was in its infancy. It would take great efforts to provide clean water and keep sewage at bay, so few tried. Much of what law and order there was, was corrupt.

Gracious living it was not, and there were worse jolts to come.

San Francisco as it appeared in November 1848, a year after the village of Yerba Buena had been given its new name. The town had already grown from a one-tent town in 1835 to a two-house city in 1836. Ten years later Americans began to arrive in force—a shipload of sailors to "secure" Yerba Buena for the United States, a contingent of 238 Mormons en route to the Promised Land in Utah. By late 1848, after Marshall found his small nugget, the town had grown even more as word spread to Mexico, South America, and Hawaii. Even so, foreigners were a rarity. The three Chinese in town—two women and one man—were objects of curiosity.

What a difference a year makes! This lithograph, made from almost the same place, shows a forest of masts in the bay and a host of new buildings in the town, with flapping tents dotted through like windblown laundry. By the end of 1849 San Francisco had a "population of twenty-five thousand—mostly men, young or of middle age, very few women, fewer children, with here and there a bewildered matron or maiden of good repute," wrote John Williamson Palmer in *Century Magazine* of 1892. "Here were British subjects, Frenchmen, Germans, and Dutch, Italians, Spaniards, Norwegians, Swedes, and Swiss, Jews, Turks, Chinese, Kanakas [Hawaiian Islanders], New Zealanders, Malays, and Negroes, Parthians, Medes, and Elamites, Cretes and Arabians, and the dwellers in Mesopotamia and Cappadocia, in Boston and New Orleans, Chicago and Peoria, Hoboken and Hackensack."

A California lodging room.

"And how did they live?" Palmer continued. "In frame-houses of one story, more commonly in board shanties and canvas tents, pitched in the midst of sand or mud and various rubbish and strange filth and fleas; and they slept on rude cots, or on 'soft planks' under horse-blankets, on tables, counters, floors, on trucks in the open air, in bunks braced against the weather-boarding, forty of them in one loft; and so they tossed and scratched, and swore and laughed, and sang and skylarked—those who were not tired or drunk enough to sleep. And in the working-hours they bustled, and jostled, and tugged, and sweated, and made money—always made money. They labored and they lugged; they worked on lighters, drove trucks, packed mules, rang bells, carried messages, 'waited' in restaurants, 'marked' for billiard-tables, served drinks in bar-rooms, 'faked' on the Plaza, 'cried' at auctions, toted lumber for houses, ran a game of faro or roulette in the El Dorado or the Bella Union, or manipulated three-card monte on the head of a barrel in front of the Parker House; they speculated in beach and water lots, in lumber, pork, flour, potatoes; in picks, shovels, pans, long boots, slouch-hats, knives, blankets, and Mexican saddles. There were doctors, lawyers, politicians, preachers, even gentlemen and scholars among them; but they all speculated, and as a rule they gambled. . . . Laborers received a dollar an hour [this when laborers in the East were lucky to get half a dollar a day]; a pick or shovel was worth $10; a tin pan or a wooden bowl, $5; and a butcher's knife, $30. . . . A small loaf of bread was fifty cents, and a hard boiled egg a dollar. You paid $3 to get into the circus, and $55 for a private box. Men talked dollars, and a copper coin was an object of antiquarian interest. Forty-dollars was the price for ordinary coarse boots; and a pair that came above the knees and would carry you gallantly through the quagmires brought around a hundred. When a shirt became very dirty, the wearer threw it away and bought a new one. Washing cost $15 a dozen in 1849. Rents were simply monstrous: $3000 a month in advance for a 'store' hurriedly built of rough boards. . . . From 10 to 15 per cent a month was paid in advance for the use of money borrowed on substantial security. The prices of real estate went up among the stars: $8000 for a fifty-vara (roughly 150-foot) lot that had been bought in 1848 for $20. Yet, for all that, everybody made money, although a man might stare aghast at the squalor of his lodging, and wish that he might part with his appetite at any price to some other man."

Hotels were quickly built in San Francisco. This one is said to have been the first. Here is the menu for dinner, à la carte, at the Ward House, October 27, 1849:

Oxtail soup	$1.00	Fresh eggs	$1.00 ea.
Baked trout, anchovy sauce	1.50	Sweet potatoes	50¢
Roast beef	1.00	Irish potatoes	50¢
Roast lamb, stuffed	1.00	Cabbage	50¢
Roast mutton, stuffed	1.00	Squash	50¢
Roast pork, with apple sauce	1.25	Bread pudding	75¢
Baked mutton, caper sauce	1.25	Mince pie	75¢
Corned beef and cabbage	1.25	Brandy peaches	2.00
Ham	1.00	Rum omelette	2.00
Curried sausages	1.00	Jelly omelette	2.00
Lamb and green peas	1.25	Cheese	50¢
Venison, wine sauce	1.50	Prunes	75¢
Stewed kidney, champagne sauce	1.25		

San Francisco was a gourmet's paradise compared to the El Dorado at Hangtown (Placerville) where one could get "hash, low grade" for 75 cents or "18 karat hash" for $1, as well as roast grizzly and jackass rabbit, whole. "Payment in advance," the hotel admonished. "Gold scales at the end of the bar." Since the coarse knives and forks the restaurants sometimes furnished (in some places it was BYOK—bring your own knife) cost $25 a pair, it's surprising they weren't chained down.

Letters from home were the most sought-after commodity in San Francisco. Men would line up the day before in the hope of getting mail from a loved one.

Some forty-niners probably did not get many letters, as they were hiding out under assumed names, as the song below suggests.

What Was Your Name in the States?

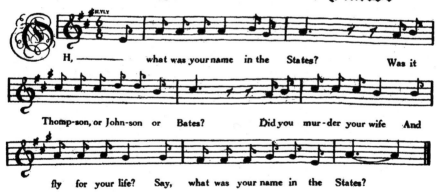

O, ———— what was your name in the States? Was it

Thomp-son, or John-son or Bates? Did you mur-der your wife And

fly for your life? Say, what was your name in the States?

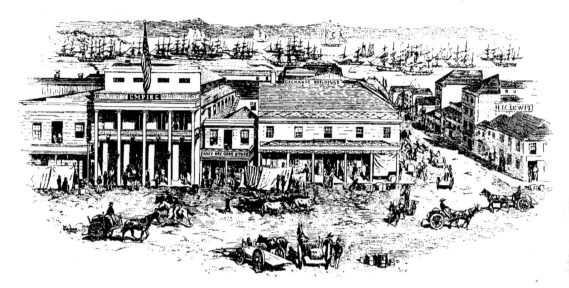

Portsmouth Square, earlier called the plaza, where, in 1846, the *Portsmouth* landed to take possession of Yerba Buena for the United States and where, two years later, Brannan waved the bottle of gold. By early 1850, as shown here, San Francisco was a tipsy metropolis. Commercial buildings flank the square, and new ones line side streets.

Some of the substantial new buildings were actually ships left rotting in the bay, hauled farther onto land and refurbished. Here the *Apollo*, whose route to San Francisco is shown on map 4, has become a saloon.

GREAT FIRE IN SAN FRANCISCO.

Navigating San Francisco's muddy streets in the wet winter of '49 was challenging. Horses and mules got stuck and were pulled out with difficulty, sometimes not at all; dogs and, we're told, even some drunks drowned. Although San Franciscans threw everything they could think of into the mire—including a shipment of iron stoves—some streets were hopelessly impassable. The Christmas season of that wet year brought an even worse disaster. The waterlogged town burned.

The chief social clubs were the barrooms and gambling halls, some in tents, some in substantial buildings like this one.

CHAPTER FIVE

Outdoor Scholars

"We are on the brink," the *New York Tribune* wrote, "of the Age of Gold." The age was ushered in by the first world-class gold rush. But the forty-niners who had come so bravely through the tribulations of ship or trail had surprises in store. Most of them had never seen gold in any form except a ring or a coin. Some had purchased books hurriedly written by purportedly rich miners returning from the gold fields. *Three Weeks in the Gold Mines*, by "Henry Simpson," supposedly an army veteran, claimed that the author had found gold everywhere he looked, one piece, he said, "as large and thick as my double hands outspread." Why he left after only three weeks, or bothered to write the book, he did not say. One guidebook claimed the riverbeds were "paved with gold" and that one could fish out "twenty to fifty thousand dollars worth" instantly. California, many of the forty-niners thought, had an "inexhaustible supply of gold." The men of one French group brought rakes to reap the nuggets, while their wives brought stools with embroidered silk covers to sit on as they gracefully picked out nuggets with silver tongs.

Many forty-niners succumbed to the blandishments of salesmen who sold them gold machines that would keep them from having to even stoop to gather gold. Or one could buy "California Gold Grease," which, when liberally applied to a miner, would allow him to roll downhill and have all the gold—and only gold—in the golden mountain stick to him. One California-bound miner even hired a clairvoyant to accompany him to the rainbow's end to pinpoint rich spots, but why he thought he needed a clairvoyant, when all one had to do was bend over, or why the gold-spotting clairvoyant did not reap all California's gold for himself is not clear.

One of the articles that at first was ignored by eastern newspapers when Brannan sent his advance copies said a "vein" of gold had been discovered on the American River that was 12 to 18 feet thick, 3 feet below the surface, and 17 miles long. All this from Marshall's handful of placer nuggets. Exaggeration, yes; but California was and is rich in gold—perhaps not as fabulously rich as such rumors made it out to be but rich nevertheless.

Henry Bigler, the Mormon who had noted the "goald" in his diary, made $11 to $30 a day prospecting—as much as a laborer in the East could earn in a month. On Mormon Island seven diggers took out $1,000 worth in fifteen days. Once the rush got started, stories of big finds came thick and fast. Pierson Reading, who hired sixty-five Indians to work on the Trinity River, got $70,000 in a few days. The French consul, Jacques Moerenhout, made a careful inspection of the mines in the summer of 1848 and concluded that miners had taken out $4 million by the end of July.

And the stories kept coming. Francisco Coronel, a schoolteacher from Los Angeles, followed a party of Indians to a ravine near the Stanislaus River. He and his two Indian employees garnered 45 ounces of gold the first day, 38 the next, 51 the third. The Reverend Mr. Colton wrote that he knew of seven men who had taken 275 *pounds* of gold from the Feather River, and another who gathered 2½ pounds in fifteen minutes. Some miners were making $1,000 a day; one man took out $9,000 worth in one day; another, $12,000 in six days.

Thirty pounds of gold came out of a claim on the Yuba River only four feet square; at Volcano, in Amador County, a single pan of gravel yielded $500 worth of gold. Near Downieville, a sixty-foot-square claim, worked by four men, yielded $12,900 in eleven days; in six months, $80,000. At the time miners were lucky to get $16 an ounce for their gold. At the Cup Diggings, also near Downieville, three owners of the claim filled a tin cup with gold each day before quitting. A sailor in Monterey, no doubt a deserter from his ship, brought 136 ounces of gold from the Yuba River, Colton reported. "It is the most beautiful gold that has appeared in the market; it looks like the yellow scales of the dolphin passing through his rainbow hues at death." Four men from Monterey who took off for the mines when they saw Sutter's gold came back after seven weeks and three days' work in the mines with $11,000 each. Another, working alone, spent sixty-four days on the Yuba River and brought back $4,534, and yet another, a boy of fourteen, spent fifty-four days on the Mokelumne and garnered $3,467. A woman from Sonora worked for only forty-six days to get $2,125—more than she would earn in several years working in the East.

According to Colton, "The capital required for this enterprise are muscle and an honest purpose." Muscle, certainly. As for honest purpose—Colton was a minister. "I met a man from the mines today [Saturday, September 16, 1848]," he wrote, "in patched buckskins, rough as a badger from his hole, who had fifteen thousand dollars in yellow dust swung at his back." Other tales to whet the forty-niners' appetites followed. On the North Fork of the American River a miner took out $1,500 in an hour; another found $2,000 worth of gold under his doorstep. Three Frenchmen dug out a stump near Coloma and netted $6,000 from its roots.

These were the stories that fueled gold fever. When a miner heard of a fabulous find somewhere else, he was likely to leave a perfectly good claim and follow the seductive rumor to another spot that was "sure" to make him rich. Since most miners followed the same will-o'-the-wisps, even a remarkably rich spot could not make everyone wealthy.

Sometimes the gold stories were outright lies, as was the Gold Lake Hoax. In 1850 rumor spread that in a deep gorge at the headwaters of the Feather River lay a lake of gold secreted among the high peaks and that along its shore one could pick up walnut-sized nuggets. The newspapers added a little local color: the inhabitants of the region, they said, used golden fishhooks and arrowheads, and a man had even lassoed a gold rock in the lake and spent three days trying to pull it out.

The rumor apparently started with a man named Stoddard, who said he had been driven from the lake shores by hostile Indians. A few hours after being run off, Stoddard was leading a band of several dozen men heading for the high country. Another party followed, and behind them thousands of prospectors struggled up the mountains. Stoddard led them high into the mountains, where they wandered about until stopped by snow. He was, he confessed, lost. Finally they reached a lake, but there was no gold. Many wanted to hang him on the spot, but others, claiming he was merely crazy, saved him. It's hard to say who was crazier, Stoddard, who started the rumor, or the thousands who followed him. The curious venture was not a total loss. On their return trip one group found gold on a tributary of the Middle Fork of the Feather River, and another located rich diggings on the North Fork. They picked out $36,000 by hand. "Rich Bar," they called it, and rich it was. One pan of gold-bearing gravel might yield $1,500 to $2,000; the richest pan contained $2,900 worth of gold.

One of the most interesting of the gold rush chroniclers, "Dame Shirley" (Louise Amelia Knapp Smith Clappe), lived in and wrote of the camp of Rich Bar in its heyday. "Through the middle of Rich Bar," she wrote, "runs the street, thickly planted with about forty tenements, among which figure round tents, square tents, plank hovels, log cabins, etc.—the residences, varying in elegance and convenience from the palatial splendor of 'The Empire,' down to a 'local habitation,' formed of pine boughs, and covered with old calico." The palatial Empire, she reported, was far from palatial. "This impertinent apology for a house cost its original owners more than eight thousand dollars. . . . At the time it was built, every thing had to be packed from Marysville at a cost of forty cents a pound." It had been built by a company of gamblers for a whorehouse, but Dame Shirley reports with righteous satisfaction that it folded after a few weeks and the gamblers sold the house for a few hundred dollars.

Dame Shirley's house was one of the better furnished, because she was one of the few women in camp and her husband was the camp doctor. In their log cabin the ceiling was of white cotton cloth, the walls covered with chintz. She had hung a curtain to separate the bedroom from the rest of the cabin. For a toilet table she used a trunk, and for a washstand another trunk, with a pail nearby filled daily with river water. Her tiny mirror had been intended for a doll's house. She had four chairs, but since the dirt floor was very uneven, none stood solidly. "I fancy nature intended me for a Nomadic barbarian," she wrote. "How shall I ever be content in a decent, proper, well-behaved house where lanterns are not broken bottles, book cases not candle boxes." "Really," she wrote in her last letter from the diggings, "everybody ought to go to the mines, just to see how little it takes to make people comfortable in the world."

Even in the halcyon days of 1848 miners did not become millionaires by mining alone, in spite of fabulous gold strikes like those at Rich Bar. By late 1849, when the multitudes poured in by wagon train, the easy pickings were mostly gone. Many of those who did make rich finds gambled away their hard-won gold. The forty-niners who did best mined the miners, not the mines—storekeepers, like Brannan, who became the state's first millionaire, doctors who learned that miners paid better than mining, and certainly gamblers.

Young Mark Hopkins, who arrived on the *Pacific* from around the Horn, took half interest in a hardware store in Sacramento, and with the profits he and his partner, Collis P. Huntington, together with Charles Crocker and Leland Stanford, financed the lucrative Central Pacific Railroad. J. M. Studebaker, who learned blacksmithing in Placerville, went into business making wheelbarrows and then, near the turn of the century, changed from one wheel to four and started an automobile empire. Although Studebaker automobiles are no longer made, they were still commonly seen a hundred years after the gold rush. Philip Armour began his meatpacking industry in the gold country. Heinrich Schliemann, the pioneer archaeologist, came to California to collect his dead forty-niner brother's gold and stayed to amass a small fortune himself, which he took back to Europe and parlayed into a vast fortune, which he used to seek and find what everyone else thought was mere legend: the ancient city of Troy.

No one knows for certain how much gold was taken out of the California mines in 1848 and 1849. The late geologist William B. Clark, in his book *Gold Districts of California*, gives 502,936 ounces as an educated guess. (See the appendix, table A4, for a list of the gold produced each year for the past century and a half.) For some years California led the nation and the world in gold production. The California total is not as great as South Africa's, but its impact on history was enormous.

The forty-niners soon found out that winning the gold was hard work. Would-be

FIGURE 14. A young Chinese miner carries his outfit and goes out to prospect.

miners grew disgusted at not becoming instantly rich and claimed they had been "humbugged." They were humbugged, the journalist Bayard Taylor said, not about the gold, but about the work. The gold was not inexhaustible, as they had thought, and it took luck and hard work to get it out of its hiding place. If the way back East had not been so difficult, most would probably have packed up and gone home at once.

Few of the forty-niners knew anything about mining, but all learned something. They had much to learn. Young males, fueled by hormones, often think they already know it all, and it must have been a shock to many of them to find whole areas of expertise of which they were wholly unaware, or never expected to need to know.

One area of expertise for which they did not foresee a need, with the exception perhaps of the sailors among them, was "women's work." Suddenly they had to figure out how to cook and sew and clean. Most were too impatient to spend much time cooking. They specialized in flapjacks, which they cooked over campfires in rancid grease. It was said that you didn't need a trail to get to Bidwell's Bar; you could follow the smell of flapjacks frying. Fresh fruit was scarce, and vegetables, had the forty-niners bothered with them, even more scarce.

Cooking was an everyday chore, but mending and cleaning were reserved for Sundays. Cleanliness was not a priority; partly for this reason disease was rife in the camps, and many forty-niners died of preventable ailments. One man even died of poison oak. Sewing was more troublesome than cooking, as few men had any idea

Enterprising Henry DeGroot was "going on 25" when he arrived in California by steamer on the last day of February 1849. He had already raised his younger brothers and sisters and put himself through school to get degrees in law and medicine but found these professions not adventurous enough, so he managed to get Horace Greeley, editor of the New York Tribune, *to send him to California to report on the gold discoveries. He caught the gold bug and spent the rest of his life following gold and silver rushes and writing both popular and technical articles about mining.*

In 1849 DeGroot tried diving for gold. Although DeGroot's efforts were not crowned with success, companies using deep-sea diving equipment did get gold from riverbeds for many years, beginning as early as 1851. Here is DeGroot's story, abridged, as he told it in the Overland Monthly *in 1874.*

DIVING FOR GOLD IN '49
By Henry DeGroot

. . . Multifarious and unique were the theories promulgated by the miners touching [gold's] origin and modes of deposit; some holding that it had been thrown up by volcanic action, while others contended that it had come down from the Sierra or been released from the quartz veins with which the country was so thickly ribbed. There was one opinion, however, in which nearly all were agreed: in its progress down-stream, [gold] must have made extensive lodgment in the deep holes along the rivers; and hence these were the places in which to find the big deposits, if only some method could be devised for getting at them.

Trudging along with my mustangs, mules, and donkeys [toward Sutter's Mill, where I was mining], I meditated much on this matter of the deep holes—pondering it now in my own mind. . . .

By the time I reached the mill that day I had my plans entirely made out: I would have a suit of submarine armor constructed, go down and clean out these receptacles, enrich myself immeasurably, advance the business of mining, and astonish the world generally. . . .

But suitable materials for the construction of an apparatus of this kind were not to be had; and then, where was I to find a person possessed of the requisite mechanical skill to put it together, or yet others sufficiently experienced to use it when completed? [I sought out Clarkson Dye, then running Sutter's sawmill] and he pronounced the proposed enterprise "a big thing," suggesting that we should take-hold of the business together—a proposition that I readily agreed to. [Soon] I saw most of the articles, including a lot of India rubber blankets and a huge pair of gum boots . . . [and shortly] he finished his handiwork. And such a fabric! I had seen many hideous and repulsive things in my day, but they were things of beauty and joy to soothe the nerves forever, compared with this. Laid on its back it looked like a huge, misshapen burial casket; turned on its side, a pauper's coffin. Long India-rubber tubes, black and flexible; two glaring eyes; dust and rubbish adhering to every pitch-besmeared seam—it were hard to say whether the thing most resembled a sleeping crocodile or a curled-up devil-fish lying in wait for prey.

[Searching for a diver, we approached a ne'er-do-well, Larry McShane, who declared himself

continued ☞

ready to dive for a price], but the instant our hero's eyes fell upon the frightful object before him, there occurred a sudden collapse of his courage. He inspected it with the deepest concern, and began, in a querulous tone, to ask a variety of questions as to its uses and the method of operating it.

"And it is mesilf that's to get into this haythenish thing, and go down undther the wather and be dthrowned intirely?" was the first inquiry made by Larry.

The persuasive Dye, perceiving the danger that our man would "back down" at the outset, proceeded, with oleaginous tongue, to expiate on the safety and comfort of his patent "life preserver," as he was pleased, for the occasion, to style this work of his handicraft, and then, getting in and adjusting it about his person, he pronounced the sensation indescribably pleasant; while, as for danger, why it was a perfect house of refuge—almost the only place one could find and be entirely out of the reach of harm—and then, the honor of being the first person to go down in one of these luxurious articles which were so soon to revolutionize mining and enrich the world at large: here was something for a brave and ambitious man to be proud of all his days! . . .

"And the wather, sure, what's to kape it from cooming into the prayzarver?"

"Ah, look you," said [Dye], exhibiting the head-piece and clapping it on the trunk, "*there!* we screw that thing on tight—can't a drop of water get in—keep you dry as a smoked herring—come out fairly roasted. And then how grand you'll look—

like an ancient knight in his armor and helmet!"

"Well thin, but the breath of me?"

"O, no trouble about the breathing," quoth the imperturbable Dye, as he seized and began working a pair of immense bellows, made from an untanned cow-hide, wherewith he sent a perfect hurricane through the air-tube. "See, see *that!* air enough to fill a balloon—could blow you clean out of the water."

"And wouldn't I then be kept just floatin' on the top o' that same, and me not able to get down at all and gather the gowld, and it just lying there on the bothom?"

When it was shown how a lot of fine large boulders would be tied to his feet to carry him down and keep him there until we saw fit to haul him up, the consternation of Larry knew no bounds. He looked upon it as clearly a plot to get rid of him by drowning; the futility of our hinting at an additional bottle of whiskey showing how completely the conviction had not only satisfied his reason but subverted every instinct of his nature.

And thus had our first effort to secure the services of a diver resulted in failure. . . .

[We then approached a young black slave, Ephriam, whom we were prepared to hire or buy.] Ephriam agreed to the project on his own until he saw the contraption, then began to make excuses, saying he couldn't be spared from his work and that it looked "turble like a coffin."

[Failing to recruit a diver, I] determined that I would take it upon myself to perform that grave service. . . . I was duly ensconced in my waterproof dress, feeling all the while very much like a wretch being prepared for public execution. If the mere sight of the machine had caused me to shudder, my frame of mind can hardly be conceived now that I was to be screwed up in it and anchored in five or six fathoms of snow-water. Though badly scared, I managed to conceal my fear so that those assisting me really thought I was in excellent spirits and even relished the operation. Gladly would I have backed out as the cold and clammy folds of the rubber invested my limbs. After I had been fairly launched, and while my companions were poking away with a couple of poles, seeking to shove me out into deep water, I was on the eve of crying out and demanding to be pulled ashore, so horrible did my situation seem to me. But all was at stake—fortune, consistency, reputation for courage—to give up at this stage of proceeding was to be branded as a poltroon, and to dissipate the gorgeous dream of wealth in which myself and partner had so fondly indulged. Better drown than this; so I restrained myself from making an outcry and . . . soon found myself at the bottom of the pool, where I lost no time in filling the two large buckets. . . . As I could no longer see after beginning to stir up the mud, I had no idea what this material might consist of, but flattered myself that a fair proportion of it, at least, was gold. Having filled the vessels, I gave the signal and was speedily hauled to the surface, [but on washing it we found] not a particle of the precious metal. . . .

Moving down to [a] more promising location, another descent was made; but nothing having been obtained—the contents of the buckets consisting in every case of only barren gravel mixed with twigs, leaves, mud, and sand—still a fourth had to be undertaken. While being submerged this last time, the signal-rope became entangled with the air-supplying tube in such a manner as to prevent either of them acting freely. Beginning to experience a difficulty in breathing soon after I was let down, I signalled for more air and at the same time to be hauled up. No attention, however, was paid to my signal. Perceiving that something was wrong, I began to tug at the signal-rope with all my might; but it was of no use, it would not work. Soon I felt myself beginning to suffocate, and in this condition I was left till my companions above, alarmed at the length of time I had been under water, pulled me up and hauled me on shore, after which they were not long in discovering what was the matter. Stripping off the armor as quickly as possible, they found me in an unconscious state, respiration suspended, my features convulsed, and my veins black and swollen. Restorative measures were adopted, and I was at length resuscitated. For a time I laid in a condition of partial stupor, but as soon as I became fully conscious of what had happened, and had strength enough to stand on my feet, I got up, and, taking one look at the accursed contrivance, without saying a word to anyone, staggered away; disgusted beyond measure with my experience at diving, yet thankful, withal, that it had ended so well: nor did I ever after inquire what had become of the machine, or seek further to explore the deep places for gold. ✕

THE COST OF GOLD

Before the gold rush California had a rich tapestry of Native American cultures, living in homes from the desert to the Oregon border, speaking a total of 90 languages that belonged to 6 major language families and had divided into more than 300 dialects. The Spanish–Mexicans, by gold rush times–had established missions and "Christianized" some Native Americans, who lived in and near the missions and worked for the padres, but the majority still lived their own lives in their own territories. The arrogant miners dismissed them all as "Digger Indians" because they ate root vegetables. The miners themselves, who subsisted chiefly on greasy flapjacks, had little access to or patience with root vegetables–not even beets or carrots.

The Californios were far less cruel than their ancestors, the fierce conquistadors. In 1851, when an abortive Indian uprising began in southern California, the Indians planned to spare the Californios but have no mercy on the Anglos (i.e., anyone not Spanish or Indian). They had had a bitter taste of miners' and settlers' cruelty.

At first the Indians found the gold that brought their destruction a blessing–mixed, perhaps. They worked for the forty-eighters and forty-niners, panning gold in bateas or reed baskets. For their backbreaking efforts, they got food and clothing for a few days–but no gold.

Soon the Indian workers realized that they were being cheated and began to demand gold, not an allowance. Gold was not, as they had been told, stuff to whitewash houses with. To keep peace– and the labor force–some employers agreed to pay gold. Even so, some Indians began prospecting on their own. Still they were cheated. White merchants weighed their gold with a special two-ounce counterweight they called a "Digger ounce," so they paid for only half the gold.

The Indians' story is fraught with atrocities. Andrew Kelsey and a man named Stone ran a ranch near Clear Lake using the labor of the local Pomo tribe. Stone and Kelsey flogged and tortured their laborers, even murdering the men and raping the women. In 1849 Kelsey led an expedition to the goldfields, taking along Pomos as slaves, few of whom survived. Finally in the fall of 1849, the much-put-upon Pomos executed the two white men. The next spring a military expedition, together with civilian volunteers, "came [to an island at the north end of Clear Lake where] a body of Indians numbering between two and three hundred [was camped]," reported the *Daily Alta California*. "They immediately surrounded them, and as the Indians raised a shout of defiance and attempted to escape, poured a destructive fire indiscriminately upon men, women, and children." Altogether they killed 135 Indians, while the soldiers had only 2 nonfatal casualties. Here is part of the tale as the Pomos told it:

> One old lady . . . said she saw two white men coming with their guns up in the air and on their guns bearing a little girl. They brought [her] to the creek and threw [her] in the water . . . and a little while later, two more men came. . . . This time they had a little boy on the end of their guns and also threw [him] in the water. A little ways away a woman [lay] who was shot through the shoulder. She held her little baby in her arms. Two white men took the woman and baby. They stabbed the woman and the baby.

The carnage was so great that the spot became known as Bloody Island. Indian massacres–massacres *of* Indians, not *by* Indians–continued to be the order of the day in California. Nearly 2,000 of the Yana tribe were purposely slaughtered by white vigilantes, even though they were the labor force for local ranches. One American official called the assault on Indians a "war of extinction," and it very nearly was.

Besides outright murder, settlers and miners brought diseases unknown to Native Americans that often proved fatal: cholera, typhoid, measles, malaria, smallpox, whooping cough, and venereal disease.

Even though by treaty Indians in former Mexican territory were guaranteed citizenship, the United States ignored the provision. Indian testimony was prohibited in court, and the killing, raping, or enslavement of an Indian was no crime at all. Moreover, the white government decided (quite unconstitutionally) that Indians had no property rights, that they were "trespassers on the public domain."

Although California proudly declared itself a nonslave state, in 1850 the new California legislature passed a law allowing any Indian to be declared a vagabond and sold into slavery. In 1861 a U.S. congressional document detailed the slave trade in northern California:

> In the frontier portions of Humboldt and Mendocino counties a band of desperate men have carried on a system of kidnapping for two years past; Indian children were seized and carried into the lower counties and sold into virtual slavery. . . . The kidnappers follow at the heels of the soldiers to seize the children when their parents are murdered and sell them to best advantage.

Sometimes the children were "adopted" rather than indentured, but the result was usually the same.

By 1880 the Native American population numbered only 16,000. In the 1840s it had been esti-

Militiamen firing on a Yuki village in Mendocino County in the 1850s, as part of a campaign to harass Native Americans or eliminate them from California. The campaign was a success. The Yuki people, who numbered 6,000 in 1850, were reduced to 300 by 1864.

mated at 150,000. Virtually every village on the coast of California was destroyed during or shortly after the gold rush. ✕

of how to do it. They did not have the repertoire of seams and stitches most women learned, so they had difficulty repairing their clothes. Their trousers took the worst beating. Many of the miners stood in water all day, doing exercises that would stress the seams of any garment.

The story is told that in the 1850s the immigrant Levi Strauss saw his fellow miners struggling with mending their woolen pants. Wool is not easy to mend— even their wives and mothers would have had trouble. Strauss devised a pair made of sturdy canvas, held together by tough double seams. On the critical points, where the pants were most likely to tear, he added metal rivets. A wonderful story, but not true. No doubt Strauss did see the miners struggling with mending their trousers, but he himself was not a forty-niner. He did not start making pants with rivets until 1873, after Jacob Davis invented rivets and joined with Strauss in making jeans.

Besides women's work, the forty-niners had much to learn about their new profession: mining. They quickly abandoned the fancy gold-mining machines they had purchased in the East. The machines simply did not work. By the time they got to California, mining methods were those the Californios and Sonorians knew. The indispensable pan, or batea, was used for prospecting at the beginning of mining and for "clean-up" to recover the gold at the end. They could use a pan—often their frying pan—for the whole mining process, but a man panning long and hard all day could barely sort through one yard of gravel to get the gold out. Two men could team up, using a rocker (also called a cradle, because that's what it looked like), and with one man bringing gravel to the rocker and the other man rocking, they could process as much as three to five yards a day. The sluice, a long wooden trough, could be used by three men or more and was even more efficient, allowing twelve yards to be worked in a day using three men. All these techniques are illustrated in "How They Mined the Gold," pages 86–93.

All of this was hard, difficult work. In the early California mines, "muscles," as someone commented, "were king." Yankees being what they are, tinkerers and inventors, they soon yearned for some mechanical methods to take over the backbreaking work. It was this desire to escape from muscles to machines that made them take the useless machines in the first place.

It did not take long for gold mining to change from an individual enterprise to one using more and more men (even, once in a great while, women). They formed large companies to move whole rivers aside to get at their beds. So many companies were formed to change the American River's course, working one below the other, that the river scarcely touched its original bed for many miles. Each dam moved it aside, carried the water in flumes or ditches, and then turned it back into its original course for the next company to divert. One newspaper writer claimed that in a ten-

THOSE HATED FOREIGNERS

Bigoted, arrogant young America, faced with men of many tongues pouring in from all over the globe, harassed the hated foreigners who were competing for "their" American gold. They called everyone who spoke Spanish "Greasers" and considered them "Mexicans" and therefore "foreigners."

In 1850 the California legislature, then only months old, passed a so-called foreign miners' tax. Americans, themselves new owners of the land of California, proposed to drive out all the hated foreigners by charging them $20 a month for the privilege of hunting for gold. The palmy days were over; most miners were barely getting by, and this was the last straw. Although the purpose of the law was said to be to enrich the state's coffers, its real purpose was to force the non-English-speaking miners out of the mines. It worked. Hundreds left for Mexico.

And foreigners had poured in. By the end of June 1849 the *Daily Alta California* estimated 6,450 had come from Mexico, 1,350 from Chile, 1,251 from Panama, 370 from Hawaii, 227 from Peru, and 120 from Tahiti. Foreigners from Europe had not arrived yet. Before the rush was over, at least 25 countries and all 31 states contributed gold rushers. (Japan and Russia refused to let their citizens go.)

Another group to suffer from forty-niner bigotry was the Chinese, who seemed very exotic. They came slowly at first. In 1848 there were only seven Chinese in California; a few years later, twenty thousand. Early ones were curiosities, but when more and more arrived and went to the goldfields (which they called Golden Mountain), American miners got nervous and impatient. From the Chinese the miners could have learned patience, but they preferred to resent them, too. Three-Finger Jack, who, legend says, ran with Joaquin Murieta (see chapter 11), was said to have hung up six Chinese by their queues and cut their throats.

Because the Chinese would work claims no one else wanted and take gold from them, white men disdained them. They were hardworking and frugal. When a Chinese miner found a good claim, he was driven off by white men. Most annoying of all was the Chinese imperturbability. No matter what was done to them, they retained their dignity and the idea that the Chinese were the brightest and most favored of races. ✕

mile stretch of the Feather River there was a dam every mile, at a cost of $8,000 each. According to the historian Rodman Paul, "In 1853 it was said that nearly twenty-five miles of the Yuba River had been turned aside, at a cost of $3,000,000, and in 1854 an Eastern mining consultant reported that over $1,500,000 had been spent for similar purposes on the American River and its branches."

Probably the most impressive of these river-turning ventures by a single company was tried on the Feather River in 1857. By that time the miners had considerable experience and were determined to use state-of-the-art techniques. They built a wooden flume 3,200 feet long and 40 feet wide and installed eight sluices and a dozen water-powered pumps, all at a cost of $120,000. When the construction was completed, 260 men prowled the riverbed, digging "dirt" and washing it through the sluices. When expenses were totaled, the cost was $176,985.63, and the company had found $251,725.45 worth of gold, leaving a profit of $74,739.82.

This was good money, but the next year when they tried the same thing, they failed to meet expenses. What they had gotten the first time was gold the river may have been pushing along for millennia, so they could scarcely expect one year's crop of new gold to be so large.

But while the rivers were being turned for gold and miners were still standing knee-deep in water, some miners looked to the sides of the river, where they saw gravel beds formed at an earlier time (how much earlier, they did not yet know). Canny miners, particularly those from Cornwall, England, recognized that these, too, might contain gold. The miners burrowed into the hillsides like animals to get at the gold-bearing beds, giving rise to the name "coyote diggings." Cornish miners showed them how to dig shafts (vertical holes) and adits (horizontal ones) and how to use winches to avoid some of the backbreaking labor of toting. The purpose of all the digging was to get at the lower part of the old gravel beds, where gold, they hoped, would have been dropped as in a modern stream. J. D. Borthwick, who visited coyote diggings in 1851, wrote:

> "Coyote" diggings [got] their name from an animal called the 'coyote', which abounds all over the plain lands of Mexico and California, and which lives in the cracks and crevices made in the plains by the extreme heat of summer. . . .
>
> These coyote diggings require to be very rich to pay, from the great amount of labour necessary before any pay-dirt can be obtained. They are generally worked by only two men. A shaft is sunk, over which is rigged a crude windlass, tended by one man, who draws up the dirt in a large bucket while his partner is digging down below. When the bed rock is reached on which the rich dirt is found, excavations are made all round, leaving only the necessary supporting pillars of earth, which are also ultimately removed, and replaced by logs of wood. Accidents frequently occur from the 'caving-in' of these diggings, the result generally of the carelessness of the men themselves.
>
> The Cornish miners, of whom numbers had come to California from the mines of Mexico and South America, generally devoted themselves to these deep diggings, as did also the lead-miners from Wisconsin. Such men were quite at home a hundred feet or so under ground, picking through hard rock by candlelight; at the same time, gold mining in any way was to almost every one a new occupation, and men who had passed their lives hitherto above ground, took quite as naturally to this subterranean style of digging as to any other.

A more elegant name for this kind of mining was drift mining. The cost of drift mining in California in the late 1800s, when independent workers were replaced by companies, ranged from about $1.00 to $3.25 a ton, while the gold they recovered was worth $1.75 to $10.00 a ton.

FIGURE 15. A large dredge working in a pond near the California foothills. Tailing is spilling out of the stern gantry, raising the height of the dredge piles flanking the pond.

Much of the gravel in these old riverbeds was cemented—that is, minerals in groundwater had sealed the gravel particles together so that the gravel had nearly become hard rock and had to be crushed to get the gold out. The miners used a variety of devices to crush the rock, then washed and worked the crushed gravel.

In 1850 the Yankee love of machinery led to the development of a steam-powered dredge, the *Phenix,* essentially a riverboat that brought up sand from the bottom of the river for miners to run through rockers. J. Wesley Jones, in the "illustrated lecture" he called "Pantoscope of California," describing California as he saw it in 1850, said, "The *Phenix* dredging machine is seen in the Yuba River, a cumbrous arrangement, by which it was designed to drag up sand from the bed of the river, and obtain gold in large quantities. It was soon found, however, that this machine dredged more money from the pockets of the owners than it did gold from the bed of the Yuba, and this kind of dredging was very soon abandoned."

Meanwhile, miners in New Zealand, Montana, and Colorado continued to work on developing a successful dredge. California reentered the dredging picture in 1897, when R. H. Postlethwaite launched a new dredge—again on the turbulent Yuba River. It sank. The next year, W. P. Hammon launched another dredge at

FIGURE 16. Close-up of line of buckets used to dig gravel for processing on board the dredge.

Oroville, and California dredging was under way. For the first two-thirds of the twentieth century dredging was the chief method of gold mining in California.

A dredge working in a field today looks much like a strange piece of building equipment, yet there are no buildings being built nearby. Closer up, one can see the pond the dredge sits in, but no streams may be running into it or out of it. The dredge is in a pond it made for itself, like a toy duck floating in a washbasin. (The duck, of course, did not make the washbasin.) Most present-day dredges are electrically powered bucket-line dredges, some as long as a city block, the topmost part (the stern gantry) reaching nineteen stories above the water. On the front of such a dredge is a series of huge iron and steel scoops, each as tall as a person, all mounted on an endless chain. The scoops dig ravenously into layers of gravel, some of it cemented as hard as solid rock. Each scoop digs its maw full, then, as it goes around the chain, drops it on board. The digging equipment, including the buckets, can weigh as much as a thousand tons, about 170 times the weight of an elephant. Once the gravel is on board, milling and processing equipment takes the gold out, pushing the unwanted tailing off the rear of the dredge. Symmetrical piles of old dredge tailing may be seen today here and there in the gold country, particularly along the

FIGURE 17. Some buckets are very large, lifting tons of gravel in one scoop.

FIGURE 18. Aerial view, taken in the mid-twentieth century, of piles of rock left by dredging near Marysville.

Yuba and American rivers, as well as in the Klamath Mountains and even the desert. Nowadays the piles are being used for building material.

After the furious rush was over and mining had turned into a business, most of the thousands of gold seekers left the goldfields. Some went home, taking with them a nest egg, not as big, perhaps, as they had hoped, but a nest egg nonetheless. Some trailed home despondently, wondering how they could ever pay off their debts. Some stayed in California and built homes, farms, and businesses in the new state. But some had caught gold fever and spent their days following one bright will-o'-the-wisp or another to fancied riches. They dashed off to the cold Fraser River in Canada, to Colorado, to Nevada, to Montana. Some heard of the fabulous nuggets in Australia and hurried there.

Wherever they went, the miners took the story of their California quest with them, as well as what they had learned about mining and about gold. The magic word *California* gave them prestige. They had been forty-niners, they had been to California, they were gold-mining men.

LIFE IN THE MINES

Charles Nahl shows as many different modes of transport and kinds of people as he can cram into his drawing. Native Americans and Chinese on foot, Chileños, Mexicans, African Americans, Hawaiians, Americans on foot and muleback, horses pulling covered wagons, all heading for the mines.

Most miners would have used horses or mules to pull this gear if they had them.

WHEN I WENT OUT TO PROSPECT

Tune: "King of the Cannibal Islands"

I heard of gold at Sutter's Mill,
At Michigan Bluff and Iowa Hill,
But never thought it was rich until
I started off to prospect.
At Yankee Jim's I bought a purse,
Inquired for Iowa Hill, of course,
And travelled on, but what was worse,
Fetched up in Shirttail Canyon.

Chorus:
A sicker miner every way
Had not been seen for many a day;
The devil it always was to pay,
When I went out to prospect.

When I got there, the mining ground
Was staked and claimed for miles around,
And not a bed was to be found,
When I went off to prospect.
The town was crowded full of folks,
Which made me think 'twas not a hoax;
At my expense they cracked their jokes,
When I went off to prospect.

I left my jackass on the road,
Because he wouldn't carry the load;
I'd sooner pick a big horn toad,
When I went off to prospect.
My fancy shirt, which collar so nice,
I found was covered with body-lice;
I used unguentum once or twice,
But could not kill the gray-backs.

Now all I got for running about,
Was two black eyes, and a bloody snout;
And that's the way it did turn out,
When I went off to prospect.
And now I'm loafing around dead broke,
My pistol and tools are all in soak,
And whiskey bills at me they poke—
But I'll make it right in the morning.

Once a would-be miner found a likely spot to stake a claim, he put up a tent or built a rough log cabin where he could sleep, prepare his food, and carry out household tasks. Camping in '49 was far from idyllic. Miners spent days in the cold mountain streams, nights on cold, damp ground. Food was scarce, and miners were indifferent cooks. Water was often impure, sewage disposal haphazard. Many miners came down with pneumonia, cholera, dysentery, or other serious, sometimes fatal diseases.

Chinese miners in camp performing their own household tasks. One chore only the Chinese performed was braiding each other's hair. Chopsticks replaced tableware American miners used, which might be only a hunting knife.

Interior of a miner's cabin. The miners shown here are far more tidy in appearance than most probably were. Mark Twain's cabin still stands along Highway 49 but seems far less spacious than this.

Miners were young and yearned for a good time with their hard-earned gold. Gambling halls did a land-office business, leaving many a miner poorer than when he arrived in the goldfields.

THE DAYS OF '49

Here you see old Tom Moore,
  A relic of by-gone days,
A bummer, too, they call me now;
  But what care I for praise?
For my heart is filled with woe,
  And I often grieve and pine
For the days of old, the days of gold,
  The days of '49.

I had comrades then, a saucy set,
  They were rough, I must confess,
But staunch and brave, as true as steel,
  Like hunters from the west.
But they, like many another fish,
  Have now run out their line;
But like good old bricks, they stood the
  kicks
  Of the days of '49.

There was Monte Pete — I'll ne'er forget
  The luck that he always had.
He'd deal for you both night and day,
  As long as you had a scad.
One night a pistol laid him out—
  'Twas his last lay out in fine.
It caught Pete sure, right bang in the door,
  In the days of '49.

There was Rattlesnake Jim who could out
  roar
  A buffalo bull, you bet!
He roared all night; he roared all day;
  He may be roaring yet.
One night he fell in a prospect hole—
  'Twas a roaring bad design—
And in that hole Jim roared out his soul
  In the days of '49.

California called many to the goldfields, and a good many she called were writers and would-be writers. Probably the best account of gold rush days was written by Bayard Taylor, a reporter for the *New York Tribune*, in his book *El Dorado*. Taylor caught the travel fever on his California trip and spent his life writing and editing travel books as well as producing novels and poetry. When he died in 1878, he was U.S. minister to Germany.

Most others wrote accounts of their days in the mines or diaries of their trip to California—it seemed like everyone who came intended to be an author. Many of these nonfiction accounts have been published, but some probably still languish forgotten in old family papers.

Two professional writers who came to the gold country wrote fiction that is still popular today. "The Outcasts of Poker Flat" by Bret Harte and "The Notorious Jumping Frog of Calaveras County" by Mark Twain are their best-known California stories. Mark Twain's story has inspired a yearly frog-jumping jubilee at Angels Camp, the setting of his story.

Bret Harte wrote many stories and poems about the gold rush, bringing to readers the flavor of the times. Here is an illustration from *Harper's Weekly*, 1881, which carried Harte's sentimental story "The Luck of Roaring Camp." The scene is the interior of a miner's cabin, where the characters from Roaring Camp have come to view a rarity in the mines: a baby. Its mother was a prostitute who died in childbirth.

The first months of the gold rush saw men's camps sprout all over the mining country. Mexicans often brought their families, but until the overland wagon parties began to arrive late in '49, very few American women were in any of the mining camps. One young miner was so homesick he walked 30 miles just to look at a woman. For entertainment miners held balls without women, as shown here, with men taking both parts. The "female" dance partner wore kerchiefs. When women did arrive, some found that although they had been wallflowers at home, they were belles of the ball in the mines.

Prostitutes, of course, came quickly, especially to San Francisco, where miners went to have a good time and spend their gold. A verse from the nineteenth century says:

> The miners came in forty-nine,
> The whores in fifty-one,
> And when they got together
> They produced the native son.

HOW THEY MINED THE GOLD

How the California mines were worked. A great many miners are at work, some picking, some panning, some washing, others shoveling gravel into a rocker. Miners in the foreground need only step out their door to go to work.

Panning. The pan was and is an indispensable tool for prospecting and mining. Californios and Latin Americans used bateas, slightly modified pans shaped like Chinese woks.

Chinese miners using a rocker, a more efficient tool for saving gold than a pan. One miner brings gravel to the rocker, while another pours water over the gravel and rocks the device with a wooden handle. Pebbles and rocks are halted on a screen at the top. Finer material passes into the body of the rocker, then over a series of slanted riffles intended to trap gold. Lighter, gold-free material and excess water pour down the trough and out the end.

The long tom, a still more efficient technique of mining, required more men. The first toms were hollowed out logs, but soon they were being neatly constructed of sawed lumber and sheet iron. A tom may be about 12 feet long and 8 inches deep, open at the top and both ends. The upper end is about a foot or two in width but widens to nearly twice that from the middle to the lower end. The bottom of the broad part is made of perforated sheet iron, with a riffle box under it to catch gold. One man shovels dirt into the upper part of the tom, while another breaks the clods apart with a hoe or shovel and stirs the mixture violently, also throwing aside rocks and pebbles too coarse to pass through the perforations. Sometimes miners would attach several feet of sluices to the upper end and shovel dirt in all along them.

A PROSPECTOR'S DREAM
Tune: "Oh, Susanna"

I dreamed a dream the other night when everything was still
I dreamed that I was carrying my long tom down a hill
My feet slipped out and I fell down, oh, how I jarred my liver
I watched my long tom till I saw it fetch up in the river.

Chorus:
O, what a miner, what a miner was I
All swelled up with the scurvy, so I thought I'd really die.

I took my shovel, pick and pan, to try a piece of ground,
I dreamed I struck the richest lead that ever had been found;
Then I wrote home that I had found a solid lead of gold,
And I'd be home in just a month, but what a lie I told!

I went to town and got drunk; in the morning, to my surprise,
I found that I had got a pair of roaring big black eyes,
And I was strapped had not a cent, not even pick or shovel.
My hair snarled up, my breeches torn, looked like the very devil.

Sluicing uses a sluice box, an open board trough, about 12 feet long and 12 to 40 inches wide. The troughs may be cobbled together to make a sluice several hundred feet in length. In ground sluicing, water is sent through a ditch instead of a trough. No carpentry is involved except at the bottom end, where a wooden sluice is fixed. Miners shovel dirt in along the length and stir it around with forks and shovels, tossing out large rocks. At the bottom are riffles arranged to catch gold, which, when full, are cleaned out and the gold saved.

Old steam dredge on the Sacramento River in 1849. Dredging was a failure in '49 but became California's chief method of mining gold in the mid-twentieth century.

Coyote diggings. Because bedrock in the California gold country was often buried under hills of gravel, yet was sometimes very rich in gold, miners undertook to reach the bedrock by means of shafts and tunnels. Since some of these looked like the dens of coyotes, that name was applied to the method. A shaft is a perpendicular opening large enough to accommodate a man and bucket. It is much like a well, except that miners were not seeking water and had to shore up the sides of the hole with boards to keep water out. Once bedrock was reached, one man stood in the shaft, filling buckets with what he hoped was gold-bearing gravel, which a man at the top pulled out of the hole, usually with the aid of a windlass. If the miner found a gold-bearing zone on bedrock, he followed it horizontally into the hillside, tunneling along like a mole in a burrow. He followed what miners called a lead, and when he tunneled he was said to be "drifting." He took the pay dirt out in a bucket, and his partner pulled the bucket out with their windlass.

Turning a river. Some miners were convinced that the bottom of the river contained enormous amounts of gold they could not reach by ordinary methods, so they formed companies to turn the river aside and get at its secrets when it was dry. To do this, they built a raceway for the water to flow down and dams to divert the river. Since dams had to be built in spring when the water came from melting snow, it was chilly work. Once the water was speeding down the raceway, the miners constructed wheels across it to power pumps to take the remaining water out of the river's bed. Then men threw out boulders, wheeled out rocks, erected toms and sluices, and took out the gold, if any. Sometimes they were rewarded richly—behind one boulder one group of men took out a pan of dirt that contained $5,227 worth of gold.

All too often, though, rains came earlier than expected, and all the workings were washed away before mining was complete. Or, as sometimes happened, there was not enough gold recovered to pay expenses.

Overleaf. More than 20 miners are occupied in a variety of tasks in this scene, drawn by J. D. Borthwick in 1851. Shown here is Kanoha Bar, 18 miles from Coloma. A company of 15 miners and 15 hired hands built this long wooden flume to divert the South Fork of the American River. It took two months and cost $3,500. Branching off the flume are several sluices for washing gold. The miners shown here are busy at a host of tasks, with the help of horses and mules. This particular effort yielded enough gold to repay the investment and a bit more. The flume could be dismantled and reassembled next year or moved to a different spot. Lumber, which cost $130 per thousand board feet, was too expensive to waste. The gold country bristled with flumes like these. Sutter and Marshall were right: supplying lumber was a good way to make money, maybe even get rich.

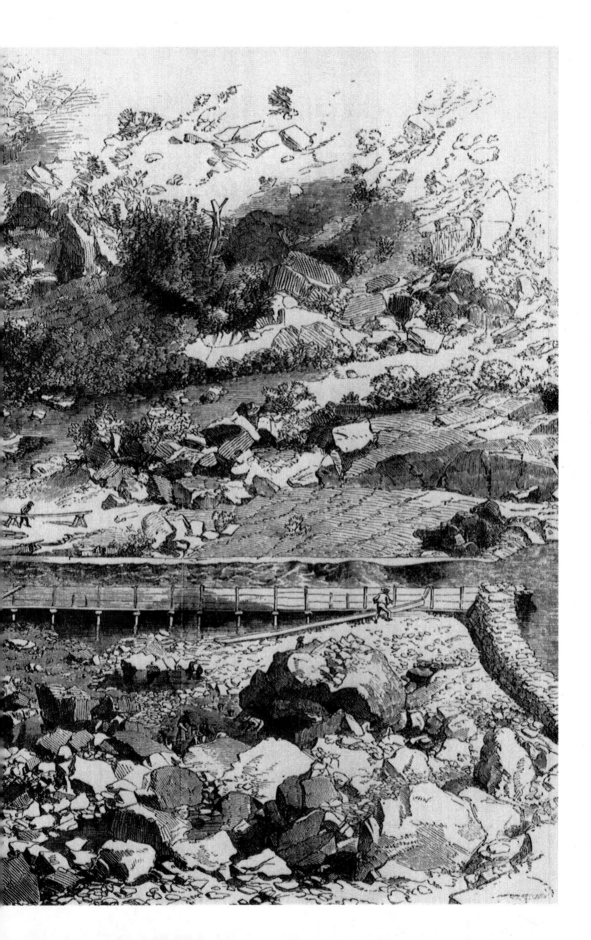

CHAPTER 6

The Natural History of Placer Gold

In 1848 and 1849 California miners were all placer miners, getting bits of loose gold washed down by streams. Placer gold is composed of dust and nuggets that have broken loose from the parent rock—probably a vein—and are now free to make their way downhill, pulled by gravity. They have been torn from the vein by weather—by storms beating on the rock and washing away broken bits; by rain and snow soaking into the vein; by freezing ice in winter expanding to break the rock apart; by wind blowing fine particles of rock away. Weathering, this constant attention by the elements is called.

Once a gold fragment has broken off, it first becomes part of the soil, then migrates downhill impelled by gravity, pushed into little rivulets that drain the hillside. These rivulets carry the gold into larger streams, then larger ones, until they come to stiller water, the sea or a lake. Very tiny gold particles—flour gold—may be dissolved or suspended in the stream water; larger ones bounce along the bottom of the streambed. A gold fragment's water journey is not steady. It may pause for an hour, a week, a century in a sandbank along the stream's course, or be pushed into a hole or behind a rock. If the stream dries, the gold particle may stay in place for a long time; if it floods, it may be whisked speedily downstream or whirled off to one side.

It was the sand and gravel banks—the miners called them bars—that the early miners worked. They gave them names: Rich Bar, Mormon Bar, Bidwell Bar. Spanish-speaking miners used "placer" to describe a gravel bank containing gold, and the word became part of the miner's linguistic currency to describe not only the gold deposits but also the act of mining them.

A gold particle may accompany the river to the sea, but it may take millennia to get there, and its journey may be interrupted not only by people pulling it out of the river but also by Earth processes that may change the river's course or destroy the

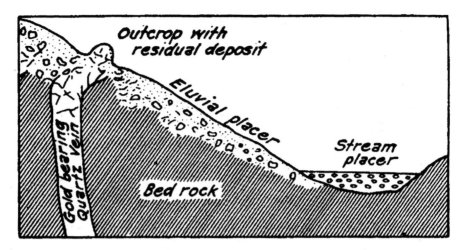

FIGURE 19. How gold, worn from the outcrop of a vein, works its way downhill to become a stream placer. A residual placer is one directly above the weathered vein. A hillside (eluvial) placer is en route to rivers, where it may become a stream (alluvial) placer.

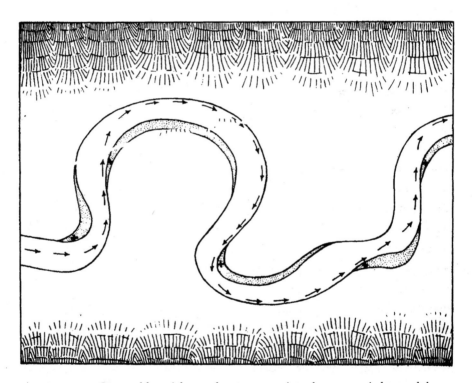

FIGURE 20. Once gold particles reach a stream or river, they are carried toward the sea by the downhill action of water. As the stream meanders, gold is more likely to be dropped on the inside of curves, where the force is less (stippled pattern).

river altogether. The saying went around among the miners that "gold is where you find it," meaning that it obeyed no discernible laws. But it does, and the law of gravity is the dominant one. Even so, knowing the laws that gold obeys did not always mean that gold was there to obey them.

Although we call them gold particles, most are a mixture of gold and silver and possibly a small amount of another metal such as copper. Gold is a noble metal, meaning it does not easily rust (oxidize). But silver does oxidize readily, and as the gold particles are carried in the water, some of the silver oxidizes and is washed away. That is part of the reason why gold nearer its source is less pure ("fine" is the word used in commerce) than gold nearer the end of its journey to the sea and why the outer rims of gold particles are finer (have less silver) than zones toward the center.

The fineness—purity—of gold is rated on a scale of 1000. Gold 1000 fine is pure gold, unmixed with other metals: 24 karat, in jeweler's terms. In placer deposits the fineness runs from about 500 (half gold) to 999. Gold from veins in the Sierra Nevada averaged 850 fine, while gold dredged from the Yuba River near Oroville, farther from the mountains, was 915 to 930 fine. Gold from beaches at Gold Bluff, Humboldt County, on the coast, ranged from 900 to 930 fine.

Gold not only does not rust, it has an additional advantage for miners: in nature, it makes very few chemical compounds. The element tellurium does bond with gold, making a series of gold tellurides. The most important ore tellurides are sylvanite ($AuAgTe_4$), a gray mineral containing 26 percent gold along with silver; and calaverite ($AuTe_2$), a bronze-colored mineral containing 40 percent gold. Calaverite was named for its occurrence in Calaveras County, but tellurides are rare in California and have not been commercially profitable as they are in Colorado.

As one might expect, gold particles are not only finer in the chemical sense (actually contain more gold) downstream, they are also finer in a mechanical sense—that is, they are smaller. Very tiny particles are easily carried toward the sea; larger nuggets require more force to move them and therefore travel more slowly. In addition, a large fragment may have corners knocked off as it tumbles along the bottom, growing smaller by attrition.

The amount of sand, gravel, gold, and trash a stream can carry—its capacity—depends on its volume and velocity. When all the particles being carried have the same specific gravity, then the rule is that if the velocity of a stream is doubled, the diameter of rock fragments it can carry is increased four times. Miners using sluices could easily see that the faster the water was moving, the larger the pebbles it moved. For example, a two-inch pebble can be rolled along by a water velocity of 3 feet per second; a one-foot rock requires 9 feet per second; a boulder two feet in diameter needs 13 feet per second.

Velocity, in turn, depends on the slope down which the stream flows, the volume of water, the shape of the stream channel, and the amount and weight of the stream's load—the sand and gravel it is carrying. All of these factors change from time to time. As the stream continues to flow, it erodes its bed, gradually reducing the slope; however, mountain-building movements may lift the land near its head, making its gradient steeper and its waters flow faster.

Volume, of course, varies with storms. Floodwaters can move prodigious amounts. When the St. Francis Dam near Los Angeles broke in 1921, blocks of concrete weighing ten thousand tons each—as well as a locomotive—were moved by the water.

Miners were less interested in what a stream could carry than what it might leave. Spring rains and melting snow push particles downhill to the streams. With plenty of water, they can move the debris along, but when summer comes and the streams have less volume, they drop some of their load—sand, gravel, and, perhaps, gold. The dropped load may remain unmolested for a week, a month, a year, or a century, until the stream once again is strong enough to pick it up and move it.

Where the load is dropped is of great interest to miners. Because the velocity of a stream is greatest in its center, the stream is less likely to drop its load there. It drops the excess it cannot carry in places where the velocity is reduced: where the stream widens, at turns, or where it joins another watercourse. The insides of bends, where suction eddies form (see fig. 21), is where the stream drops what it needs to, forming the river bars beloved of the forty-niners. On the outside of bends, where pressure eddies form, the stream is more likely to erode its banks than to deposit its load.

It is easy to see why this is so. If a marching band makes a right-angle turn and wishes to keep its lines straight, players on the inside of the turn must take mincing steps, nearly marching in place, while those on the outside must take long strides and hurry. Anyone stepping in the path of the band would find being hit by a player on the outside much more forceful than being struck by a pivot player.

Because the stream flows downhill, the force of gravity is urging it toward the sea. Gravity is also pulling the gold toward the bottom of the channel, because gold is very heavy—the heaviest of the metals. The density of pure gold is about 19 grams per cubic centimeter, that is, nineteen times more than water's. Gold's specific gravity (density) is therefore 19. The specific gravity of quartz is 2.7. In water, gold has roughly eight times the effective specific gravity of quartz (which is what much sand is made of). For this reason, gold tends to be deposited with pebbles and to work its way through the gravel and sand to the bottom of the streambed toward bedrock. The churning action of the stream aids the gold particles in their vertical trip. As the sand and gravel in the bed load of the stream are roiled, gold particles sink rapidly toward the bottom. This is essentially what happens in a gold pan: as the gravel is

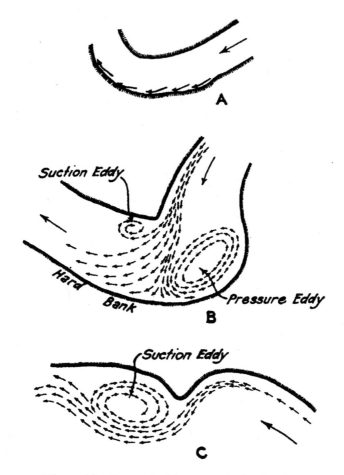

FIGURE 21. Where eddies form and gold may stop in river bends.

A. As a river bends, the place of greatest erosion is on the outside, as marked by arrows. Where the stream is eroding, gold cannot settle.

B. Another view of a river bend, showing where pressure eddies and suction eddies form. Gold is more likely to be dropped in a suction eddy than a pressure eddy.

C. When a stream hits an outside curve, the force of the water against the bank is unlikely to allow gold to drop, but where there is an impediment—such as a hard rock projecting into the stream—just beyond the curve, the water will be deflected out into the stream, allowing a suction eddy, a place where gold might drop, to form shoreward of it.

shaken and the pan whirled, particles with higher specific gravity head toward the bottom, while lighter grains are floated off the top. Table 1 gives the specific gravity of a few common minerals, as well as gold.

When the gold reaches bedrock, it is most likely to remain if the streambed is not perfectly smooth. Potholes, natural riffles, and irregularities in the bedrock are places where gold can get caught and perhaps remain even if the velocity of the stream

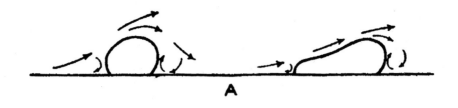

FIGURE 22. How irregularities in a streambed affect water current.

A. As the current strikes the round boulder to the left, an eddy forms, and some of its load—including gold—may be dropped before passing over. After the water passes over the boulder, another eddy is formed. It, too, may contain dropped gravel and gold, though probably not as much. As the current strikes the second, more elongated boulder to the right, no eddy forms on the currentward side of the rock, but eddies are formed on the lee side, where some gravel and gold may be dropped. The eddies are all likely spots for the accumulation of gold.

B. The direction in which pebbles are tilted reflects the direction of stream flow (shown by arrows). Geologists and miners use the alignment of pebbles in ancient stream channels to determine which way the stream flowed when water was running in it.

TABLE 1. *The Specific Gravity of Some Common Minerals*

The listing below shows how much heavier gold is than other minerals. Because gold is so dense, it tends to work its way to the bottom of sand lenses to form pay streaks.

Specific Gravity	Mineral	Specific Gravity	Mineral	Specific Gravity	Mineral
2.07	Sulfur	2.80	Talc	8.94	Copper
2.20	Graphite	3.00	Mica	10.50	Silver
2.30	Gypsum	3.51	Diamond	11.37	Lead
2.70	Quartz	4.68	Zircon	14.40	Mercury
2.75	Beryl	7.20	Tin	19.30	Gold

increases. Many gold particles finding the same hiding place become pay streaks for a future miner. One particularly good place with natural riffles was along the foothills of the Sierra Nevada, where ancient beds of schist (rock with a layered structure, often derived from shale) stand nearly vertical, uplifted during mountain building. These upended beds give a washboard effect, and gold particles tend to get trapped in the troughs.

If a gold particle reaches the sea, it may remain in a delta, move on to a beach, or, if extremely fine, continue into the ocean. Delta is the fourth letter of the Greek alphabet; a capital delta is shaped like a triangle (Δ). When the Greek historian Herodotus saw the fan-shaped deposit at the mouth of the Nile, he called it a delta, and *delta* has become a physiographic term.

California rivers have not built huge deltas where they enter the sea, as have the Mississippi and the Nile. California's delta country is inland, where the Sacramento and the San Joaquin rivers meet and hesitate before entering San Francisco Bay. As both of these rivers are fed by streams from gold-bearing areas (the Sierra Nevada and the Klamath Mountains), it is likely that particles of gold were deposited in the delta muds. However, this is California's prime agricultural land, and no amount of gold would make it worthwhile to destroy the topsoil.

The gold particles on the beach may form streaks or lens-shaped deposits of gold, because gravity separates the heavier minerals into layers on the beach as it does in the streambed. Particles that go out to sea are often washed back on shore during storms or even high tide, joining the particles that stayed on the beach. The washing-machine action of the surf tends to winnow out the less dense particles and enrich the pay streak on the beach. Miners, aware that storms sometimes brought in gold, erroneously concluded that gold comes from seawater. The truth is just as strange, as we shall see in chapter 9.

Prospectors have searched the California beaches for gold for a long time. This type of mining was especially popular during the Great Depression of the 1930s, when many people were out of work (see chap. 13), but their efforts yielded only small amounts of gold. The beach deposits of Nome, Alaska, have been the world's richest.

So gold is being carried from its source in the veins of the mountains downhill and then downstream toward the sea. All of it does not reach the sea—if it did, we would have no gold placers. The sea itself contains one part of gold in 600 million parts of water, but so far no one has found an economical way to remove it.

We have seen that gold particles get smaller the farther they travel: as they are knocked about in the tumbling gravel beds, they become rounded, and their edges get clipped off. Larger placer nuggets are more likely to be found close to the source, as there hasn't been time to wear them down, and large nuggets resist traveling far.

How does this fit with the miner's notion that "gold grows"? Those engaged in moss mining (see below) were convinced that gold grew, that it was an annual crop. Others pointed out that because gold is malleable (an ounce of gold can be hammered into a thin sheet that will cover 100 square feet) and ductile (it can be stretched into a wire 50 miles long), grains might stick together when pounded in the riverbed, making nuggets out of smaller pieces.

To test whether gold particles do get smaller as they are hammered, in 1975 U.S. Geological Survey geologist Warren Yeend tumbled them in the laboratory with cobbles and sand, as they would be in a natural stream. He found that yes, they did get smaller—10 grains were broken into 68 grains, and a portion of the gold was broken into fragments too fine to save by panning. He found, too, that wet sand (as in a streambed) broke up the gold better than dry sand did and that how fast the water ran was more important than how far it traveled (in the laboratory, how long they were tumbled). When he increased the water velocity, and therefore the rate of tumbling, the particles were broken up ten times as fast. Yeend's experiment showed that grains do not clump together to make nuggets—quite the opposite. Gold particles get smaller, not larger, as they are hammered in the riverbed.

Until recently most scientists thought that all nuggets were simply large chunks of gold that were worn out of the vein in big pieces and not yet broken completely apart. Gold nuggets were the product of attrition; they just hadn't yet been worn down to gold dust or flour. Nuggets, in other words, simply started out larger. Most nuggets are, without doubt, detrital—that is, the product of weathering. And not just California nuggets. Researchers working in New Guinea, Canada, and elsewhere in the United States came to the same conclusion.

But that is not the whole story. As early as 1908, a mining engineer pointed out that moss mining showed that gold was probably both detrital (worn from the vein) and chemical (added to by chemical action):

> On the Trinity river, in California, a stream which runs through some of the best gold-bearing ground in the State, and has rich placer ground on both banks nearly over its whole length, there occurs during the summer season of low water a heavy growth of algae in the low pools along the banks, and a species of dense moss covers the banks. These plants are constantly being submerged during local floods, and again on the water retiring, subjected to the burning heat of the sun, so that partial decomposition is always going on. During the rainy season these growths are entirely covered by high water. . . . Now it has been discovered that these plants contain considerable gold, and every spring, towards the end of the rainy season, the miners . . . collect the mosses and wash them for their gold contents. . . . [T]he function of the plant life in these cases is probably to a great extent mechanical, as the fine gold caught on their surfaces, while flaky and excessively fine, does not show sharp edges. . . . [But under the microscope] we find bright hair-shaped particles bent at

FOOL'S GOLD

During the century and a half after James Marshall's discovery of gold in California, miners found other minerals in California streams that closely resembled the much-sought-after gold. A bright golden gleam from the bottom of a pan of gravel caused gold hunters' hearts to skip a beat. But all too often when the assayer tested it, the mineral was not gold but merely a gold-colored mineral. The disappointed miner returned to his claim empty-handed, having been fooled by worthless "false" gold—"fool's" gold.

The mineral that fooled could be any of a number of common California minerals. The most common masqueraders are iron sulfides: pyrite, chalcopyrite, pyrrhotite, and marcasite. Surprisingly, weathered flaky biotite, a mica, is also a fooler.

One good way to tell gold from these fool's gold minerals is to check its streak—the color of the powdered mineral. It can be checked most easily by rubbing the mineral against a piece of unglazed white porcelain or tile. Only gold makes a golden mark; the others have blackish marks, except for mica, which is too flimsy to make a streak at all.

Pyrite is the mineral most often mistaken for gold. It is found in veins or as scattered grains in many types of rocks. Seen on exposed rock surfaces or as grains in a stream, pyrite often appears brown on the outside, because the exposed parts have been rusted to limonite, another iron mineral. The crystal faces of pyrite may be striated parallel to the edges of the face. It can be distinguished from gold by its greater hardness, its lower specific gravity, its greenish black streak, and the striations on its crystal faces when they are present.

Chalcopyrite, pyrrhotite, and marcasite are less common than pyrite but can be found in veins or as scattered grains in California rocks. These minerals, like pyrite, all have a dark streak and are lighter in weight and harder than gold. Pyrrhotite, when pure, is magnetic, which gold and the other fool's gold minerals are not, and can be picked out of gravel (along with magnetite) with a strong magnet. Because none of these minerals, unlike pyrite, commonly occurs in crystalline form, they are most often found as irregularly shaped, homogeneous masses, as gold is. All tarnish easily, going from bronze or brassy yellow to yellowish or grayish brown.

Biotite is common in granitic rocks of the Sierra

different angles and all having the appearance of embryonic crystallization. This would tend to prove that the river waters carry gold in actual solution as well as in suspension, and that this gold is precipitated [on the plants].

Some geochemists from Russia and North America agree. True, the gold particles are smaller downstream, but they also become purer—finer in the chemical sense. Some of this can be accounted for by the loss of silver when it oxidizes in the water and is washed away, but not enough silver is lost to account for the increase in the percentage of gold. What is more, geochemists have shown, crystals of gold are more common in placers than in source rocks. They see this as chemical action—precipitation—of gold in placers, the gold coming from the vein and being dissolved by groundwater. The gold crystals have sharp edges, not at all what one would expect in placer deposits, where pebbles and rocks are being rounded by the stream.

Gold and Fool's Gold Compared

Mineral	Color	Specific Gravity	Hardness	Streak	Chemical Formula
Biotite	Black*	2.7–3.1	2.5–3	None	Complex silicate
Chalcopyrite	Brassy yellow	4.1–4.3	3.5–4	Green black	$CuFeS_2$
Marcasite	Pale bronze yellow	4.85–4.9	6–6.5	Brown black	FeS_2
Pyrite	Pale brassy yellow	4.95–5.1	6–6.5	Green black	FeS_2
Pyrrhotite	Bronze yellow	4.58–4.64	3.5–4.5	Gray black	$Fe_{(1-x)}S$
Gold	Golden yellow	19.3	2.5–3	Golden yellow	Au

*Turns dull, brassy yellow when exposed to air and water.

Nevada. As these rocks erode, the small black flakes of biotite are washed into streams and, after a short exposure to air and water, turn a dull brassy yellow. Because of their light weight and flat shape, biotite flakes may be concentrated in quiet eddies and along sandbanks. Flakes of biotite have fooled many gold panners in the Sierra Nevada foothills.

Gold is very heavy, the heaviest of the metals. Although it occurs in small flakes like biotite, and is as soft as biotite, it has a golden yellow streak. Gold, unlike the brittle iron sulfide minerals, is malleable, as Marshall and Sutter proved with their tests of Marshall's gold nugget. ✕

In 1920 a man working in British Columbia found an old, square nail on bedrock that was festooned with clusters of gold crystals. Proof, miners said, that gold does indeed grow in placers. More recently Russian geologists working in the Ural Mountains have discovered stream-worn nuggets that have crystal faces, and gold rims on other minerals, and films and threads of gold on pebbles in the gravel.

Gold is nearly insoluble in most liquids. The alchemists used aqua regia, a mixture of nitric and hydrochloric acids, to dissolve it. But given enough time, gold can be dissolved in groundwater and streams, particularly if the water carries organic and inorganic acids. This dissolved gold will then precipitate on other fragments of gold in placers. Time is what is needed, and time the Earth has.

Gold may grow also with the direct help of organisms. Scientists of the U.S. Geological Survey put spores of the soil bacterium *Bacillus cereus* in a solution of gold chloride in water and shook the mixture. When the spores were examined under an electron microscope, they were found to be coated with gold. The researchers thought that the gold bonded chemically with the spore surfaces, forming "a foundation for growth of crystalline gold." Once crystals started growing they continued to do so long after the spores were dead.

But crystals are rare in gold deposits of any kind, vein or placer. Although researchers found that gold accumulated chemically on bacteria cells, the gold took the shape of bacteria, not crystals. Even so, all bacteria-shaped gold fragments are not truly bacterial. Experiments showed that the appearance of gold-coated bacteria could be achieved in the laboratory inorganically, either by accident or by design.

If some nuggets do indeed grow, why aren't the largest ones found farthest downstream in the quietest settings, where they have the most uninterrupted time in which to grow? The answer, I think, is that attrition works to make large pieces of gold broken from the vein smaller faster than chemical or organic processes add to them. The stream simply is not powerful enough near its mouth to carry large nuggets, so they are dropped along the way, perhaps to grow a little more in their new home. If we can determine exactly how nuggets form, we might know better where to find them. Or perhaps we should just wait for nature to make us some new ones.

MINING THE DEAD RIVERS

Much of California's gold came from the channels of rivers that no longer flow. They, like the modern stream deposits the miners first worked, are alluvial; but because the deposits had been so long deserted by the ancient streams, they became hardened—cemented—and required more Herculean measures to recover their gold. The answer was hydraulic and drift mining.

Someone early in the history of mining in California told the miners these old beds were of Tertiary age. Perhaps it was J. B. Trask, a forty-niner with Audubon's party, or some other forty-niner who had geological expertise. Even Dame Shirley had taken several geology courses in the East before coming to California. Wherever they got the idea, it was correct. The old streams ran during epochs of the Tertiary Period—in Eocene, Oligocene, Miocene, and Pliocene times (see the geologic time scale below). The oldest channels, those of Eocene age (50 million years old), were richest.

In late Cretaceous time, 70 million years ago, the Sierra Nevada was a low mountain range that drained into a nearby shallow sea. The climate was subtropical, allowing deep weathering of the mountains. Then in the Eocene, the mountains began to rise again, shedding debris—including sand, gravel, clay, and gold—that millions of years of quiet weathering had accumulated and washed down the streams toward the sea. The clay traveled farthest because it was finest, piled up in seaside deltas, and today is mined by ceramics industries. It took longer for the larger pieces—the gravel—and the heavier gold to make their way to the sea. Much was still in the rivers when volcanoes from higher in the mountains began to erupt, throwing out ash that dammed the rivers and formed small lakes, forcing streams to find new routes. As Tertiary time went on, volcanoes spewed out different kinds of materials—lava, coarse volcanic detritus, and mudflows—that covered much of the ash as well as the streams. Again the streams had to find new channels, and they finally settled on routes very close to those of today. Stream channels of this volcanic episode are called intervolcanic channels.

The oldest channel gravel deposits—those of Eocene age—the miners called "blue gravels." They were the deepest, richest, and most sought after. Natural riffles in the bedrock in these old channels halted the gold, creating very rich gold pockets. Where the old streams flowed over limestone, the pockets were exceptionally rich. Limestone is basically calcium carbonate ($CaCO_3$), soluble, and easily scoured by sand and pebbles, forming deep potholes that are perfect resting places for gold fragments. The towns of Volcano and Columbia are on limestone. Today, now that hydraulic mining has done its work, one can visit these towns and see the river bottom as it was in Tertiary time, bereft of its water.

Above the deep gravel deposits were what the miners called bench gravels—floodplain deposits of yesteryear. In places, these beds were as much as three hundred feet thick. Sometimes revitalized streams cut through the bench deposits and left deposits of their own, deeper down than the bench gravels, although younger. In some places these streams stole gold from the deep, "blue" gravel beds, causing the miners headaches to sort it out so they could steal the gold back from these Tertiary "sluice robbers."

At Mokelumne Hill there is a complicated series of eight channels ranging in age from Eocene to Pliocene. At Oroville Table Mountain (where the Cherokee hydraulic pit is) the

The Geologic Time Scale			
Era	Period	Epoch	Millions of Years Ago
Cenozoic	Quaternary	Holocene	0.01
		Pleistocene	2
	Tertiary	Pliocene	5
		Miocene	24
		Oligocene	36
		Eocene	54
		Paleocene	65
Mesozoic	Cretaceous		144
	Jurassic		208
	Triassic		245
Paleozoic	Permian		286
	Pennsylvanian		330
	Mississippian		360
	Devonian		408
	Silurian		438
	Ordovician		505
	Cambrian		570
Precambrian			4,000

whole gravel sequence is covered by basalt, while at Tuolumne Table Mountain a covering of lighter-colored volcanic rock fills the streams and caps the gravel beds. Where the volcanic cover was too hard to be hydraulicked away, miners used drift methods, tunneling into the hillsides below the volcanic cap to reach the old river channels.

Gold particles in the gravel beds ranged from flour size to large nuggets, some weighing more than one hundred ounces, but much was about the size of a mustard seed. Most of the grains were flat, having been pounded by the cobbles in the stream. The chemical fineness of the gold ranged from 840 to more than 950. The gold was in black sand, composed chiefly of the mineral magnetite with some other minerals, including pyrite. A few grains, even some nuggets, of platinum went along for the ride, as well as diamonds.

In the Sierra Nevada Tertiary channel deposits extended from Butte and Plumas counties in the north to Tuolumne County in the south, and reached nearly to the crest of the Sierra Nevada range. The Tertiary counterparts of many of today's rivers that drain the western slope of the Sierra Nevada—the Yuba, American, Mokelumne, Calaveras, and Tuolumne—were rich in gold, as were some of the isolated channels, like the Magalia, no longer related to the streams. In terms of richness, the short Magalia channel, mined chiefly by underground drift methods, heads the list, followed by Cherokee and Bangor (all three in Butte County); branches of the Tertiary Yuba River, including, among many others, Poker Flat in Sierra County and North Bloomfield in Nevada County (where the Malakoff mine was); the Tertiary American River, Gold Run, Placerville, and Iowa Hill included; the Tertiary Mokelumne River, including Volcano; and the Tertiary Tuolumne River, where the Columbia diggings proved enormously rich.

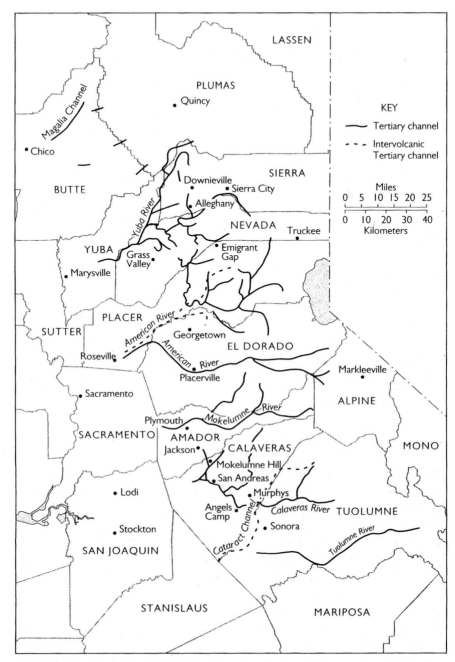

Sierran rivers of Tertiary time. The older channels, called here "Tertiary channels," are those of about 50 million years ago. The "intervolcanic channels" are younger, dating from approximately 30 million to 2 million years ago (but also Tertiary).

How a Tertiary stream was dammed and rerouted by volcanic ash and volcanic mud.

A. A stream of about 50 million years ago meanders through the gentle western slope of the Sierra Nevada. In the lower foothills, it had encountered a ridge of tough, resistant rock; it has cut through the ridge and is plunging over a waterfall to the region underlain by softer rock below and to the west. A cutout of the stream channel shows gravel in the bottom of the bed. Mixed with the gravel are nuggets and tiny fragments of gold, worn from the higher mountains and being carried by the stream toward the sea.

B. About 20 million years ago, ash, falling from volcanoes erupting higher in the mountains, has clogged the stream. Where once the stream poured over the resistant ridge in a rushing waterfall, a dam of ash has ponded the water behind the ridge. In the cutout, ash may be seen covering the gravel of the river bottom.

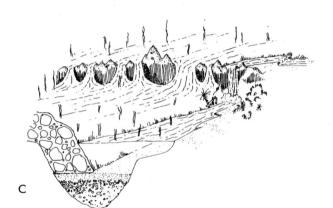

C

D

c. During the next 18 million years, steaming volcanic mudflows rolled downhill from near the Sierran crest, covering much of the landscape. Here the stream has been forced to seek a new route through the resistant ridge; parts of the ridge and about half of the streambed in the foreground have been covered by the mud. The cutout shows a succession of deposits, including the original gravel in the bottom of the channel, followed in turn by ash, and then partly covered by a mixture of volcanic mud and rock.

d. The mud has cooled, and a new river has established its way though the resistant ridge. The original route of the stream behind the ridge is now abandoned. The new stream course crosses the abandoned channel in the background; where it crosses, the stream may steal gold from the older channel. Where the channel lies buried and untouched by the new stream, gold may be locked beneath the ash and volcanic mud.

    The cutout shows an older, buried gravel deposit, an ash bed, a volcanic mud layer, and new gravel layers. Since the stream now has more water, and therefore more erosive power, the new deposit is actually lower than the older one. Part of the older gravel in the bottom of the bed and part of the covering ash have been reworked by the modern stream.

Cross-section of present-day topography in a portion of the foothills of the northern Sierra Nevada showing how complex the relationship between the various stream channels can be. The bottom of the first, primary channel is not as low as that of the secondary channel not far from it. The primary gold-bearing channel was covered by ash, and then both it and the two gold-bearing secondary channels were covered by andesitic (a type of lava) volcanic mudflows and lava flows; then a new channel was cut that has no gold, and it is covered by more lava. The modern topography is "reversed."

A

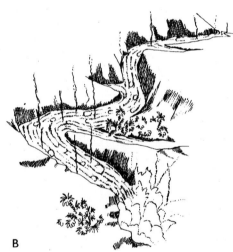

B

C

Stages in the creation of Tuolumne (Stanislaus) Table Mountain.

A. The Tertiary Stanislaus River flowed through moderately rolling hills, flanked by subtropical vegetation.

B. Nine and a half million years ago, steaming lava followed the easiest course downhill— the bed of the river. It filled, but did not overflow, the river valley.

C. The lava flow, being much harder than the surrounding hills, still marks the course of the ancient river. The softer rock of the enclosing hills has been eroded away, leaving a high, sinuous ridge where once there was a river valley.

Miners in search of gold could not break apart the hard, tough lava flow, so they tunneled under it to reach the ancient Stanislaus River bed, most of which had been preserved by the lava flow, gold and all, as it was 9.5 million years ago.

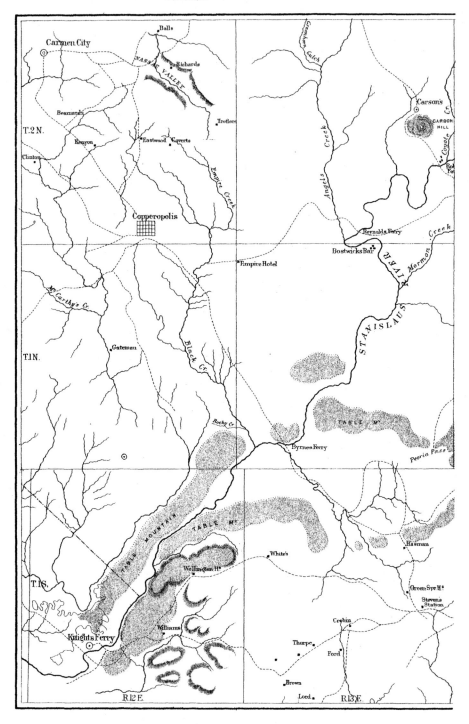

Map showing extent of Tuolumne (Stanislaus) Table Mountain, made by J. D. Whitney, the California State Geologist, and published in 1880. What is left of that long lava flow is shown here in pattern.

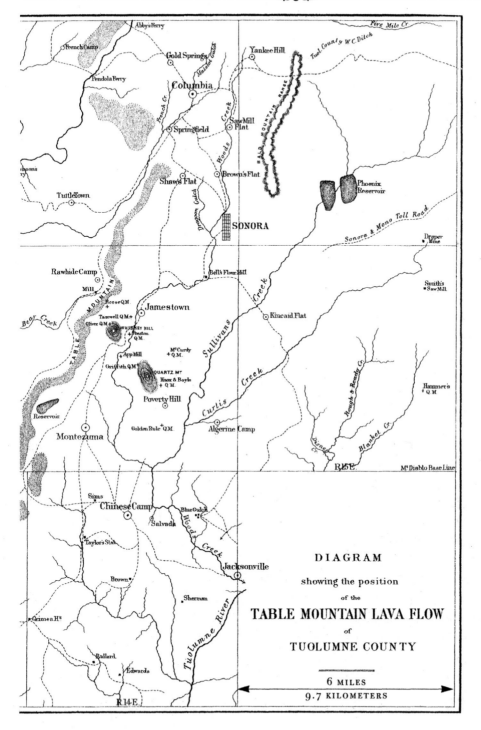

DIAGRAM

showing the position

of the

TABLE MOUNTAIN LAVA FLOW

of

TUOLUMNE COUNTY

6 MILES
9.7 KILOMETERS

CHAPTER SEVEN

The Mud Flood

The most spectacular method of placer mining, hydraulic mining, or hydraulicking, was, the miners insisted, invented in California. Whether it was or not, hydraulicking nearly split the new state in half, pushing it into a civil war whose salvos were fired in the courts and the legislature and which culminated in a private militia. The environmental conflict pitted miners against farmers, rich against the not-so-rich, absentee owners against residents, mountain dwellers against valley dwellers. It split both political parties and almost created a third.

The principles of hydraulic mining are simple, so simple that some writers have maintained that it was not invented at all but developed as a natural consequence of mining. Most miners and reporters asserted that Connecticut Yankee Edward E. Matteson (spelled in a variety of ways) invented hydraulic mining by attaching a nozzle to a canvas hose made by his partner, Anthony Chabot. The Romans used a primitive system of ground sluicing, as Pliny, science's first martyr (he died observing the eruption of Vesuvius in A.D. 79), recorded. He did not, however, mention a nozzle, which is essential to hydraulic mining as we know it today.

In order for this type of placer mining to work, there must be a large supply of water located a considerable elevation above the mine, a large supply of gravel to be worked, and some place for the debris—the tailing, or "tailings" as the miners called it—to go. All of these conditions were admirably met in the northern California gold country. Nineteenth-century companies owning large hydraulic mines obtained water high in the Sierra Nevada; they claimed, bought, or leased vast tracts of gold-bearing land. The argument came over the last requirement: someplace for the waste to go.

Mining was given top priority and unusual privileges in California. California had been founded on gold, and many of its legislators were, or had been, gold min-

FIGURE 23. Edward E. Matteson as a young man, probably about the time he added a nozzle to a hose and thereby "invented" hydraulic mining.

ers. For example, miners could take water from the mountains and use it as they wished, with no regard for those downstream. The lawyer and historian John S. Hittell, writing in 1858 on the mineral resources of California, summed it up:

> There is no limit to the amount [of water] which a man may claim. He may take the largest river in the mountains; he may take a dozen of them and hold them all. He may not only take all their water, but he may take all the land necessary to use it. He may make reservoirs covering hundreds of acres. He may make ditches a hundred miles long. All that is necessary to give him a possessory title to the water and the land, is that he should drive stakes along the route of the ditch, post up notices of his intention, and commence work in building the dam and cutting the ditch.

Here is how this new hydraulic mining system worked, as William H. Brewer, a member of the California Geological Survey, saw it in 1862:

> The river here makes a curve. A stratum of soil twenty or thirty feet thick forms a flat at the curve of the river, of limited extent. The "bed rock" beneath this is . . . much twisted, contorted in every shape . . . and much of it very hard. The soil above is *very* hard, like rock itself, made up of loose rounded bowlders, cemented by a firm red clay into a mass as hard as ordinary sandstone. In this the gold is found.
> Deep ditches are cut, not only through this, but deep down into the hard bed rock beneath, often twenty or more feet into the latter, and running out in to the river.

In these are the "sluices"—merely long troughs for conveying the water. The bottoms of these sluices are made of blocks sawed from the ends of partially squared timber, so that the end of the grain is presented to the surface, sometimes of a double row, sometimes, however, of but a single row of blocks. These do not lie perfectly square and level, so, as the water flows swiftly over them, they cause a ripple, like water flowing swiftly over the stony bed of a stream. The bottom of the box or trough, below these blocks, is perfectly tight, and quicksilver [mercury] is poured in and collects in all the holes between the blocks.

Ditches, from miles back in the mountains, bring the water up against the hillside, far above the surface of the flat, and a flume, or "raceway," built on high stilts, over seventy or one hundred feet high, brings the water directly over the "claim." A very stout hose, often six inches in diameter, conducts the water down from this high head, and has at its end a nozzle like that of a fire engine, only larger. Now, this stream of water, heavy and issuing with enormous force from the great pressure of so high a head of water, is made to play against this bank of hard earth, which melts away before it like sand, and all flows into the sluices—mud, bowlders, gold. The mud is carried off in the stream of thick, muddy water; the bowlders, if not too large, roll down with the swift current; the heavier gold falls in the crevices and is dissolved in the quicksilver, as sugar or salt would be in water. In some mines these sluices are miles long, and are charged with quicksilver by the thousands of pounds. This washing down banks by such a stream of water under pressure is "hydraulic mining." After a certain time the sluices are "cleaned up," that is, the blocks are removed, the quicksilver, amalgamated with the gold, is taken out, the former then driven off by heat—"retorted"—and the gold left.

From a miner's point of view, hydraulic mining was a gift from the gods.

From Matteson's small beginning, hydraulic mining methods gradually improved. In 1870 the simple nozzle was replaced by the "Little Giant," or monitor—an enormous metal contrivance shaped like a cannon with a 6- to 10-inch bore, mounted so a miner could swing it easily and balanced with rocks so he could aim it vertically. In place of powder and cannon balls, this cannon projected water, but the noise it made was as loud as that of a military cannon, and *steady*. Instead of a simple canvas hose, one was constructed of sheet iron that would withstand immense pressure. With these new improvements miners could aim and shoot a stream of water forceful enough to rip apart a hillside from a distance of hundreds of feet. It may have been the most powerful erosive force in the 570-million-year history of the Sierra Nevada.

No one knows precisely how much gold was won from hydraulic mines in California. In 1878 Hamilton Smith, of the North Bloomfield Gravel Company, one of the largest hydraulic mining companies, estimated in court testimony that hydraulic mines were producing $11 million to $13 million a year. Of course, he was on the side of the mines and may have been exaggerating. State Geologist Josiah Whitney, in his tome, *The Auriferous Gravels of the Sierra Nevada of California*,

FIGURE 24. Miners engaged in hydraulic mining in the very early days. Here one man is able to hold the hose and point it toward the bank while others prepare to shovel the wet gravel. No one here appears to be afraid of the bank caving. When stronger jets of water were used, miners stood hundreds of feet away from the unstable bank.

echoed this estimate, giving $12 million to $14 million yearly as the figure for drift and hydraulic mining. For the late 1870s the state's annual gold production was $15 million to $19 million, making hydraulic mining's contribution at least two-thirds. During the thirty-year period 1854–1884, hydraulic and drift mining contributed about a third of the gold produced. A good guess for the total overall production by hydraulic and drift mining, when gold was officially $20 an ounce, is $300 million.

At $100 per ounce, the figure would be raised to $1.5 billion; at $800 gold—nearly the highest price in recent years—$12 billion.

To produce much of this, miners along the Feather, Yuba, Bear, and American rivers ripped up 1,295 million cubic yards of gravel—enough to cover Washington, D.C., with a blanket of debris nineteen feet thick. In 1880 alone the debris washed into the Sacramento and San Joaquin rivers was calculated at more than 46 million yards. Just the amount thrown into the Yuba during an eighteen-month period could have completely filled the Erie Canal.

"The amount of soil removed in hydraulic mining must be seen to be believed," wrote Brewer in his diary in 1864. "The mud not only muddies the Sacramento River for more than 400 miles of its course but is slowly and surely filling up the Bay of San Francisco. In the sierra, the soil from hundreds of acres together has already been sluiced off the rock, which it formerly covered even to a depth of 150 feet! I have seen works and effects that one would imagine would take centuries to produce, instead of the dozen years that have elapsed since the work began."

To wash these mountains—literally—of material, miners used an enormous amount of water. No longer would a ditch dug by a few men suffice. Already, water companies had constructed ditches from the higher mountains down to the mines and charged miners—not just hydraulic miners—for its use. To meet the requirements of hydraulic mining, huge projects were undertaken, requiring the work of hundreds of men and the expenditure of many dollars.

The Giants discharged as much as 1,500 "miner's inches" of water per minute, or about a million gallons an hour. In 1879 the mines of the North Bloomfield Gravel Company used more than 15 billion gallons of water. The Spring Valley mine, at Cherokee Flat, required 36 million gallons every twenty-four hours, or about three times what the city of San Francisco needed. All of this water came from the Sierra Nevada, through an expensive network of dams, reservoirs, and artificial watercourses. Dams upstream on the American, Bear, Yuba, and Feather rivers could impound 50 billion gallons and supply it to the miners through 6,000 miles of main line ditches and 1,000 miles of subsidiary ones.

This required capital. New, permanent companies were formed, not seasonal ones as the miners were used to, both to supply water and to do the actual mining. A whole new industry began: the buying and selling of mining stocks. It even had its own stock market, the Mining Exchange, which operated in San Francisco for nearly a century. Part of the bad feeling during the long years of the hydraulic mining controversy arose because farmers saw the mining interests as being controlled from afar, by rich men from San Francisco and England who had speculated in the market but had never even seen the mines or the farms.

As far back as 1856 miners had begun to wonder, if not worry, about what would

TABLE 2. *How Much Water It Takes for Placer Mining*	
For	Water Needed
Rocker	4–5 gallons per minute, or 80–100 gallons per cubic yard, if water is reused
Ground sluicing	22,000–162,000 gallons per cubic yard
Bucket-line dredge	3,500–10,000+ gallons per minute (cubic yards worked varies with pressure system of dredge)
Hydraulicking	2,000–32,000 gallons per cubic yard.

ultimately happen to the tailing they were so blithely washing into the streams. In 1862 they found out. Early that year the heavens opened and the rains came—more than anyone could remember or imagine. In just two months, between November 11, 1861, and January 14, 1862, 72 inches—6 feet!—fell on Sonora, in Tuolumne County. By February the total had reached 102 inches—8 ½ feet—and similar amounts were falling up and down the Sierra. It rained for twenty-eight days straight in dry Los Angeles. The entire Central Valley—the Sacramento and the San Joaquin—was underwater. Thousands of farms were cut off, leaving cattle stranded or dying. Even the tops of the new telegraph poles were underwater.

Poor Marysville, county seat of Yuba County, and its twin, tiny Yuba City, county seat of Sutter County, were even harder hit than Sacramento. (California has a way of displacing names that should go together. Mount Lassen is in Shasta County, Mount Shasta in Siskiyou County.) Time after time the two towns were to take the brunt of devastation, and to be the focus and the leader of the farmers' fight. It was a difficult time for Marysville, particularly for the merchants, as they supplied goods not only to farmers but to miners as well.

Marysville is cradled in the arms of a pair of pliers where the Yuba River joins the Feather. Across the Feather River lies Yuba City. So sediment from both rivers—derived, the farmers claimed, from mine tailing—was dumped on the towns. The Feather carried debris from mines near Oroville, including the Spring Valley mine at Cherokee, while some of the biggest and richest hydraulic mines, including those of the North Bloomfield Gravel Mining Company, of which the largest was the Malakoff pit, lay between the Middle and South forks of the Yuba River northeast of Nevada City.

By 1868 the beds of the two silted-up rivers were higher than the streets of the town. Marysville built levees to hold back the waters of the swift rivers, but the riverbeds kept rising, and Marysville kept building the levees higher. By 1874 the bed

FIGURE 25. Hydraulic mining at Michigan City, California, in 1853. Although the practice of hydraulic mining had only been under way for a couple of years, already the process had dug a deep hole.

of the Yuba was sixteen feet higher than it had been when hydraulic mining started. Eventually the levees circled the town, as high as the housetops. Over the next ten years Marysville spent hundreds of thousands of dollars on this safety net, eventually well over a million dollars.

Then, in 1872, farmers in Butte County along Dry Creek pooled their assets and brought suit against the Spring Valley mine at Table Mountain near Cherokee in the name of a farmer whose peach orchard, eight miles downstream from the mine, was buried. It was a trial balloon that would lead to what today would be called class action suits. What the farmers asked for was $2,000 in damages for the orchard and an injunction to stop the mining.

Because there were more than fifty companies whose operations may have contributed silt to the orchard, the courts could not say who should pay damages. What was more, halting hydraulic mining at the Spring Valley mine left other mines in the mountains free to continue to dump debris. More important, perhaps, to the trial was the fact that mines were there before farms and that mines enjoyed special status. The Spring Valley mine, for example, was worth hundreds of thousands of dollars and the peach orchard very little. The jury found for the defendant.

FIGURE 26. The Cherokee pit in the early days. The mine took a huge bite out of Table Mountain. Most of the diamonds—between 400 and 500—found in the hydraulic mining days were saved from the flumes at this mine. It is difficult to say whether Gardner Williams, the engineer in charge, was more alert to diamonds (he later went to South Africa to run the diamond mines there) or whether there were a great many more here than at other hydraulic mines. In almost forty years of operation, Spring Valley produced about $10 million worth of gold, when gold was about $20 an ounce.

But rain kept coming. Roads vanished, fields turned into lakes, crops were destroyed as the silt-laden brown water surged toward the valley.

In 1874 angry farmers tried the courts again. The actual rights involved had not been decided by the previous case. The farmers issued a manifesto declaring that the Spring Valley Mining Company had "impoverished the weak . . . and are inclined to continue by use of might." The owners of the Spring Valley mine and their engineer, Gardner F. Williams, moved quickly, and by so doing kept hydraulic mining going for more than a decade. They bought the land destroyed by hydraulic mining debris along Dry Creek. Then with farsightedness and goodwill, they went a step further. They constructed a long ditch, the Cherokee Canal, to carry debris to Butte Creek and from there to the tule swamps along the Sacramento River in Sutter County. Here they made a huge settling basin, ringed by levees. From then on the Spring

FIGURE 27. The mine at work at Cherokee. In the mine's rich years, 18 monitors shot 400-foot streams of water against the bluffs, washing gold, diamonds, sand, and gravel down deep shafts into the Eureka Tunnel, which was lined with sluice boxes to capture the gold. In 1876, the year that Spring Valley attained the stature of the largest hydraulic mine in the world, the company poured the world's largest gold bar, weighing 317 pounds troy (216 pounds avoirdupois) and worth $76,000 when gold was $20 an ounce. It was exhibited at the Philadelphia Exposition.

Valley mine was not part of the hydraulic mining controversy. It continued to operate until 1887, when costs exceeded the amount of gold recovered. All told, about $10 million worth of gold came from the gravels at Table Mountain.

But this did not solve all of Marysville's problems, or the problems of the farmers of the Sacramento Valley. The hydraulic monitors in the mountains kept roaring, and silt kept pouring down the rivers. After the flood of 1862, farmers were already beginning to move out. The Sacramento Valley was on its way to becoming a ghost land. Marysville built its levees higher.

Then, in 1875, winter rains again flooded the valley, topping Marysville's levees. Desperate townsfolk tried to sandbag, but the waters cut through near the cemetery and poured down on the town. Marysville filled like a bathtub. Houses floated, people were hurriedly rescued (all except one little boy, who drowned), buildings filled with water and sand. There was no food for two days, until a steamer from Sacramento braved the turbulent floodwaters. When the water receded, the enormity of Marysville's calamity could be seen. Sand and mud had filled streets, houses, and stores. Nothing was untouched. Marysville built its levees higher, until it was dubbed "The Walled City."

The winter of 1876 was a repetition of 1875. The farmers laid plans to petition

MORE THAN GOLD

Miners of the nineteenth century occasionally found diamonds in their placer workings. Unfortunately, they frequently tested diamonds by hitting them with a hammer, under the mistaken impression that because diamonds were the hardest natural substance they were also unbreakable. If they had stopped to think, they would have realized that facets are cut into diamonds by judicious use of a hammer. Until the 1980s about six hundred diamonds had been saved from being crushed or going down the sluices in the hydraulic mines. The largest was 6 carats. Then in the 1980s, the geologist Edgar J. Clark searched the Klamath Mountains in Trinity County and discovered several more, including his first, the Jeopardy, 3.90 carats; the Serendipity, 14.33 carats; the Enigma, 17.83 carats, found in 1987; and the Doubledippity, 32.99 carats, the largest recovered in California so far.

In 1995 the second-largest diamond ever to be auctioned, the 100.1-carat Star of the Season, was sold for a record price of $16,548,322, making it the most expensive piece of jewelry in the world. The famous Hope diamond weighs 44 carats. Both the Star and the Hope are cut diamonds; the 33-carat Doubledippity is not, and would lose size in cutting. Billed as the world's largest uncut diamond,

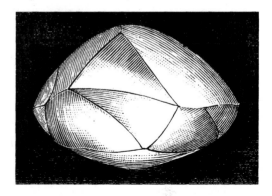

Diamond found in Cherokee hydraulic pit, Plumas County, during hydraulic mining.

the Giant Sefadu, found in 1970 in Sierra Leone, weighs 620 carats.

Most of the diamonds found in the nineteenth century came from hydraulic pits. No doubt many were washed away as worthless. However, Gardner F. Williams, engineer at the Spring Valley hydraulic mine at Cherokee, was alert to them, and his mine recorded the greatest number. With this experience behind him, Williams went to South Africa to be in charge of developing the great diamond mines there. ✗

---

the legislature for a bill to stop hydraulic mining altogether, pointing not only to the suffering and loss it had caused but also to the major rivers, which were being silted up so much that river traffic could no longer move. This had already ruined the Feather River. Soon the Sacramento, also, would be lost.

The miners argued before legislative committees that agriculture depended on the miners for customers; that of the $1.1 billion in gold won from the Sierra, about 90 percent had come from hydraulic mines; that they had made a huge investment and eventually would employ as many as 120,000 people; that the damages could not be more than $3 million; and that anyway, all this debris was good for the soil and could be used for levees.

No man, the farmers replied, should use his property so as to damage another. Where "once stood fine mansions, pleasant homes, rich orchards and fields smiling with golden grain is now to be seen only barrenness and desolation." Hydraulic mining, they said, was in its infancy, and things could only get worse. Furthermore, farm production already exceeded the value of gold mining.

The farmers got a bill submitted to the legislature, but the bill—merely to examine the question, not to do anything about it—lost in formal vote. Discouraged with a legislature that put politics and self-interest before justice, the farmers turned again to the courts, asking for a restraining order to prevent eighteen mining companies (three of them English owned) from throwing tailing into the Bear River basin.

Alarmed, the hydraulic mining companies grouped together and formed the Hydraulic Miners Association. The association not only pooled resources but also, astonishingly, pooled company information, including how they worked, what equipment they used, how much gravel they moved, all the statistics about reservoirs, and any information on new discoveries or improvements "or anything connected with hydraulic mining." Only the owners of hydraulic mines and the ditch companies that served them could belong, and virtually all did—officers of ninety mines and ditch companies. In the Articles of Agreement, the new association proposed to defeat passage of any state or federal laws "which would tend to interfere with, or embarrass the operations of Hydraulic Mining in California."

The battle was joined. On one side were the millionaires who owned the mines; on the other, poor but angry farmers. When the new suit brought by the Bear River farmers reached the state court, miners' attorneys successfully argued that the suit belonged in federal courts, and so the process was delayed for another two years while the suit worked its way up to the U.S. Supreme Court and back.

In 1877, while the suit was inching its way through the courts, the farmers built the levees higher along the rivers and around Marysville. The miners even helped. They contributed $30,000 and the labor to construct a long levee. Everyone breathed easier. Now the farms would be safe for many years to come.

For part of a year, anyway. In February 1878 heavy rains caused the Sacramento River, whose bed was now much higher thanks to the tailing in it, to burst through the new levee downstream from Sacramento and flood a huge area. The farmers were furious. The only good thing about the devastation was that at last there could be no pretense that the mines were not to blame.

Once again a bill to investigate the problem was proposed in the legislature and voted down. Lester Robinson of the North Bloomfield mine said farms, not mines, were producing most of the silt. Besides, the miners said, if hydraulic mines were shut down in the Sierra Nevada, the coyotes would take over the land. At last the legislature acted, creating the position of State Engineer, empowered to investigate and recommend a solution.

Meanwhile, the farmers' suit, which had gone to the U.S. Supreme Court, had been returned to local courts. Farmer after farmer told of his disasters. The miners countered with figures on the enormous gold production of the mines and the men who would be thrown out of work. The miners said also that because they had always discharged tailing into the rivers they had a right to do so, a right buoyed up by the federal government in granting them patents, making the mines their private properties.

Two months later, the judge handed down a permanent injunction against mines dumping debris into the Bear River or its tributaries. But the Bear was only one river in the mountains. Mindful of the rich and powerful Hydraulic Miners Association, the farmers organized the Anti-Debris Association. The miners appealed the court decision, successfully staying the injunction, and the mines continued to operate. Marysville built its levees higher.

The Anti-Debris Association decided to sue all mines on the Yuba in the name of the City of Marysville. Alarmed, the Hydraulic Miners Association offered to pay half the cost of levee building in Marysville and half the expense of building a levee north along the Yuba to the mountains. In addition, they said they would urge the passage of a law to force the mines to contain their tailing behind dams in the mountains, or whatever else the new State Engineer might recommend. All this if Marysville would not allow its name to be attached to the suit.

Marysville, angry and tired, refused this astounding offer, and on September 15, 1879, the suit went to court, asking for a complete ban on all hydraulic mining. Although an injunction was granted and papers were served on North Bloomfield and other mines, the Nevada City *Transcript* opined that the miners would pay "about as much attention to these writs as to the blowing of the winds." The San Francisco *Stock Report* wrote, "The idea of the city of Marysville bringing suits to abate hydraulic mining . . . is preposterous."

Just as the Marysville writs were being served, the California Supreme Court invalidated the Bear River case on the grounds that the suit was "misjoined"—too many defendants (all of the mines) were lumped together and one might not be guilty. The farmers were in a dilemma. It was not possible to show which mine had produced which lump of mud, and now it was not possible to sue them as a group. It looked as if the farmers had ultimately lost.

But they did not give up. In 1880, once again, the farmers went to the legislature. This time the newly appointed State Engineer had his report ready. He detailed mile after mile of canyon choked with mining debris and which mines it came from. The biggest problem was at the junction of the Yuba and Feather rivers, just where Marysville lay. "By the rapid accumulation of the sands, the natural channels of the Yuba and Bear Rivers were first obliterated, and the beds of the streams raised to a level with the top of their former banks. Levees that were thrown up to confine the waters [caused] the beds to rise still higher by the constant deposition of detritus between them, until they were finally overtopped by the floods, and the bottom lands were submerged from rim to rim of the adjacent plains with sand and clay sediment, to such depths that in places orchards, gardens, fields, and dwellings were buried from sight, landmarks were lost, and the course of the devastating flood was marked out by broad commons of slime and sand." Unless something was done, the State Engineer warned, more and more of the Central Valley would be ruined for agriculture. Suisun Bay was shoaling, San Francisco Bay in danger.

Finally the legislature acted. After a great deal of wrangling, it passed a statewide drainage bill. Opponents said the whole state should not be taxed to help the farmers of the valley. The farmers retorted that they did not want a drainage bill; they wanted hydraulic mining to stop. Finally the bill passed, despite fireworks, charges of fraud, and one senate member being jailed overnight for refusing to tell who tried to bribe him.

For the first time, a government agency was set up to represent the state's interest for all citizens. It began to build dams and levees. More hearings, more debate, more field trips, and more rain.

Once again the Anti-Debris Association went to the courts to obtain a total ban on hydraulic mining. Injunctions were issued again, forbidding hydraulic miners to dump debris into the Yuba or its tributaries. This time the injunction was not suspended. The Yuba River mines had to shut down, including the North Bloomfield.

To stop other mines from throwing debris into the river system, the Attorney General of California brought suit against the Miocene Mining Company, which discharged its debris into the Feather River above Oroville. Its mud was encroaching even on the Sutter County Hospital. The court issued a preliminary injunction against the mines. The miners burned an effigy of the judge issuing the injunction at Columbia Hill after shooting it to pieces with a cannon ball. (A blast from a hydraulic monitor might have been more symbolic.)

In June 1881 Gen. John Bidwell, who had a farm near Chico, urged all farmers to join the fight. The editor of the Colusa *Sun* wrote, "No one has any feeling against the miners. The farmers are willing to do almost anything to avoid injuring the mining interest except to give up their farms."

The fight went on. More court battles, more injunctions. In 1891 the California Supreme Court declared the Drainage Act invalid. Neither the miners nor the farmers bemoaned the demise of this compromise act. They were joined in a death struggle. More injunctions and more invalidations of injunctions followed. Sheriffs trying to serve writs against the hydraulic mining companies found no officers at work. But the mines, injunctions or not, continued to operate.

On June 12, 1882, the judge hearing the case against Gold Run gave his decision. He issued a perpetual injunction against the mine, prohibiting it from discharging "coarse debris" into the North Fork of the American River. The mine could build dams to restrain tailing. He also ruled, at long last, that the miners never acquired the right to use the rivers as dumps simply because they always had, since that prevented the use of riverside lands and free navigation. Here, at last, the farmers had legal support for their position. But the farmers had not won total victory. Hydraulic mining had not been outlawed—and never would be. Although the miners could no longer send "coarse debris" down the rivers, the water would still be muddy, unfit for irrigation or drinking by people or animals. Miners said they were willing to build dams. Farmers said, fine, just shut your mines down while you do. No mine shut down. More suits were filed, this time by county supervisors. The farmers sent observers—"spies" the miners called them—into the mountains to see who was working and whom to sue.

The two political parties had assiduously avoided getting into the fray, but when asked, the Democrats declared Washington ought to take care of it. (This from a state where almost every major river rises and flows within its boundaries.) The Republicans refused to comment at all.

The Anti-Debris Association formed a special unit of about seventy young men called the Anti-Debris Guard. They were issued uniforms with sky blue sashes (symbolizing water in its pristine condition) and red, white, and blue trim (signifying they would uphold the law). They were not issued arms. Their duty was to report to the "proper authorities" any infractions of the law.

The Anti-Debris movement then held a convention to form a third party, since neither Republicans nor Democrats had come to their aid. General Bidwell was elected permanent president of the convention. Being permanent president was not as permanent as it sounded. Within a few days quarreling among the delegates disbanded the convention, and the third-party idea died.

The farmers filed another suit against North Bloomfield and all the other mines along the Yuba, asking for a permanent injunction. The case lingered for a year and a half before the judge, Lorenzo Sawyer, gave his decision. Since Judge Sawyer had been a forty-niner, miners felt he was sure to be on their side.

Curiously, in the late 1870s Lester Robinson, chief investor in the North Bloomfield mine, had himself gone to court. He owned a farm along the San Joaquin

River, where a coal company had been dumping tailing that spread out over his land. He won restitution, thereby setting a legal precedent for the principle that owners did not have the right to dump tailing without regard for other landowners.

Judge Sawyer did his homework well. He made several field trips to the rivers, the mines, and the farms. He did not go alone; men from both sides accompanied him. He found many state-built and other dams full of tailing, in some cases where the mines had not even been working. At North Bloomfield, the timber dam built to restrain tailing had already broken. While the judge was considering his decision, the farmers again appealed to the legislature. Three bills were entered; none passed.

In early April 1883 Judge Sawyer gave the first part of his decision. There was, he said, no "misjoinder" (i.e., defendants were not erroneously grouped together). "[The defendants] pour their debris into several streams, which they know must, by the force of currents, be carried down into the main river, where they comingle into an indistinguishable mass long before they reach the point where the nuisances complained of are committed and damages created. . . . The final injury is a single one . . . and all defendants cooperate in . . . producing it." This decision removed the previous stumbling block—that of not being able to attack all the mines at once. Now the state and the farmers could begin again.

The Hydraulic Miners Association was in other trouble, too. Earlier they had collected money not only from rich mine owners but also from individual workers, yet refused membership to all but owners. Although they had changed their name and their policy, the miners pressed for an accounting. The association replied that the money had been used to bribe officials and legislators (!), and couldn't be accounted for. The association had gathered $10,000 from workers in 1882, but it collected nothing in 1883.

The legal cases poked their way through the courts. Testimony was taken in the latest suit—twenty thousand pages of it. It brought some comic opera arguments from the lawyers. Because the mines had been discharging tailing onto one person's land for ten years, the miners, they contended, now owned the land. "In other words," ridiculed the Marysville *Appeal*, "because the miners have been pouring debris on Mr. Woodruff's land for ten years, it is no longer his and has become the property of the mines. They won't even let him have the debris! Can legal fiction any farther go?"

Although hydraulic mines were shutting down, orders for monitors came from all over the world as California-trained engineers took the techniques to new fields. The monitors were manufactured in—of all places—Marysville.

On Friday, January 7, 1884, Judge Sawyer handed down his final decision. His field trips had taught him, he said, that dams were ineffective and that unless dump-

FIGURE 28. Malakoff hydraulic pit, North Bloomfield gravel company, in its heyday. The town of North Bloomfield was first known as Humbug City, but the mine proved to be anything but a humbug. Hydraulic mining began here in 1851, shortly after the system was invented, and shut down when Judge Sawyer issued an injunction against dumping mine debris into the Sacramento and San Joaquin rivers and their tributaries. The Malakoff pit grew to be more than 7,000 feet long, 3,000 feet wide, and as much as 600 feet deep. Altogether, the pit produced $3.5 million in gold (at $20 an ounce). The gravel bed was more than 600 feet thick, but most of the gold came from the blue gravel layer in the lower 130 feet. Even so, the blue gravel contained only four to ten cents of gold in each cubic yard. When mining ceased, the Malakoff had processed about 30 million yards of the gravel, and an estimated 130 million remained. (A later, more conservative estimate gave 40 million yards removed and 50 million remaining.)

ing mining debris into the rivers was specifically authorized by law, it was a "general, far-reaching and most destructive public and private nuisance." He ended by saying that the companies were "perpetually enjoined and restrained from discharging or dumping into the Yuba river . . . any of the tailings, bowlders, cobble stones, gravel, sand, clay, debris or refuse matter." Nor could the companies allow anyone else to use their water supplies for hydraulic mining. It was the final word.

There was great jubilation in the farmlands. Marysville blew all her steam whistles, rang all her church bells, lit bonfires, and called out a marching band; the town went on a toot. Grass Valley, Nevada City, and the mining towns were in mourning. Most hydraulic miners still working prepared to leave. It was the end.

But it was difficult to shut down the mines. The big ones stopped first. North Bloomfield issued its last statement, showing a net loss of $800,000 for eighteen years of mining. Up and down the mining country, towns were abandoned, houses were left vacant, and the tax rolls were cut back drastically. The state's gold production took a nosedive.

Some hydraulic mines did not cease operation. Those along the Trinity River in northern California did not have the same problems and continued to operate legally. Others in the Sierra Nevada worked surreptitiously and illegally—some miners operating even in the abandoned North Bloomfield pits.

In many places the injunction was violated. The miners cried "Spy" when they suspected someone was checking on them. One man, a wagon driver from Marysville, was brutally beaten in North San Juan and forced to walk out of town. One storekeeper from a town near Nevada City was even tried in a kangaroo court to determine if he was a spy.

Slowly, the mines shut down, but not without legal action, this time by the federal government. The 1890s brought depression, and farm prices dropped to a new low. What was needed, some said, was a revival of hydraulic mining. It looked for a while as if the whole controversy would start anew. Then U.S. Congressman Anthony Caminetti, formerly an assemblyman from one of the mining counties, proposed a bill that passed in 1893 authorizing establishment of the California Debris Commission, giving it authority to license hydraulic mines provided tailing was properly restrained. So California, unable to clean its own house, passed it to the federal government, thereby setting a precedent for federal interference.

Through the years the miners continued to push for high dams to contain the tailing. The rise in the price of gold from about $20 to a government-guaranteed $35 per ounce in 1933 made hydraulic mining once again look promising, and two high dams were actually built, one on the American River and one on the Yuba. But by the time the dams were completed, $35 gold was not so enticing, as the cost of mining was rising precipitously, and little tailing was dumped in them.

The waterworks constructed for the mines met a different fate. They found uses in electric power generation, irrigation, and general water supply. Pacific Gas and Electric Company bought the Spring Valley waterworks, which still serve San Francisco.

Today the vast pits are silent. No longer does the roar of the great monitors thunder through the mountains. No longer do the rivers roil with the slime of the mountains as the mountains themselves are ripped apart and thrown away. It is even difficult to locate some of the pits of these monsters, so overgrown have they become.

FIGURE 29. Malakoff pit in 1953, over a century after hydraulic mining began. What remains are cliffs reminiscent of Bryce Canyon National Park, except that the cliffs were eroded by miners, not nature. Today the area has become Malakoff Diggins State Historic Park.

The farmers were, of course, morally correct. No one should have the right to damage another person's property or the Earth's environment, no matter how handy it may be to do so. Even the *London Mining Journal*, which no doubt numbered among its subscribers some of the "foreign, plutocrat" owners of the hydraulic mines, praised Judge Sawyer's injunction against the mines. It was, the *Journal* said, "unquestionably correct in law and equity." What no one in the controversy seemed to consider is that we, and they, are merely stewards of the land, "owning" it only in our lifetimes, and that it behooves us to husband it well for our children and their children.

What is our legacy from hydraulic mining? Clearly, mining produced jobs for the miners, profits for the stockholders, and gold for the world. The techniques of hydraulic mining were exported to other gold-producing states and nations, and used also for big engineering projects that had nothing to do with gold. The water systems constructed for mining were converted to give us water and power. The court fight set legal precedents. The whole struggle taught us a lesson.

The most obvious physical legacies are the pits in the landscape and sediment-congested streams. Some pits have been used for garbage dumps, as we Americans seem to feel that we should throw garbage into anything that is lower than our feet. U.S. Interstate 80 runs through the Gold Run pit, where travelers at a rest stop can see the vast expanse left by the now-defunct ogre. One pit, the Malakoff at North Bloomfield, has become Malakoff Diggins State Historic Park, which preserves the pit and part of the nearby town of North Bloomfield. This huge pit, more than 7,000 feet long, 3,000 feet wide, and as much as 600 feet deep, was probably the largest in California. When the mine stopped operating, it had removed about 40 million yards of gravel, which contained about ten cents worth of gold per cubic yard. Perhaps 50 million yards of gold-bearing gravel remain.

The miners were right about one thing. The last time I was there, a coyote rummaged through a campground garbage can, just as the miners had predicted.

CHAPTER EIGHT

Mining in the Deep Dark

In 1850 George McKnight stubbed his toe against a rock outcrop while chasing his cows near Grass Valley and broke off a piece of quartz glittering with gold. That stumble solved a puzzle that had been troubling the miners since Marshall's gold strike. All of them could see that although the rivers carried gold, it likely didn't hatch there. It must have come from somewhere else—some fabulously rich source. At first they thought of Noah's flood, but if that brought the gold, its source could be anywhere—near Babylon or Mount Ararat, or even mysterious India. Most miners thought the gold came from the mountains behind them and was washed down by streams, and they were correct. McKnight's accident showed them that some of it, at least, was coming from close by.

The gold McKnight found was in veins in hard rock, and to get it involved breaking up the rock. Since McKnight's vein, and, as it proved, many others, contained principally the mineral quartz (SiO_2)—the same mineral that makes up most of the sand of our beaches—with gold held tightly inside the quartz, mining these veins came to be known as quartz mining. Hard rock mining and lode mining are other names for it.

Many miners had been hoping to find the gold source, but they didn't desert their claims along the rivers to prowl the mountains—not until McKnight found his quartz vein. Then once again they followed a rumor—this time true—and began searching for more rich veins. And they found them. Not just one but many, scattered through the hills and mountains. In the Sierra Nevada many of the veins ran more or less parallel to faults and parallel to the crest of the range, that is, north or northwest.

Early miners weren't hoping to find the "Mother Lode"—that term didn't come into vogue until the 1860s. They were looking for the "Great Blue Lead." "Lead" (rhymes with "need") was the miner's word for what geologists and professional miners call "lode." It is synonymous with "vein," although geologists recognize veins, meaning mineral-filled fissures, that may not contain ore. Veins are thin sheets, not tubes like blood vessels, and they may extend vertically in the Earth or at any angle from the horizontal.

Whatever his motives, or wherever he got his information, Richard Hakluyt, who wrote about Drake's voyages, was exaggerating when he said there is scarcely any place in California where one could dig and not find gold. California is rich in gold, but this does not mean that every shovelful of dirt is minable, or that one could pan any gold at all out of it. Gold is extremely scarce compared to the rocks that house it. In igneous rocks (those that cooled from hot molten rock and, as we shall see, are the ultimate source of gold) the amount of gold averages about five ten-millionths of one percent (0.0000005%). Most gold mines that produce enough ore to pay the cost of mining are in places where nature has concentrated the metal twenty thousand times that much, yet the ore may contain less than a third of an ounce of gold per ton of rock! In many modern open-air mines, worked by huge machines, a third of an ounce per ton would be considered rich, and many of today's mines produce gold no miner can see with the naked eye. Efficient dredges, working in California during the twentieth century, could make a profit from gravel that contained only five cents' worth of gold per cubic yard. That is a concentration of about 1/800 of an ounce per yard, or about one part in 32 million.

McKnight's discovery catapulted Grass Valley into one of the richest and most famous of California's mining districts. Not only was it the first of the state's lode mining districts to be worked, but when its mines ceased operating in the 1950s, it held title as the nation's longest lived—nearly 106 years of continuous operation. Gold was so plentiful at first in Grass Valley that claims were limited to one hundred square feet, for fear the price of gold would drop too rapidly.

Grass Valley is in the Sierra Nevada gold belt. Although the entire belt is often called the Mother Lode, the term, according to many miners and historians, should be used only for the 120-mile-long strip in the central part from El Dorado to Mariposa. The Grass Valley mines would lie in the "Northern Mines" portion.

The veins of much of the Mother Lode proved rich, too, with gold concentrated in astounding quantities. The richest segment of the Mother Lode Belt has been the 10-mile-long portion between Plymouth and Jackson, in Amador County, including such famous mines as the Kennedy and the Argonaut. The entire Sierran gold belt extends from Plumas County, where it is nearly 70 miles wide, southward to Tulare County, where it nearly dies out, only to reappear briefly in Kern County.

Millions of years ago the entire Sierra Nevada was under the sea, and limestone and sediments were accumulated on the seabed. Undersea volcanoes cut through the beds and poured lava over the sediments. Later, all of this was uplifted by Earth

FIGURE 30. Grass Valley about 1850. This is a copy of a lithograph, probably made from an artist's rendering, although it may have been taken from a photograph or a daguerreotype. Forty-niners headed for the gold rush had their likenesses taken by daguerreotype, a method that used copper plates coated with silver iodide and made only one image, no negative. One enterprising daguerreotypist made a tour of the gold mines, carrying his equipment in a covered wagon. Photography was just coming into its own in 1850, when the Grass Valley mines had their beginnings—explorers were taking cameras or photographers with them to record scenes unfamiliar to most people. Most of the early illustrations in this book are from drawings, as that was the most common rendering in forty-niner days. After the Civil War (1861–1865), the first American conflict documented by photographers, photography became the dominant medium.

forces into mountains. The old sea sediments, now consolidated and metamorphosed (changed by heat and pressure) into hard rock, were bent upward, allowing molten rock to invade them. In the mountain core the molten rock cooled to form granitic rock. The gold veins crystallized from hot waters percolating through fractures in this mixture of granite and old metamorphosed sediments. As time went by, erosion wore the mountains down. At times the mountains were uplifted again, giving renewed strength—because of steeper slant—to streams that were the major erosive agents. The gold in the old rocks covering the crest was washed down the rivers, forming placer deposits. But some of the veins in the old rock along the edges were not completely eroded, allowing miners to become the erosive agent and tear out the gold. This story of the building of the Sierras is told in more detail in chapter 9.

These old rocks and the veins in them are the principal sources of gold. In Grass Valley two sets of veins cut the rocks, one set that dips gently east or west from the surface outcrop into the Earth, another that dips steeply. The gently dipping veins are in granitic rock, the steeper ones in rocks related to granite but containing more iron and magnesium than ordinary granite. Ore was found not only in the veins but also in adjacent rocks.

Most veins in the Grass Valley area were from one to ten feet thick and filled small fault zones. The zones are cut by many small fractures, which have served as avenues for ore-bearing fluids and boundaries for the ore bodies. The profitable zones within the veins, the "ore shoots," vary in size and shape. Some veins in Grass Valley have been mined to an inclined depth of eleven thousand feet. Although miners uncovered numerous rich pockets, the average grade of ore was from one-fourth to one-half ounce of gold per ton. Besides gold, the ore contained considerable pyrite (iron sulfide) and some galena (lead sulfide) as well as small amounts of copper- and zinc-containing minerals.

If one vein can be followed for eleven thousand feet, and there are literally hundreds of veins and mines in the Sierra Nevada gold country, imagine how thoroughly honeycombed the foothills are underground. Map 6 shows the locations of the Grass Valley mines. It is not easy to count the mines, as they frequently change names and ownership, or are combined with other mines. Underground, too, they run into one another.

Much of American mining law is based on mining practice in California. Some of this has worked out well, but one law, known as the Apex law, has been the cause of many headaches for mine managers and enriched the pockets of mining lawyers. According to the Apex law, a person or company who claims the apex—the outcrop—of a vein owns it underground. You cannot claim the entire length of a vein on the surface, only a portion the size of your legal claim, but you do own it underground to the sides of your claim, providing you have laid out a claim with straight lines. If a vein runs underground past the surface limits of the side lines of your claim, you have the right to pursue it underground even though it continues under someone else's property. So if you owned land or mineral rights next to a miner who was following a vein, you could dig straight down on your own property and perhaps discover him hammering away in your deep basement. He would be within his rights. This rule worked fairly well in California, particularly in the Sierra Nevada, where some veins were easily followed, but in places like the Comstock Lode in Nevada and in Butte, Montana, where intersecting veins are faulted and tangled like a skein of yarn tossed by a kitten, it caused a nightmare of litigation.

In 1918 two of Grass Valley's largest mines got into a legal hassle. The North Star, whose surface plant was a mile west of the Empire's on Wolf Creek, brought a $15,000 suit against the Empire for encroaching on North Star's claims underground. Fortunately for both mines, a boundary was settled on, and the matter never

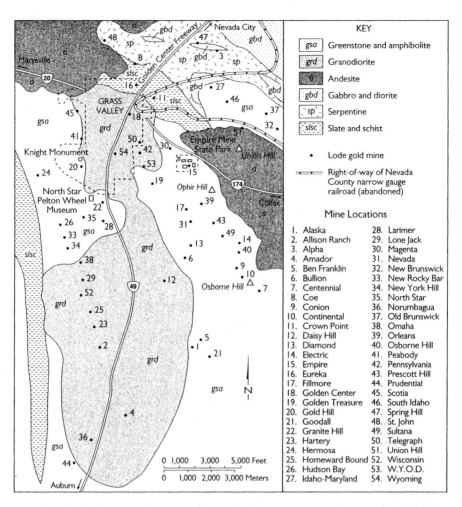

MAP 6. Geologic map of the Grass Valley Gold District, showing mines, the Empire Mine State Park, and the North Star Pelton Wheel Museum. The rocks shown are andesite (a volcanic rock), granodiorite (a type of plutonic rock, a member of the granite family), gabbro and diorite (dark plutonic rocks), serpentine (metamorphosed rock from the Earth's mantle—the California State Rock), greenstone (a metamorphosed volcanic rock), amphibolite (a dark, highly metamorphosed rock, originally basalt or gabbro), slate, and schist (metamorphosed shale). Hydrothermal quartz veins, many of them carrying gold, cut through these rocks.

went to trial. Eleven years later Newmont Mines acquired both the North Star and the Empire and consolidated them as Empire-Star Mines Company, Ltd. By then the holdings of the two giant mines encompassed 3,700 acres, making the Empire-Star the largest of all western gold mines at that time.

When underground mining began few of the forty-niners knew anything about lode mining—they had barely learned about placers—but they quickly took to the idea. Gold Hill and nearby Allison Ranch were the two leading producers of the 1850s. In 1857, after the Allison Ranch mine was a going concern, a writer for *Hutchings' California Magazine* made a visit to the underground workings and described his journey for his readers:

> Under the guidance of Mr. Daniels, of the far-famed Allison Ranch Lead, we descended their shaft—but not before the workmen had offered and we had accepted the loan of an India rubber suit of clothing—and on reaching the bottom of it we found a considerable stream of water running in the centre of the railway, constructed along the tunnel to the shaft. This water was removed by a pump in one corner of the shaft, working by steam power, both day and night.
>
> On, on we went, trying to keep a sure footing on the rail track, inasmuch as water-tight boots even then became a very necessary accompaniment to the India-rubber clothing. Drip, drip fell the water, not singly, but in clusters of drops and small streams so that when we arrived at the drift where the men were at work, we had a sufficient supply of water for drinking purposes (!) in the pockets of our coat. The miners who were removing the quartz from the ledge, looked more like half-drowned sea-lions, than men. We did not make ourselves inquisitive enough to ask the amount of wages they received, but we came to the conclusion that they must certainly earn what ever they obtained. Stooping, or rather half lying down upon the wet rock, among fragments of quartz and props of wood, and streams of water; with pick in hand, and by a dim but waterproof lantern, giving out a very dim and watery light, just about bright enough, or rather dim enough, and watery enough, as Milton expresses it, "to make darkness visible," a man was at work, picking down the rock—and which, although very rich, was very rotten, and consequently not only paid well, but was easily quarried, and easily crushed, and although the rock was paying not less than three hundred and fifty dollars per ton, we could not see the first speck of gold in it, after a diligent search for that purpose.
>
> At the bottom of the drift another man was employed to shovel the quartz into a tub standing on a railway car, and push it to the shaft, where it was drawn up and taken to the mill. . . . We had the satisfaction of descending the Osborne Hill lead, under the guidance of Mr. Crossett, and, after bumping the head against the rocky roof above, and holding on by our feet to the wet and slippery roof of rock below on which we were descending, at an angle of forty-two degrees; now clinging to the timbers at the side; (to prevent the lubricity of our footing from taking advantage of the back part of our head, and making us to "see stars in a dark passage", from the tripping up of our heels) now winding among props, and over cast-iron pump tubes; now making our way from one side of the inclined shaft to the other, to enable us to travel as easy as possible . . . we again crossed over to and entered a side drift. . . .
>
> Now, reader, let us rest for a moment, and look around a little. . . . Except for the lights in our hands it is all dark, and is still almost as the tomb; with the exception of the distant creaking of a pump, and the steady dripping of some water at our elbow. Rock here, there and everywhere. For several years men have been picking and drilling and blasting through solid rock; by day and night; in winter and summer; led forward by the talismanic power of gold—or at least by the hope to obtain it. Hard

FIGURE 31. Miners tramming ore (pushing an ore car, or tram) at the Kennedy mine, Amador County.

rock, hard work, and often very hard prospects; although combined with difficulty and danger, have never for a moment daunted or dismayed them. Above ground or under; by daylight or candle light, – onward – ever onward – has been their unswerving resolve – and the guiding star of hope has ever shone with cheering light upon their labors. May their reward be near.

"As it is getting rather chilly, suppose we ascend."

"All right; shall we ascend by the ladder, or by the same way that we came?" inquired our excellent guide.

"Oh, by the ladder, by all means," was the response.

Lights were then fastened on our hats; as "in ascending we shall have need of both hands perhaps!" suggested our guide.

"What pleasure there is in seeing daylight after one has been for some time in darkness; and inhaling the cool fresh air above ground after some time spent underneath," we remarked, as we wiped the sweat from our brow, when we had reached the top.

Mark Twain, who had a poor opinion of the hard labor involved in quartz mining, was acquainted with a pocket miner whose cat, Tom Quartz, hated it even more. Once Tom got accidentally blown out of the mine when a charge of dynamite was set off, and after that he could never be broken of his "cussed prejudice agin quartz-mining."

Through the years Grass Valley became the world leader in gold mining know-how. Engineers used to work at Grass Valley just to add it to their résumés to impress prospective employers. Among those who learned their trade in the Grass Valley mines was a future U.S. president, Herbert Hoover, who shoveled ore at three of the mines just after graduating from Leland Stanford, Jr., University. Hoover, a geology major, was in the first Stanford graduating class. His wife, Lou Henry Hoover, was the first woman geology graduate in the world.

Early on, expert help was brought in from overseas. It is said that John Charles Frémont, the explorer, suggested the plan: use miners from Cornwall, England, who knew about deep mining from working in the Cornwall tin mines. It proved to be just what the mines needed, and just what the Cornishmen wanted. So many came over and they stuck together so tightly that it was said when one was hired, he would ask if there wasn't a job for his "Cousin Jack," and so all Cornishmen became known as Cousin Jacks. They brought with them a store of mining knowledge and skills, as well as their tasty Cornish pasties (a turnover great for miner's lunches), tales of friendly mine ghosts called Tommy-Knockers, and a love of music. The Grass Valley Cornish Carol Choir, started in the 1850s, sang throughout California. In 1940 they serenaded the whole country on radio from the two-thousand-foot level of the Idaho-Maryland mine. The response was enthusiastic, but World War II intervened, so encore performances were not heard until 1951 and 1952.

Cornishmen also brought with them one of the most unusual pieces of mining equipment ever devised: the Cornish pump. Many of the Grass Valley mines had Cornish pumps, including the North Star and the Empire. Their purpose was to take groundwater out of the mine—the water the writer from *Hutchings' California Magazine* found so troublesome. (An operable Cornish pump is on display at the North Star Mining Museum at the North Star mine.) The "pump" consisted of enormous timbers that ran from the surface to the bottom of the mine, moved by a steam engine at the top. The rod, which had to go around many corners, was hooked up to several smaller pumps that lifted the water by stages out of the mine. The Cornish pump was a remarkable piece of equipment, weighing more than 135,000 pounds and moving six feet at a stroke four times a minute. It ran night and day, and seemed to go on forever.

Sometimes a miner would "walk the beam" up from the level he had been working on that day. The miner rode the upstroke of the rod, stepped to a platform, and waited until the downstroke brought the next higher step to him; this he rode to the next higher platform in the shaft, and so progressed to the surface. "There must be no hesitation," wrote the Frenchman L. Simonin in 1869. "If the place should happen to be already occupied on the ladder or on the stage fixed against the shaft, by one miner who is going up as another is going down, he should remain quiet in his place and wait for a second movement. The slightest embarrassment may cause the

FIGURE 32. Miners working underground at the Kennedy mine, in one of the richest segments of the Mother Lode. The mine produced $34.28 million (at earlier prices) before it was shut down in 1942. For a time, the Kennedy was the deepest mine in the United States, burrowing more than a mile into the Earth, but it has been surpassed by the Homestake mine in South Dakota, down more than 6,000 feet.

The superintendent's house and remaining mine buildings, as well as the huge wooden tailing wheels, visible from Highway 49 and accessible from the road to Jackson Gate, have all been preserved as part of a historical museum. What has not been preserved is the horrendous noise that must have reverberated through the valley. The Kennedy's mill had 100 stamps, and its neighbor, the Argonaut, which adjoins the Kennedy underground, had 60. It is difficult to imagine as one walks through the quiet pastoral scene today what decibel 160 stamps crashing night and day must have reached.

most serious accident and the brutal engine, by its sudden return-motion, may kill the traveller on the spot or break a limb."

Through the years the mining equipment, so modern when it was installed, was replaced by newer and better machinery. Rock was crushed by stamp mills, in which metal posts were repeatedly lifted and let fall by rotating steam-driven cams. At the Empire mine, the mill, which crushed the rock to a powder so that the fine gold could be extracted, was replaced by a new thirty-stamp mill. Unlike most gold mills, this one did not exhibit its rough-hewn timbers. Everything was sealed and painted and uncommonly neat. Rossiter W. Raymond, writing in his *Mineral Resources of the States and Territories West of the Rockies*, called it the "most magnificent in the state." In 1870 it burned. It was replaced by a steam-powered mill with a battery of stamps each weighing nine hundred pounds, dropping nine inches seventy-two times a minute.

A fine new mill, but by the end of that decade, quartz mining was at a low ebb. Most of the Grass Valley mines were no longer working; only the Empire and Idaho continued to operate. But new management brought in new ideas and new money. Water power was brought to the Empire in 1884, the surface plant was refurbished, and the stamp mill was enlarged to forty stamps. The mine had gone down 750 feet vertically (1,700 feet on the incline), and the reliable Cornish pump was pulling out 18,000 gallons of water an hour. The Empire was back in business, employing between 120 and 160 men at $3 a day. By 1900 the Empire was the showplace of all the California mines. The principal owner, W. B. Bourne, Jr., had a San Francisco architect, Willis Polk, create a "cottage"—actually a mansion—on thirteen acres of lawn, complete with pools and an artificial lake.

Over at the North Star, it became clear that some power beyond men's and mules' muscles would be needed to continue mining. Near the turn of the century the president of North Star Mines, James D. Hague, wanted something modern, perhaps an electric plant to power the mining equipment. But the engineer he hired, Arthur deW. Foote, thought electricity was not yet safe or dependable enough to run the whole mine. Instead he devised a system using water to drive a metal water wheel connected to an air pump that would produce compressed air to run the jack-hammers and other machinery.

The Pelton Engineering and Shipbuilding Company of San Francisco was chosen to build the wheel, but they refused to build one 30 feet in diameter, the size Foote wanted. Fifteen feet, they said, was as large as would work. Foote persuaded them to build an 18-foot wheel, which, for a time, was the largest in the world. But its distinction did not last long. By 1898 a much larger wheel was needed for the mine, and this time the company agreed to provide a 32-foot one. This monster, the largest in the world, was made of steel and had bronze buckets. Today the Pelton wheel is on display at the North Star Powerhouse on Wolf Creek, now a mining museum.

Electricity did reach the North Star, allowing the old Cornish pumps to be worked either by water or electric power. But in 1925 the Cornish pump was retired after forty years of work, night and day, and electrically driven turbines took its place.

Compressed air and electric power greatly improved the efficiency of mining. Instead of miners working in pairs, one hammering, the other holding the bit for drilling, each could operate a jackhammer. Unlike jackhammers used in street work,

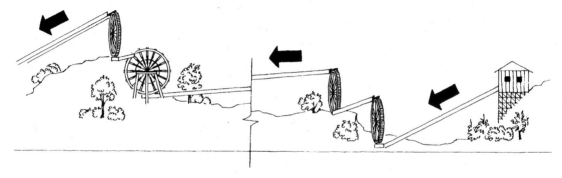

FIGURE 33. How mining wheels of the Kennedy mine worked. These now-ruined wooden wheels were used to carry the finely ground waste rock—tailing—from the 100-stamp mill near the mine entrance to the dump. From a hill to the north of the Jackson Gate road, one can see two of the pine wheels and, beyond, the headframe and remaining buildings of the Kennedy mine and mill. Two other wheels are on the hill to the south of the road, and over the hill is the old tailing dump.

This diagram (not to scale) shows how the wheels carried the tailing. Wet tailing from the mill (right), lifted to near the top of the building, was pushed into a flume, down which it flowed toward the first wheel, where it was dropped into a well at the bottom of the wheel. (Arrows show direction of flow.) Each wheel was equipped with 176 little redwood wells, or buckets, along its perimeter. Each bucket picked up its share of wet tailing, and as the wheel was rotated by the electric motor and belt drive that powered it, the tailing was lifted to the top of the circle. There it was dumped into another flume, angled slightly downhill toward the bottom of the second, higher wheel. From there it was again lifted to the top, where it was dumped to slide toward the third, and similarly, to the fourth and highest wheel. The gap in the middle of the diagram indicates a much longer trip for the tailing from the second to the third wheel than between wheel one and two or three and four. Each wheel was 68 feet in diameter and lifted the waste 48 feet vertically. Of course, each wheel actually lifted it 68 feet, but since part of the elevation gained by the preceding wheel was lost in dumping the waste in the well and part was lost in sliding it down the flue to the next wheel, the total amount gained was 48 feet. From the top of the fourth wheel, the ground-up rock slid down a series of long flumes to a dump, where it grew into a flat-topped, artificial hill.

The purpose of the enterprise was to protect the environment—to move the tailing away from the local water supply.

drills underground were lubricated by water to keep the dust down. Doubtless this also saved miners' lungs, but it meant they emerged completely enveloped in mud.

In 1933, when the price of an ounce of gold was raised by the government to $35, mining boomed, and Grass Valley and the Empire continued to flourish until 1942. President Franklin D. Roosevelt, who had been responsible for the gold-mining boom in the midst of the Great Depression by raising the price of gold, now signed War Production Board Order L-208, causing all American gold mines to shut down. The purpose, the board said, was to shift miners from gold to coal and other mines needed for World War II. They did not realize that a gold miner is a gold miner and a coal miner a coal miner and that shifting from one to the other is like being asked to sing tenor if you are a bass.

Many mines, which produced gold as a by-product in the mining of lead, zinc, and other sorely needed metals, were ordered to stop working. That rule was soon changed, as the other metals were vital to defense. Because the North Star also produced tungsten, a part of the mine was allowed to remain open, and in 1944, the Empire-Star mines were given permission to run, using no more than 175 men.

No doubt another purpose for the order was to wean the United States away from gold and the gold standard. The 1933 law made the owning of gold by private citizens illegal, except for jewelry and certain other exemptions, and all gold mined in the United States had to be sold to the government. This worked well during the depression, when $35 was a high price for gold. But after World War II, when the price of gold in other countries rose while U.S. gold was still pegged at $35, it proved a great trouble to the U.S. Secret Service, which was kept busy trying to apprehend smugglers attempting to move gold *out* of the country.

The L-208 order was a disaster for the gold mines. Only a few with adequate capital could afford to keep the mines pumped clear of water. When the order was lifted in 1945, only gold dredges and a few California lode mines reopened.

But the Grass Valley days were numbered. The companies limped along, mining at a loss, hoping the price of gold would be adjusted, but it was not. In 1956 the North Star shut down for good, and in 1958 the machinery and equipment of the Empire-Star mines were sold at public auction. No one knows for sure how much gold the Grass Valley mines produced, but it has been estimated that the lode mines yielded nearly 13 million ounces, worth $1.3 billion when gold is only $100 an ounce.

Today, the Empire grounds are a state park, where one may visit the mining days of yesteryear. The mine itself, however, is still owned by Newmont Mines, one of the nation's most aggressive and progressive mining companies, so its future may not be wholly settled.

ALL DRESSED UP

Miners working in the streams in the days of '49 took nearly uncontaminated gold from the gravel using gravity to separate it—gold pure enough that merchants and gamblers would take it in place of coin. It was not that easy for hard rock (lode) miners. The ore had to be "dressed"—first crushed finely enough that the ore would pass through screens, then separated from other constituents of the rock in a variety of ways. Crushing was a problem the miners solved in different ways, using man, mule, water, and later electric power to beat the rock into small pieces. Today mechanical crushers of various types, all powered by electricity, do not call on muscles.

The constituents of the ore were separated in various ways. Amalgamation with mercury was a favorite method for the first half century after the gold rush. In early mills, water was added to finely ground gold ore to form a pulp. Mercury was added to that, and the pulp passed over mercury-coated copper plates. The mercury picked up gold from the pulp, and the amalgam of mercury and gold stuck to the plates. The plates were scraped at intervals and the mercury squeezed out of the amalgam through a bag. If gold still remained in the mercury after squeezing, the volatile mercury was driven off by heating. Since mercury was expensive, the heating process included a method for capturing mercury vapor and cooling it back to liquid mercury.

Toward the end of the nineteenth century a new gold separation process using cyanide was developed. Cyanide is one of the few chemicals that will dissolve gold. At first cyanidation was used on tailing to recover gold that had been missed, then it was applied to the ore itself. At the present time, slow, open-air cyanidation, or heap leaching, is the method used in most large American gold mines. Another process used in many American mines before

Mexicans of the early days using a backbreaking method to crush ore-bearing rock, as shown in this drawing by the nineteenth-century artist Charles Nahl.

heap leaching was flotation, a process that depends on separating gold out by its specific gravity, just as in panning. However, chemicals of a certain specific gravity are used instead of water, which permits the constituents of the ore to be separated from one another, not just gold from waste rock. Flotation cells churn like washing machines, forming froth at the top like soap bubbles. The lighter ingredients are caught in the froth and scraped off.

Once the ore is dressed and concentrated, it is taken to a refinery, where gold may be chlorinated. In this process the gold is melted, then chlorine gas is passed through to take out impurities. Or acids can be used. These acids attack the gold, but not until they have removed all the impurities.

The U.S. mints purify gold by electrolysis. Gold bars (serving as anodes) are suspended in an electrolyte of gold chloride and hydrochloric acid, where sheets of pure gold (serving as cathodes) are also suspended. Slowly, the gold is removed from the anodes and deposited on the cathodes, while impurities remain behind. Electrolysis is a slow process, but the gold it yields is 999.9 fine. Once gold has been refined, it is poured into bricks. Official U.S. bricks weigh about 28 pounds (12.7 kilograms), although larger, heavier bricks are common.

An arrastra (called "raster" by Americans), a slightly easier method (for people, if not for mules) of breaking up quartz. A circle of stones was arranged for the ore, then a heavy stone was dragged over it to crush the ore into powder. A batch of about 500 pounds was dumped into a 10-foot arrastra, and the mule set to about eight revolutions per minute. It took the mule three to four hours to grind the ore down. About three-quarters of an hour before the batch was done, quicksilver was added. Ten minutes before crushing was complete, about sixteen buckets of water were tossed in and the mule urged around a few more times. The water was then allowed to run off and the mercury-gold amalgam picked up and panned, or the mixture sent to a larger mill. If steam or water power replaced mule power, the work took about half as long.

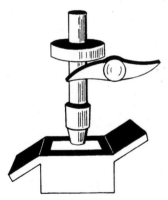

A mill employing stamps that were dropped on the ore in rotation took some of the labor out of crushing. It still had to be fed by hand—more backbreaking work. The inset shows how a stamp worked. Ore shoveled down the incline on the right dropped into a trough. The heavy iron- or steel-clad stamp—the knob on the bottom—was fastened to a long rod (shown here much shortened) driven by a rotating cam (the flange shown offset). The cam was power driven—in early days by steam or water—forcing the rod up and down, crushing the ore as it dropped. The crushed ore washed over the trough to the left, where the gold would be separated out.

Interior of a quartz mill, Grass Valley, in the 1850s. Within a few short years after the gold rush, gold mining had turned into big business, requiring numerous laborers and considerable money. In the background here is a stamp mill. After being crushed by the stamps, the water-laden ore passed over a screen. The part of the ore that could not pass through the openings returned to the stamps. The part that could moved on to an apron or amalgamating box, where mercury took out gold. To be certain the gold was all recovered, the mixture went to blanket tables, a form of flat sluice. Blankets were kept on the tables from 10 to 30 minutes, then rolled up and washed in a tub, as the man in the foreground is doing. But before the rolled-up blanket was moved to the tub, another was quickly put in place so that the stamps did not have to stop. Gold not caught on the blankets continued down a series of inclined tables, each having a trough or pan with quicksilver beneath it where gold was caught, while lighter material floated over the top.

PLATE 1. Gold leaves from the Eureka mine, Tuolumne County, an exceptional example of the California State Mineral. Most gold recovered from underground mines is in small grains—some too small to see with the naked eye—scattered through rock. The rock must be crushed to get the gold out. Very rarely, miners find gold in crystals or leaves. This specimen is about seven inches high and weighs 454.7 grains (0.95 troy ounce).

PLATE 2.   *Above:* Marshall's original
nugget. This tiny piece of gold, shown
here on a finger, weighs 7 grains (0.015
troy ounce, a little over one one-hun-
dredth of a troy ounce), yet it sparked the
historic gold rush that changed the face of
the United States and brought California
to the world stage. The nugget does not
look the way it did when Marshall found
it. He and Sutter hammered it flat and
subjected it to various tests to be sure it
was gold. Marshall's nugget has been a
part of the Smithsonian Institution's collections since 1848.

PLATE 3.   *Right:* Three gold nuggets
and an 1852 octagonal $50 gold "slug"
minted at the United States Assay Office.
Each of the nuggets is far larger than
Marshall's original. The coin contains
2½ troy ounces of gold, making the bullion value—the value of the gold alone—
$250 when gold is $100 an ounce. On the
numismatic market it is worth several
thousand dollars.

PLATE 4. *Above:* Plant of the McLaughlin mine at night. Here the lights of the busy plant shine as golden as the gold it recovers.

PLATE 5. *Left:* Workman at the McLaughlin mine pouring liquid gold into molds to make gold doré bars. Doré bars still contain some impurities, especially silver, and must be further refined.

PLATE 6. A sea of modern gold coins produced by the U.S. Mint.

PLATE 7. Stacks of gold bars produced by the U.S. Mint in the twentieth century.
The mint produces gold bars that are 999 fine, or 99.9 percent pure.

CHAPTER NINE

The Big Picture

It was easy enough for miners to see that flakes of gold were being worn from veins in the mountains and then being washed downhill and finally downstream, forming placer deposits. They realized that the beds they called the "Auriferous Gravels" had been laid down in ancient, fossil rivers, the "dead rivers of the Sierra Nevada," but they did not realize that much of the gold in them came from dead mountains, too, mountains no longer there, and not all of it from the high, snowcapped peaks behind their claims.

Experts studying the veins from which the gold rush rivers got their gold could see that it was the process of weathering that loosened the gold fragments so they could become placer deposits. Weathering begins when groundwater penetrates the vein. The water starts as meteoric water (water that comes from the sky), which has picked up natural chemicals—oxygen and carbon dioxide—in the air and ground, allowing the water to attack the vein. As the groundwater oxidizes sulfide minerals it becomes dilute sulfuric acid, increasing its chemical power. Most of the acid is from the weathering of the mineral pyrite (FeS_2). Pyrite often contains atoms of gold hitch-hiking in the crystal lattice (that is, within pyrite's crystalline structure), so the dis-solution of pyrite may release bits of gold floating in the water, either as dissolved ions or in submicroscopic colloidal particles. This makes it possible for the gold to move very easily from place to place. If some of the gold is larger than one hundred microns—larger than a quarter of ten-millionths of an inch—it is probably tiny plates, spangles, or minute nuggets. These pieces may then become centers that even smaller, ionic gold will latch onto, thus forming larger pieces.

The chemistry of the gold, the oxidizing waters, and their reactions with other minerals is quite complex. So far as gold is concerned, it is most mobile—likely to migrate farthest—in water that is either strongly alkaline or strongly acidic. If the waters are more weakly acidic or alkaline, or even neutral, gold may stay where it is.

Below the oxidized zone, in the weathered gold lode, a very rich secondary sulfide zone may exist just beneath the water table. (The water table is the level below which the ground is saturated. When digging a well, one wants to penetrate the water table to have a reliable supply of water.) This zone may be enriched in copper and sometimes gold. Below is the unaltered primary ore.

If deeply penetrating groundwater—the meteoric water—meets a source of heat in the ground, such as might be provided by hot, fluid rock (magma), the process is immensely speeded up; in fact, many ore deposits the world over are classed as hydrothermal deposits because they resulted from the action of hot water, and as we shall see, much of the world's gold is ultimately hydrothermal, that is, precipitated from hot water. But the problem remains: how did gold get into the hydrothermal fluid in the first place?

Based on earthquake waves and other data, the Earth appears to have a thin crust that ranges from 5 to 70 kilometers (3 to 45 miles) in thickness, depending on whether it is measured in the deep sea (the thinnest part) or on the continents (the thickest part). The crust contains the rocks and the veneer of "dirt" we know—all the granite, all the sandstone, all the soil; for that matter, all the gold. Even so, the crust is so thin in comparison to the rest of the globe that it could not be shown to scale on a piece of paper the size of this page. Below the crust is the mantle, a region extending halfway to the center of the Earth, making it some 2,900 kilometers (1,800 miles) thick. Farther down is the Earth's core, first the outer core, about two-thirds of the whole core, intensely hot and liquid. By volume, the Earth's outer core is 96 percent of the total core. The very center of the Earth, the inner core, is solid, and is thought by most scientists to be chiefly nickel and iron. (Harrison Brown, scientific adviser to presidential candidates, suggested in 1949 that the nickel-ion core may be

TABLE 3. *What the Earth Is Made Of*	
Iron	34.6%
Oxygen	29.5%
Silicon	15.2%
Magnesium	12.7%
Nickel	2.4%
Silicon	1.9%
Titanium	0.05%

Eighty-five elements, including gold, are not plentiful enough to warrant a ranking on this list.

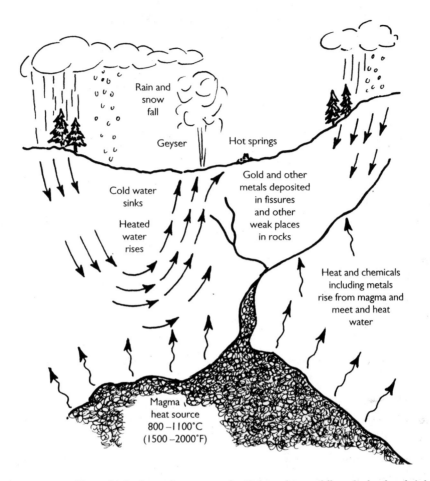

FIGURE 34. How a hydrothermal system works. Rain and snow fall on the land and sink into the ground. If the water goes deep enough, it may encounter heat rising from a magma body beneath. When the cold water is heated, it, too, begins to rise, and if it gets hot enough, it may become superheated—heated beyond the boiling point of water—and on reaching the surface may erupt as a geyser. Once the superheated water is expelled, the now-cooled water flows back into the ground to recharge the system, as coffee in a percolator does as it perks. Hot water that does not become superheated may spill out at the surface as hot springs.

Besides heat, the magma exudes chemicals that rise with the heated water to be deposited in fissures, fractures, and other planes of weakness in the rocks above, forming mineral deposits. If the chemistry is right, some of the mineral deposits may contain gold.

rich in gold and platinum—enough, if we could dig a hole down to it, to cover the Earth in a blanket several meters deep.)

The origin of gold ores involves the principles of global plate tectonics (from the Greek *tektōn*, meaning "builder")—the idea that Earth's crust and part of its mantle is divided geophysically into several large plates and a number of smaller ones. These plates include and underlie continents and seas. The South American plate, for exam-ple, extends from the western coast to the middle of the Atlantic Ocean. We can see only portions of the plates and can identify and locate them only by geophysical clues. What we see is what is on the plates—the continents, islands, and seas. In only a few places in the world can we see plate boundaries, as most are covered by water. What we can see clearly are the Earth features that we interpret as being produced by plate movement—mountains, rift valleys, volcanoes, and much else.

It was not until the cold war in the 1950s that we began to know the whole globe, especially to understand what the oceans were like beneath the waves. Neither the U.S. Navy nor its Soviet counterpart wanted its submarines bumping into undersea cliffs, so both began to map the ocean floor. The results were secret for some time. However, the U.S. National Science Foundation funded a project to traverse the oceans, mapping and taking samples. What resulted from this project and the U.S. Navy's efforts was a picture of the ocean bottom that was entirely unexpected.

Ocean waters covered not a dishlike surface but many more mountains than even the submarine captains suspected. There were seamounts, flat-topped volca-noes as much as 4,000 meters (2.5 miles) high; ranges and valleys crisscrossed by faults, not unlike the Basin Ranges country of the western United States; and through the middle of the seas a 65,000-kilometer-long (40,000 miles) volcanic mountain range, the longest on Earth.

Along the central ridge of this mountain range volcanoes periodically erupt. Molten lava flows to either side of the ridge, making stripes of basalt on the ocean floor. The lava probably comes from deep within the Earth, in the Earth's mantle. Responding to this periodic injection of lava and to other forces, the seafloor "spreads apart," moving away from the central ridge on either side. Most of the range is underwater, but it does break the surface of the sea in a few places. Iceland is one such place, where new rock is being constantly added from the island's numerous volcanoes. Proof that this has been occurring for millions of years lies in the fact that a stripe on one side of the ridge has a twin on the other that is the same age and has the same magnetic orientation. In other words, the lava (basalt) layers and sediments that covered them are older as one progresses farther away from the ridge symmetrically on both sides.

The Mid-Ocean Ridge is one type of boundary between plates, where plates are moving apart, or spreading. Other types of plate boundaries are subduction zones, horizontal displacement zones, and collision zones, all of which play a part in Earth's present and past, as we shall see.

The continents do not slide around on the ocean floor, like rafts on a lake. The moving plates contain both continents and ocean floor fragments. Based on an enor-mous amount of geophysical data, present theory is that the plates consist not only of the Earth's thin crust but of part of the underlying upper mantle as well, the more solid part. Scientists call the crust and this rigid part of the mantle the lithosphere (from Greek *lithos,* "stone"). These lithospheric plates slide on the plastic lower part of the upper mantle, which is referred to as the asthenosphere (from Greek *aesthenēs,* meaning "weak"). Below the lithosphere and the asthenosphere lies the lower mantle, which, on the basis of earthquake waves, is thought to be rigid and stiff. It, in turn, overlies the outer and inner core. Thus, a soft, plastic layer (the asthenosphere), which lies 60 to 200 kilometers (40 to 100 miles) deep within the Earth, is what the plates slide on; and, as we shall see, the asthenosphere is also what provides new material for the rocks of the Earth, as well as Earth's gold.

Early in Earth's history continental centers, called cratons, formed slowly, dozens of them, finally rising above the sea waters. The cratons became parts of the plates, which slid around, occasionally crashing into one another at collision zones. Where the plates collided, ancient mountains formed, and volcanoes were active. The cratons, containing the oldest rocks on Earth and some of Earth's richest gold deposits, still form the interiors of today's continents. North America, for example, is made up of seven ancient cratons that stuck together about two billion years ago.

Once the cratons formed, bits and pieces of new land and seafloor were added to them. After much jostling, several pieces eventually coalesced into one gigantic continent (Pangea), which then split apart into the modern continents. California, for example, is made up of a number of fragments that were pasted (in plate tectonics parlance, "docked") onto the beginnings of North America at various times from various places. These Earth fragments are referred to as terranes. They consist of what we normally think of as terrain—an area of land—plus parts of the seafloor and all the Earth's crust below, and perhaps even a fragment of Earth's mantle. In this way, an American scientist and an Argentinian scientist have concluded, a terrane broke away from the American South and docked in Argentina, leaving a gap in the South that became the Gulf of Mexico and creating the Precordillera of South America. And if plate motions continue as at present, the Taiwan terrane will soon (geologically speaking—it will take millions of years) dock at mainland China, thereby unifying what is now a politically torn country.

As the Earth does not appear to be expanding, seafloors cannot continually widen without the new crust—the new basalt stripes—going somewhere. The Atlantic Ocean is less than 200 million years old, younger than a twentieth of the age of the Earth, so that ocean has not been expanding indefinitely. In some places the plates dive (by being pulled or pushed or both) back down into subduction zones and then into the Earth's mantle from whence they came. In this way, Earth conserves its area. These modern subduction zones are the deep-sea trenches; the deepest, the Mariana Trench, near the Marianas Islands, east of the Philippines, is 11,040 meters (36,198 feet) down. It is here that recycling takes place. Rock is pulled downward into the subduction zone, to be shipped down to the mantle, partially remelted, and, eventually perhaps, to rise again through volcanoes. This keeps the ocean crust geologically youthful. Old rock is cremated and reworked, while young magma is born. The process is not quick—it takes millions of years. The plates move at speeds of a few centimeters per year.

Some of the subducted plate is recirculated to the spreading centers. Some stays closer to the subduction zone and supplies molten magma for volcanoes on island arcs or on the continents. The volcanoes that rim the Pacific Ocean, the so-called Ring of Fire (including Mount St. Helens, Washington), have this origin. The oceanic crust of the Pacific plate is subducted under the continents that surround it.

Not all plates are moving outward, propelled by new lava. Some are gliding past one another, not always smoothly, at horizontal displacement zones. This sort of movement is common along the San Andreas Fault in California—mostly horizontal, with one side of the fault slipping past the other. The San Andreas Fault is about 950 kilometers (590 miles) long, and has generated earthquakes for millennia. It is a major plate boundary, separating the Pacific plate to the west from the North American plate to the east. It is one of the few boundaries between plates that we can see on land. Most lie beneath ocean waters. It is particularly well displayed at Point Reyes National Seashore, where the fault line is clearly visible and the plates are marked by signposts (NORTH AMERICAN PLATE ⇒, PACIFIC PLATE ⇐) so that you can stand with one foot on the North American plate and one on the Pacific. The two plates are moving past each other at a rate of five centimeters (two inches) per year, but the boundary appears to be stuck, and will remain so until enough stress (manifested as elastic strain) has accumulated to overcome friction. Then an earthquake will occur. If you were to stand on the east side of the fault at Point Reyes for a long enough time (say, about a year), you could see that objects on the opposite side are moving north. Eventually, if you stood there long enough (millions of years), Los Angeles would pass by.

The concept of plate tectonics has led geologists to reevaluate long-known gold deposits. Among others, California's Sierra Nevada gold country has been restudied. The western belt of this area, the Foothills Copper Belt, contains copper and gold ore deposits in volcanic rocks, now metamorphosed (changed by heat and pressure). The volcanic rocks were originally erupted under the sea in an oceanic island arc similar to the present-day Aleutian chain. The eruptions took place in the Jurassic Period, roughly 150 million years ago. Since then the whole countryside has been moved to its present position by plate tectonic activity.

Copper and gold deposits like these are termed volcanogenic (formed by volcanoes). Geologists have seen such deposits actually forming undersea along the mid-ocean volcanic range and have recognized more than a thousand such volcanogenic deposits on land. These deposits are in volcanic flows, domes, and other volcanic material originally formed undersea. Much of the gold ore within them is in pyrite-rich bodies, below which are gold-rich feeder veins that extend downward.

Plate tectonics may help us understand how gold got into the veins in the first place. No one knows for certain, but some geologists who have studied this problem think the story goes like this: Gold is carried upward from the depths of the Earth, probably from the Earth's mantle, as a part of the lava that pours out along the mid-ocean rifts. As the lava cools, it cracks and seawater moves downward through the crack network. The seawater is heated by the hot but cooling lava and reacts chemically with it. This process is hydrothermal action, but this time it is seawater, not groundwater, that is the "hydro" part. Chlorine from the salt of the sea (common salt is sodium chloride, $NaCl$) aids in dissolving the metals. The hot, metal-enriched seawater rises toward the seafloor, where cooling causes the metals to be precipitated (separated out of solution as a solid). Metals are concentrated at and below the seafloor in this way, making such metal sulfides as pyrite and forming metal-rich chimneys, mounds, and sediments, with gold ions hitchhiking within the lattices of sulfide minerals.

This hydrothermal process keeps working on the minerals, concentrating them until the new ocean crust is cool. The minerals may become part of a plate that is subducted, going back into the mantle (as in the Ring of Fire), where the valuable metals may enter the new magmas and rise back toward the surface again, contributing metals to the new hydrothermal systems that develop in and near the subduction-related volcanism. There is eyewitness testimony that this might be so. Many submarine hydrothermal hot springs have been seen in action. In 1979 John Edmond and Karen Von Damm, scientists aboard the tiny research submarine *Alvin*, found an active hydrothermal vent only fifteen centimeters (six inches) in diameter on the seafloor surrounded by large blocks of sulfide minerals. They measured the temperature of the water in the vent: about 350°C (660°F). If this were a vent at sea level, the water would boil explosively, as Old Faithful does in Yellowstone, but being 2,500 meters (8,000 feet) under the sea, the pressure of overlying water kept it liquid.

The solutions left the vent as clear, homogeneous fluids a billion times richer in iron, zinc, copper, and nickel than ordinary seawater. In addition, the vent water contained 210 parts per million of hydrogen sulfide—again, far more than ordinary seawater. The hydrogen sulfide provided food that sustained an extraordinary community of strange organisms. And the silica content was also very high: 1,290 parts per million.

In 1983 researchers aboard *Angus*, another tiny undersea research vessel, dis-

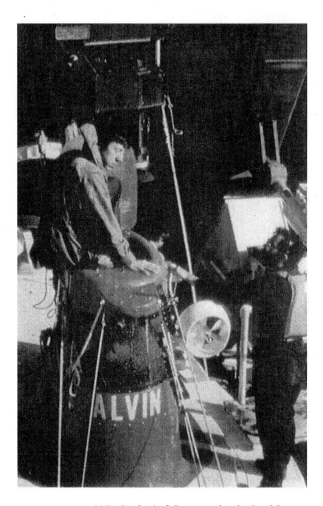

FIGURE 35. U.S. Geological Survey scientist Jan Morton climbs aboard the submarine *Alvin* to begin a research dive.

covered fields of hot springs in the sea, most of them inactive. Then *Alvin*'s crew found a live hot spring near the Gulf of California. "Black smoke" was shooting out of hydrothermal vents. The vents were built up from chemicals recycled by the hydrothermal waters, as hot springs on land have mineral "collars" like those at Yellowstone National Park. The center of the vent was open, like a volcanic neck, allowing the black smoke to pour out, back into the sea.

The black smoke forms when the mineral-rich water is thrown out of the mouth of the vent and quickly mixes with cold seawater. The "smoke" is iron sulfide, precipitated out of solution. Much of it is wafted away by the sea, but some falls back to the bottom as a metal-rich sediment. It, too, cracks and is penetrated by seawater, and hydrothermal action begins on the metal-rich sediment.

FIGURE 36. A hungry spider crab feasting on tube worms.

Since the 1980s many metal deposits formed by black smokers have been found along spreading seafloor volcanic ridges. Two of the deposits are especially rich in gold. One in the Atlantic part of the Mid-Ocean Ridge is 580 meters (1,900 feet) in diameter and 50 meters (165 feet) high. Its large size suggests that it has been venting gold-rich black smoke for a long time.

Surprisingly, animals live in and near the undersea hydrothermal vents in warm waters—as close as they can get without cooking themselves. In 1991 the marine geologist Rachel Haymon dived in *Alvin* to a volcanic caldera (crater) on the East Pacific Rise she had seen fifteen months earlier—a place where hot springs teemed with animal life, especially tube worms, some of which were as long as two meters (six feet). When Haymon reached the caldera this time, all was changed. No animals anywhere. Just inky blackness of lava. The *Alvin* continued to dive, and on the fourteenth dive Haymon found the remains of tube worms and mussels, all dead—scorched and shredded. They had been too close to the vent when it erupted. "It was absolutely pitiful," Haymon said. She and her fellow researchers called it Tube Worm Barbecue.

Eleven months later the team returned to Tube Worm Barbecue and found the tube worm meat gone. Small fish were there, and little white octopuses and crabs. Like the walrus and the carpenter in *Alice in Wonderland*, "they'd eaten every one." In 1995, when the team returned again, there were no tiny crabs, just big fat ones.

In the Atlantic researchers found black smokers surrounded by blind, eyeless shrimp, crowded together around the hot vents. And in 1991, on the Juan de Fuca Ridge in the Pacific, scientists, again aboard the *Alvin*, found reddish brown "sulfide worms" less than an inch long that live *inside* the chimney walls of the hot smokers. Their life at home is a hot one, as the temperature of the vent is much more than 100°C, and the sulfide concentration is enough to kill 99 percent of the species of life on Earth. "They also seem to travel well," wrote Robert Kunzig in *Discover* magazine in December 1993. "A Canadian geologist named Jim Franklin once collected a piece of black smoker from the Juan de Fuca Ridge and, several weeks later, decided to use it as a prop in a lecture he was giving. A sulfide worm crawled out of the rock, which by then was cold and bone dry, and started nosing around the podium."

But, although the black smokers in the sea emit gold, no one mines gold on the seafloor. The mines are in terrestrial mountain belts, within or along the margins of continents. This is where plates have collided or subducted; it is where the mineral-rich rock from old central vents has been incorporated into one plate, then crashed into another. It is here that mountains are lifted up, earthquakes take place, and new volcanoes erupt. Here again the great pressure of large, moving plates, interacting at plate boundaries, brings with it high temperatures. Where plates are subducted, rock is melted as one of the plates plunges beneath the other and mixes with continental rock, once again changing its chemistry. Metals formed at the midocean vents and concentrated during their journey are further concentrated here. Volcanoes form, and beneath them, large bodies of granitic rock gradually solidify. This remelted hot rock once again cracks, and water enters and is heated and again reworks the metals within the rock. This time the water is from the land—meteoric water, derived from rain and snow, sometimes mixed within the Earth with "magmatic water" sweated out of solidifying magmas—and the process of making ore for gold lodes has begun.

THE MOVING EARTH

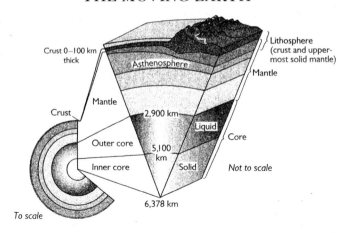

Crust 0–100 km thick
Asthenosphere
Lithosphere (crust and uppermost solid mantle)
Mantle
Crust
Mantle
2,900 km
Liquid
Core
Outer core
5,100 km
Inner core
Solid
Not to scale
6,378 km
To scale

INSIDE THE EARTH

No one has yet made a journey to the center of the Earth. The deepest anyone has gone has been in a gold mine in South Africa, which is more than 3,700 meters (12,000 feet) deep. Using information from measurements made by various instruments, particularly those registering earthquake waves, scientists have developed a picture of Earth's interior. The picture inferred is that of a ball made up of layers, like an egg or a golf ball. Where the layers begin or end, the instruments register a change in the speed or direction of earthquake waves.

The outside layer, like the egg's shell or the golf ball's cover, very thin in comparison to the other layers, is the crust. It is brittle and can break, like an eggshell, and is only about 5 kilometers (3 miles) thick under the oceans and an average of 30 kilometers (19 miles) thick under the continents. Thirty kilometers does not sound "thin," but when compared with the radius of the Earth, 6,375 kilometers (3,961 miles), it is a small fraction. The crust is made up principally of the elements oxygen, silicon, and aluminum, with smaller amounts of iron, magnesium, calcium, and others. Gold constitutes 0.0000002 percent of the crust.

The bottom of the crust marks the top of the mantle, a dense, hot layer of semisolid rock about 2,900 kilometers (1,800 miles) thick. Here, scientists think, the chemistry, too, changes, making the mantle richer in iron, magnesium, and calcium than the crust.

The upper part of the mantle, cooler and more rigid than the lower part, together with the crust, is the lithosphere, or rocky portion of the Earth, more solid than the lower mantle. The lithosphere, vital to the plate tectonics concept, averages 100 kilometers (60 miles) in thickness. Just below the lithosphere, at the top of the lower part of the mantle, is the asthenosphere, a 100-kilometer- (60-mile-) thick zone of semisolid material. Most of the mantle below the asthenosphere is solid.

Below the mantle is the beginning of the core. It, too, is divided into two parts, a liquid outer core some 2,200 kilometers (1,400 miles) thick and a solid inner one, about 900 kilometers (560 miles) in radius, that may be as hot as 7,200°C (13,000°F) in its center, hotter than the Sun's surface. It is probably composed chiefly of iron. As the Earth turns, the liquid portion of the core turns, too, creating the Earth's magnetic field. Like the Earth, the inner core spins, but at a rate slightly faster than the rest of the Earth, possibly gaining about a quarter turn per century.

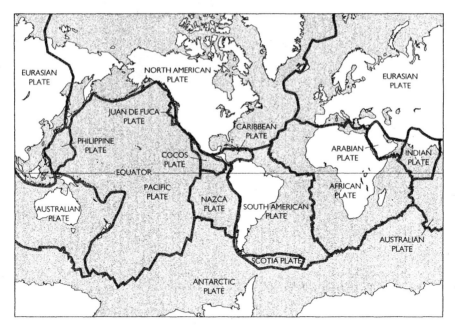

THE EARTH'S PLATES

According to plate tectonics theory, the Earth's lithosphere is divided into several large "plates" and twenty or so small ones. Each plate carries oceanic crust, and most have continents on them as well. The eight largest plates are

- *North American plate*, carrying North America, the western North Atlantic, and Greenland;
- *South American plate,* carrying South America and the western South Atlantic;
- *Antarctic plate*, carrying Antarctica and the so-called Southern Ocean;
- *Eurasian plate*, carrying the eastern North Atlantic, Europe, and Asia excluding India;
- *African plate,* carrying Africa, the eastern South Atlantic, and the western Indian Ocean;
- *Indian-Australian plate*, carrying India, Australia, New Zealand, and most of the Indian Ocean;
- *Nazca plate*, carrying the Pacific Ocean near South America; and
- *Pacific plate*, carrying most of the Pacific Ocean, including a sliver of California.

The plate boundaries are like political divisions—they are invisible unless one's attention is called to them, as along the San Andreas Fault at Point Reyes, California. Otherwise, to recognize plate boundaries, one needs to look at a map of earthquake epicenters and volcanoes around the Pacific, which delineates those plates clearly.

Plates can be thousands of kilometers across or only a few hundred. They vary in thickness from 200 kilometers (125 miles) or more (plates containing continents) to less than 15 kilometers (10 miles) (young, fresh oceanic plates). All of them move about on the asthenosphere.

The plates have been in motion, although they have changed direction, size, and shape many times, for at least hundreds of millions of years. Some geologists have suggested that plate motion began shortly after the birth of the Earth, and plates have been moving, connecting, and disappearing throughout most of Earth's time.

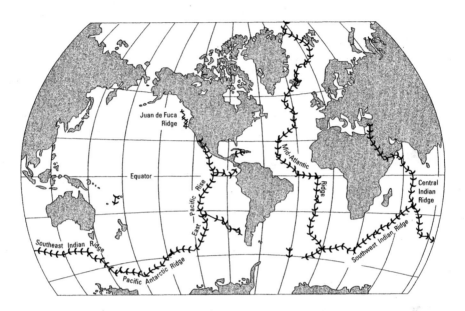

One surprising feature almost entirely covered by Earth's waters is an enormous mountain range, the Mid-Ocean Ridge, some 80,000 kilometers (43,000 miles) long. Along this ridge liquid rock pours out, forming new layers of dark-colored basalt lava and adding to the ocean floor. The layers diverge from the ridge in both directions. One segment of the ridge, running from the Arctic Ocean to the tip of Africa, is called the Mid-Atlantic Ridge (right). It is the plate boundary in the Atlantic Ocean and is marked by a central rift valley. The volcanoes of Iceland are part of this ridge; they are one of the few places on Earth where the ridge projects above water.

PLATES: HOW THEY MEET AND MOVE

Earth's plates move in three ways: away from each other (divergent), toward each other (convergent), and alongside each other along transform faults. As we shall see, plates also plunge under one another and ride atop one another, so up and down, although by-products of horizontal plate motion, are not ruled out.

Divergent boundaries   The Mid-Atlantic Ridge is a prime example of a divergent boundary. The ridge is a spreading center, along which new crust is created by hot molten rock (magma—which cools into basalt lava) pushing up from the mantle. As each new lava layer is added and flows to each side of the ridge, other older, cooler layers are pushed and pulled toward the side. Here the ocean crust is spreading, moving apart at the ridge axis at the rate of about 2.5 centimeters (about an inch) per year, or 25 kilometers (16 miles) in a million

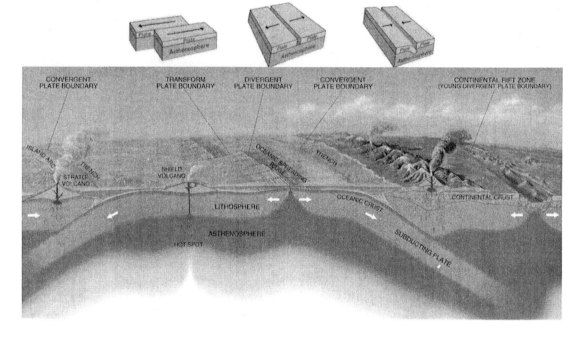

CONVERGENT PLATE BOUNDARY · TRANSFORM PLATE BOUNDARY · DIVERGENT PLATE BOUNDARY · CONVERGENT PLATE BOUNDARY · CONTINENTAL RIFT ZONE (YOUNG DIVERGENT PLATE BOUNDARY)

years. Over the past 100 million to 200 million years it has caused the Atlantic Ocean to grow from a tiny inlet to a vast ocean that now separates the continents of Europe, Africa, and the Americas. This does not mean that the ocean crust is entirely lava, even though much of the surface of the ocean floor is. Near shore, sediments from the land form a wedge out to sea, and even in the deep sea there is a dusting of debris falling from the surface of the sea. Beneath the ocean floor, the crust includes solidified rocks from the mantle as well as fluid rock that feeds the volcanic centers and provides heat for the submarine hot springs.

All rocks are composed of minerals, and lava is no exception, even though the minerals may not be visible to the naked eye. In the 1960s scientists discovered that iron-containing minerals within the lava (basalt) stripes were oriented toward Earth's magnetic pole—known as the North Pole—so that the tiny compass minerals within fresh lava point north. When older lava beds on either side were checked, however, their minerals, which had been locked in position at the time the basalt cooled, pointed in the opposite direction, indicating that the Earth's magnetic pole had flip-flopped through the ages, and each flip was recorded by a pair of magnetic stripes, one on each side of the ridge, while another adjacent pair recorded flops. Since scientists now have a method of measuring the actual age of a lava flow in years, they can tell precisely when each magnetic stripe was formed.

Convergent boundaries Plates moving toward each other are convergent, colliding very slowly. If an oceanic plate meets another oceanic plate, one of them generally is pulled and pushed (subducted) under the other, forming a trench. The world's deepest trench, the Mariana, at one spot as much as 11,040 meters (36,198 feet) deep, is the site where the relatively speedy Pacific plate converges with the slower and smaller Philippine plate.

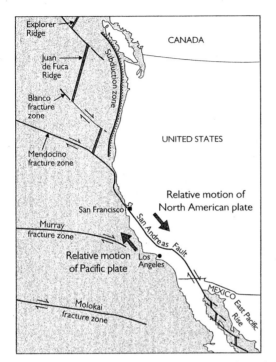
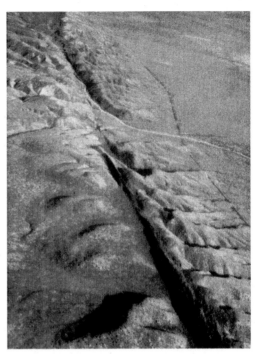

Left: *Some of the many fracture zones (transform faults) on the ocean floor, including both fossil (Murray) and active (Blanco). Very few transform fault lines are visible on land. The most striking exception is the San Andreas Fault, separating the Pacific and North American plates in California.* Right: *The San Andreas Fault from the air.*

If an oceanic plate meets a continental plate, as along the South American coast, the oceanic plate subducts under the continental plate—here the Nazca under the South American plate. This occasionally causes earthquakes generated deep within the Earth along the plate boundary and within the cool, brittle subducted lithosphere, often lifting the Andes even higher.

When two plates carrying continents converge, the results can be dramatic. Because both continental blocks are light compared to oceanic plates, neither is deeply subducted. Instead, the Earth's crust buckles and is pushed upward or sideways. A collision like this between the Eurasian plate and the Indian plate beginning 50 million years ago lifted the Himalayas and the Tibetan Plateau to their great heights. Here the continental crust is about twice as thick as normal. The Himalayas are the highest mountains in the world, reaching over 9,000 meters (nearly 30,000 feet). The Tibetan Plateau has an average elevation of 4,600 meters (15,000 feet), higher than any mountain peak in the United States south of Alaska.

Transform fault boundaries   In some places, two plates slide past one another along faults, without either one being pushed or pulled into a subduction trench. Many such boundaries exist in the ocean, breaking the magnetic basalt stripes into a checkerboard pattern.

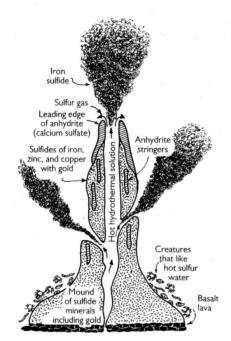

Iron
sulfide

Sulfur gas
Leading edge
of anhydrite
(calcium sulfate)

Anhydrite
stringers

Sulfides of iron,
zinc, and copper
with gold

Hot hydrothermal solution

Creatures
that like
hot sulfur
water

Mound
of sulfide
minerals
including gold

Basalt
lava

Diagram of a black smoker, showing how chemical compounds spew out. Eventually these compounds may become mineral deposits rich enough to mine when the plate tectonics process has moved them to the land. Although the seafloor itself contains valuable minerals, the cost of mining has so far kept mining companies from exploiting them.

One black smoker, the tallest yet found, rises 50 meters (160 feet) above the seafloor near the coast of Oregon. "Godzilla," researchers called it.

Two sites in the ocean were found to be particularly rich in gold, the southern part of Explorer Ridge and Axial Volcano, on Juan de Fuca Ridge. "Particularly rich," however, was not a bonanza.

The black smoker chimneys consist partly of the mineral anhydrite ($CaSO_4$). It forms at high temperatures, and when the temperature drops it dissolves quickly. Old, extinct chimneys have little anhydrite. As the smoker expels its "smoke," some of the iron and other sulfur-bearing minerals of the smoke fall to the seafloor, forming a heap of sulfides around the vent. Such heaps are incipient ore deposits.

The environs of the hot springs in the sea, of which black smokers are one type, are surprisingly rich in life. No one expected any life at all where the vents could reach a temperature of 350°C (660°F), enough to cook most land animals quickly. In addition, the mineral-rich waters would be toxic to most creatures; yet by 1985 researchers had identified 58 new species in 33 new genera from the vent areas. The hot springs were the center of a whole new ecosystem, previously unknown to science. To show that life could indeed endure at high temperatures, scientists John Baross and Jody Deming grew bacteria in the laboratory under high pressure at a temperature of 250°C (482°F). Under such pressures, water may be very hot but does not boil.

Tube worms living near the hot springs—strange creatures with shiny white tubes and protruding red, plumelike tips—proved to be so unusual they were put in a phylum all their own—placing them on an equal rank with all vertebrates. The odd "worms" had no mouth, no gut, and no anus, but they did have red blood, which is what made the tips—which proved to be a sort of gill—red, looking, as the writer Joseph Cone put it, "like lipstick coming out of a tube." How could they live without eating? The puzzle was solved when scientists noted that they were filled with bacteria, on which they lived. But what did the bacteria live on? Whole mats of bacteria were growing on the seafloor, packed so tightly together that a million would fit in one cubic centimeter (¹/₂₀ of a cubic inch). Clams, tube worms, and mussels all lived nearby and apparently dined on the bacteria. The bacteria themselves, instead of feasting on other creatures as we do, or being powered by sunlight, as plants are, lived by chemosynthesis; some actually thrived on a diet of dissolved hydrogen sulfide (which smells like rotten eggs) delivered to them, in the case of the tube worms, by the blood in the red tips of the tubes. How a baby tube worm acquires its bacteria when adults, at least, have no mouth, was a puzzle, but by careful study of juvenile worms, biologist Meredith Jones showed that the babies did have rudimentary mouths and guts, which disappeared when the worm became filled with bacteria and grew up.

There were living fossils, too, stalked barnacles that, according to paleontological records, had died out at the end of the Jurassic, when dinosaurs roamed the land. Yet here they were, alive and well.

The exotic hot spring animals in their strange environment caused several researchers, particularly geologist Sarah Hoffman, to consider the possibility that hot springs in the sea might be a source not only of gold and other mineral deposits but of life itself.

WHAT MAKES THE PLATES MOVE?

Almost as soon as geographers were able to put the Earth together, with the Americas taking their proper place, thinking people began speculating that South America and Africa looked as if they had once been joined and had moved apart. Even the Elizabethan scientist Sir Francis Bacon entertained the thought, but he could not prove it. The most vocal advocate of "continental drift" was the German meteorologist Alfred Wegener, who thought about the Earth while he was in a hospital bed recovering from his World War I wounds. He assembled a great mass of evidence but stumbled on the question "What makes the continents drift?"

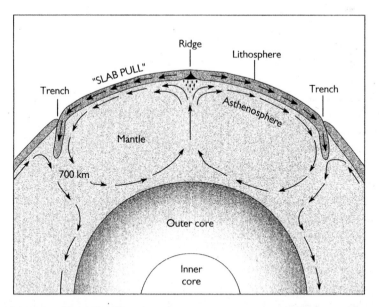

How convection cells in the mantle might power plate movement. When a cold plate slab descends into the mantle through a subduction zone (trench) to a depth of about 700 kilometers (435 miles), the Earth's internal heat softens it so that it loses form and flows, producing convection "currents" in Earth's mantle.

Even today the problem is not solved. Details as to how and why the plates move are not wholly agreed on, but it seems clear that they *do* move. Most scientists agree that convection in the mantle is the driving force. The mobile mantle rock is heated, perhaps from radioactive heat and from hot areas left over after the Earth's formation, rises toward the surface, spreads out, cools, and sinks back down. In this way, convection cells form, the mantle heating, rising, cooling, and falling back, in the process moving the plates along. Also, as the inner core crystallizes, enough latent heat is being released to provide enough energy to keep the mantle convecting long into the distant future.

Some plate tectonics experts emphasize that subduction zones are the keys to plate movement. As the cold, dense oceanic slabs sink into subduction zones, they pull the rest of the plate with them, stirring up convection in the mantle, and are thus the driving engines of plate tectonics. Possibly, as some researchers suggested in 1996, the independently spinning inner core, which whirls faster than the rest of Earth, also exerts a force that contributes to plate movement.

CHAPTER TEN

Gold Comes to California

Where was California during all this sliding and diving and docking and making of gold ore? For many millions of years California wasn't there at all. Certainly the latitude and longitude that California now occupies existed, but there was no fragment of the land we call California—only the deep blue sea.

Even so, this is where the story of California begins. Rocks that date back nearly two billion years can be seen in the Transverse Ranges and the Mojave Desert. They have been changed through the ages from whatever they were to hard, crystalline rock. But where they originated and by what route they came to California is not completely known.

Whatever its location on the globe, by about 400 million years ago, during the early part of the Paleozoic Era, the western margin of the North American continent extended roughly from today's southeastern Idaho across central Nevada and into southeastern California. Most of California was underwater. In basins along the shore, most of which was beyond the state's present boundaries, a wedge of sediments accumulated. Seaward, beyond the basin and the continental mass, were islands, forming island arcs near where the northern Sierra Nevada and Klamath Mountains are today. These arcs would be accreted (pasted) to the continent by action related to subduction. The drawing on page 178 shows one interpretation of how this might have happened. Rocks that did not plunge into the subduction zone were scraped off and pasted onto the continent (obducted).

Toward the end of the Paleozoic Era, in Devonian and Mississippian time (about 360 million years ago), mountains were lifted in central Nevada in an event called the Antler Orogeny. A great fault, the Roberts Mountains thrust, pushed older rocks on top of younger ones as the marginal basins were closed. Today the younger rocks beneath the Roberts Mountains thrust are being mined for gold, and have made Nevada the nation's current leading gold producer.

By 240 million years ago North America had grown. It was now joined to South America and Africa, with what would be Eurasia looming to the north. For about 200 million years after the Antler Orogeny—until about 160 million years ago—sediments continued to accumulate as a wedge along the west side of North America, in a new basin called the Nevadan geosyncline. As you can see from map 7, this included most of California's gold country. The whole area of the thick sedimentary wedge was more than 320 kilometers (200 miles) wide and extended from Alaska far down into Mexico. Although the layers of future rock that filled the basin to a thickness of 21 kilometers (13 miles) were laid down more or less horizontally, they were deformed about 150 million years ago and now are bent, twisted, and faulted.

Within these faulted and twisted beds is a group of rocks initially referred to as the Smartville complex, more recently, the Smartville block. (The name comes from the village of Smartville, which is west of Grass Valley and east of Marysville. Former president Herbert Hoover helped make the first geologic map of the Smartville area—called Smartsville then.) The belt is as much as 40 kilometers (25 miles) wide and lies below the high Sierra Nevada from about Auburn to Oroville and westward beneath the Central Valley.

The block came from the ocean depths, moved to an island arc, and then found its way to future California, bringing gold with it. Off the California shore were two ocean trenches (subduction zones), one dipping east, the other west. Both were destroyed by the arrival of the Smartville block. Either the trenches were stuffed so full of rock already subducted that part of the Smartville block (what we can see today) rode right over the trenches instead of diving into them, or, in the process of diving into one of the subduction zones, a piece of the Smartville was shaved off and left resting on the new continental edge. In any case, the Smartville is a piece of ocean crust, a very surprising batch of rocks to find in today's Sierra Nevada. To identify the Smartville suture (the line along which the Smartville block was joined to the American continent), you need only look at a map of the Mother Lode, because the docking of the Smartville created California's Mother Lode.

By 150 million years ago (Jurassic time) the North American continent had moved closer to its present position. Europe and Africa were beginning to move away, but there was still very little dry land in California. For that reason the state is not rich in dinosaur fossils. The big animals lived on dry or swampy land east of California. However, in 1991 a fossil of a small hypsilophodont dinosaur was found in Shasta County, indicating there was land there for the creature to walk on. Other dinosaur fossils found in California Jurassic rocks were sea-dwelling ichthyosaurs and the sacrum of a hadrosaur, an amphibious dinosaur with webbed feet and a duckbill.

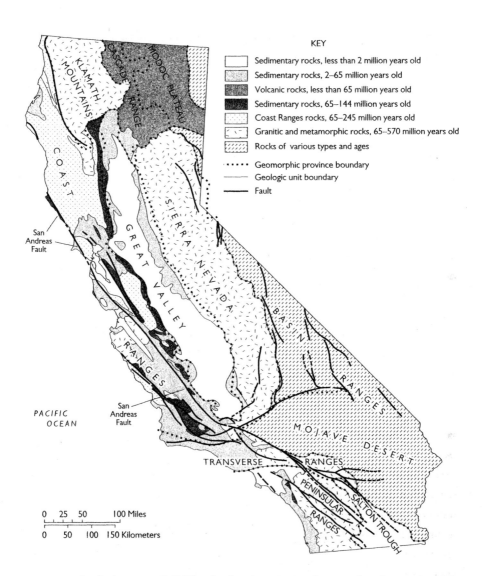

KEY

▢ Sedimentary rocks, less than 2 million years old
▦ Sedimentary rocks, 2–65 million years old
▓ Volcanic rocks, less than 65 million years old
■ Sedimentary rocks, 65–144 million years old
▒ Coast Ranges rocks, 65–245 million years old
⌇ Granitic and metamorphic rocks, 65–570 million years old
▨ Rocks of various types and ages

······ Geomorphic province boundary
——— Geologic unit boundary
——— Fault

MAP 7. Geologic map of California showing type and ages of rocks, geomorphic provinces, and principal faults.

From about 140 million years ago (late Jurassic) to 108 million years ago, the geosyncline was caught in the jaws of a great nutcracker. One jaw was the North American plate to the east, carrying the North American continent, the other the oceanic Pacific plate to the west. The pressure exerted by this nutcracker bent, twisted, and folded the rocks, lifting them up into mountains. The squeezing was accompanied by a great deal of heat, which melted some rocks and greatly changed others. This mountain building, which created the Ancestral Sierra Nevada, is called the Nevadan Orogeny.

Mountain building also caused the emplacement of granitic bodies. Most people know "granite" when they see it: a speckled, hard rock. Geologists think of granite as one of a number of different members in a family of rocks. Here I refer to the whole granite family as granitic rock. Part of the magma that formed the granitic bodies came from melting of rocks of the geosyncline, and part from gold-bearing rocks that had been subducted and melted. It was during the emplacement of granitic rock that the gold found its way into the veins of the mountains.

By the time the Ancestral Sierra Nevada had been fully constructed, North America had a mountainous region reaching from Alaska far into Mexico, a much longer range than the one we call the Sierra Nevada today. No one knows where the highest peak in this range was, or how high it might have been. It was a vast range, one that made a profound difference in North American geography.

As the mountains rose, they were attacked by erosion. For 40 million years erosion worked, eventually wearing the mountains down to mere stubs. (The mountains and foothills were dry land by 80 million years ago. The bones of a young, meat-eating theropod dinosaur were found near Granite Bay.) This long erosive period masked whatever else was happening. So profound was the gap in the rock record that early geologists called it the Great Unconformity and labeled the rocks beneath the unconformity the Subjacent Series and those above the Superjacent Series. These terms, though superseded, are still useful and still used.

The Ancestral Sierra Nevada was largely washed away, into valleys, into river-beds, into the sea. Fragments of the rocks of these old mountains lie deep under the Central Valley and are brought up in drill cores. Rocks that formed from sediment deposited near shore, perhaps as deltas, as well as some originally deposited in coastal lagoons may be seen along the edge of the Central Valley. Some of these rocks may carry invisible, "no-see-um," gold.

The rocks derived from the Ancestral Sierra that made the deepest impression on the miners (though few of them knew they did not come from today's mountains) were beds of gravel, boulders, sand, and clay they called Auriferous Gravels. Although there were other gold-bearing gravel beds in the mountains, it was the Auriferous Gravels the miners remembered. The miners thought they were the remnants of ancient streambeds, or "channels." At first geologists and miners thought they were Miocene in age (20 million years old); in fact, one company called itself the Miocene Mining Company. Later the beds were found to be even older, about 50 million years old (Eocene).

The gravel had filled gently sloping valleys of the foothills to a depth of as much as four hundred feet. More than filled the valleys—it extended across the valleys as far as two miles. The gravel covered an even older stream channel, the original river channel before the gravel swung its wide floodplain over the land. It was this narrow, original channel that was the richest in gold. The pieces of rock—the gravel—within the original stream channel came from rocks in the vicinity, and no doubt the gold in the channel did, too. This inner channel contained fine particles of pyrite, the iron in which gave the gravel a bluish or greenish tint, the miners' Deep Blue Lead. Gravel in the channel sides they referred to as "bench gravel" if it contained gold; if it did not, they damned it as "bastard gravel." Today, no gold-bearing blue gravel beds can be seen in the Sierra Nevada: the miners tore them up, every piece.

The miners thought they were digging into a tropical landscape, but in fact they were not. Plant fossils show that the climate when the beds were laid down was like that in parts of Mexico. The average temperature was about 18°C (65°F), with no frost but heavy rainfall.

Certainly the rivers drained down from the crest of the range, but where was the crest? Unlike the gravel of the Deep Blue Lead, the rocks making up the Auriferous Gravels are partly from neighboring mountainsides, including granite from the mountains east of the channels, and partly from elsewhere. The ancient rivers were bringing broken pieces of rock from somewhere to cast on their floodplains, but probably not all from California. Chances are they were picking up Nevada material, and possibly some of Nevada's gold, too.

It is no wonder the miners thought of Noah's flood when they saw the thick beds of gold-bearing gravel. But it would have taken a mighty storm to carry all that detritus—a storm like the world has never seen. Yet good-sized storms, repeated many times over millions of years, would accomplish the same purpose. The late geologist Cordell Durrell, in his excellent book, *Geologic History of the Feather River Country, California*, calculated that during the 10 million years or so it took the gravel to accumulate, a sizable flood every twenty years would total 500,000 floods. If such a flood deposited only two feet of sediment (including gold), only half that many floods would bury the ten northern counties of the Sierra Nevada (some 12,500 square miles, or 32,400 square kilometers) to a depth of four hundred feet.

After the floods that left the Auriferous Gravels subsided, the area that is now the Sierra Nevada was covered with lava flows, volcanic mudflows, and ash, thus burying the ancient gold-bearing riverbeds (but not fooling the persistent nineteenth-century miners, who found them anyway).

It was not until about 3 million years ago—just yesterday in geologic time—that the present Sierra Nevada began to rise as a great fault block. As it rose, erosion stripped off much of the volcanic rocks and the remaining older rocks from the crest, leaving granite that Ice Age (Pleistocene) glaciers pruned into sharp peaks and ridges, beginning about 2 million years ago. The glaciers left the debris from their efforts as long, sinuous moraines below them. A glacier is rarely a carrier of gold, unless there is a very rich vein in its path, or glacial streams find a gold pocket; but gravel from an Ice Age lake in Plumas County did yield placer gold.

The Sierra Nevada was lifted higher in the south than in the north, so that the highest peaks are in the south (Mount Whitney and its neighbors). Because the mountains are not as high as one goes northwestward into the Klamath Mountains (geologically similar to the Sierra Nevada), far more of the old rock of the Nevadan geosyncline is to be seen in the Klamaths, as it has not been so thoroughly stripped by erosive forces. Between the Sierra Nevada and the Klamath Mountains, beds of lava from the Modoc Plateau and the Cascade Range, emplaced from 20 million years ago to today, cover the rocks connecting the two ranges. Beneath this lava cover there well may be untapped gold deposits.

The Mojave Desert and Peninsular Ranges, too, contain gold deposits, most of them related to the granitic rock that occupies many of the ranges and is a continuation of the Klamath-Sierra story. The desert is so filled with rock debris that the mountains are merely terrestrial islands. For example, the Mojave-Rosamond District in Kern County produced gold from five buttes south of the town of Mojave near the Rosamond Hills. Here it is easy to see the island effect: only the buttes have been gold producers; in between the desert is filled with alluvium. The Tropico mine on Tropico Hill, one of the buttes, is now a museum. A good time to visit is in the spring of a wet year, when the buttes, particularly Soledad Mountain, are exploding with wildflowers.

Geologically, the Sierra Nevada may be considered the westernmost range of the Basin Ranges province, but it is not the only range in California belonging to that province. A corner of Modoc County to the north and portions of eastern California and the southern deserts, including Death Valley, are part of the Basin Ranges. The Bodie mining district northeast of Mono Lake produced an estimated $30 million in gold (at $20 per ounce), plus a million ounces of silver. The town of Bodie had a reputation for wildness—particularly for murder—in the nineteenth century. Today it is a state park.

East of the Klamaths are Mounts Shasta and Lassen, which, together with Medicine Lake Highlands, are active volcanoes—the southernmost volcanoes of the Cascade Range. These volcanoes are the result of the subduction of the Juan de Fuca plate under the North American plate. Although volcanoes and volcanic rocks are the ultimate source of gold, neither the Cascades nor the Modoc Plateau has yielded rich bonanzas, as there has not been time for nature to concentrate it. However, there well may be no-see-um gold in the rocks.

The Coast Ranges, as we know them, are also recent additions to the landscape. Their rocks are so soft in comparison to the tough granite of the Sierra Nevada and the desert mountains that a few million years from now, they probably won't even be mountains. Erosion will have worn them away, barring, of course, nature lifting them up again. Much of the Coast Ranges consists of rocks of the Franciscan group (named for its outcrop near San Francisco), a mélange of rocks that were gathered up in many places and scrambled together. The rocks within the Franciscan are far older than the mountains themselves, which rose only about 3 million years ago. The Franciscan first appeared as offshore islands. The islands were shoved against and over the coastal plain, pushing the sediments of the coastal plane upward, deforming them.

The pusher in this case was the Farallon plate. It lay between the North American and Pacific plates, and has mostly disappeared in a subduction zone. As it was being consumed by the subduction zone, the Franciscan mélange was scraped off its top and left as a wastebasket of confusing rocks. This action brought the Pacific plate in touch with the North American plate, first in southern California some 29 million years ago. Here the plate action changed, becoming a lateral motion along the new San Andreas Fault, as it is now.

Coast Ranges volcanoes, such as those in the Napa Valley, resulted from the new San Andreas Fault pulling the land apart at bends, while some of the volcanoes of the Sierra Nevada—the Sutter Buttes, for instance—may be the final volcanic outburst of the dying Farallon plate. As the last of the Farallon plate moved east and down, basaltic magma rose to take its place, creating the Clear Lake volcanic and geothermal field.

Where the San Andreas bent in one direction, mountains rose—the Santa Cruz mountains and the Transverse Ranges, for example. By measuring the magnetic orientation of mineral needles within the volcanic rocks near the bend of the Transverse Ranges, scientists have shown that there was a 75° rotation of rocks as they were being moved along the San Andreas fault system.

The story of California and its gold may never be accurately or completely known, because as new facts surface parts of it will have to be corrected and the story expanded. Neither science nor the Earth stands still.

CALIFORNIA THROUGH THE AGES

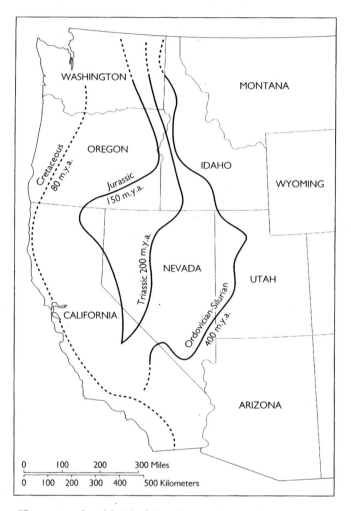

The western edge of the North American continent as it was 400, 200, 150, and 80 million years ago. For most of the time, California as we know it was under the waters of the sea.

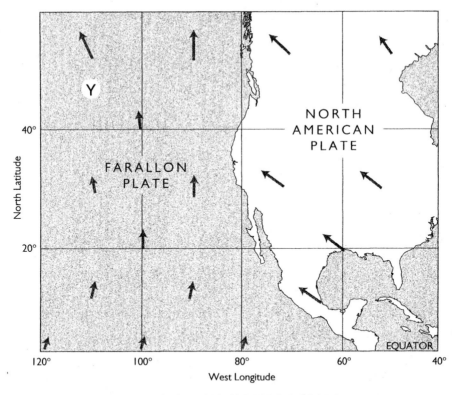

TRAVELS OF THE FARALLON PLATE:
NOW YOU SEE IT, NOW YOU DON'T

One hundred million years ago two great Earth plates were in the vicinity of what is now the California coast, moving in slightly different directions. Arrows show direction of movement: the Farallon plate nearly north, the North American plate northwest. The length of the arrows indicates the amount of movement (scaled to the map) during 10 million years. The continent, shown here in its present configuration merely for reference, was 40 degrees east and a little south of the position it occupies today. The "Y" marks the hot spot that created the lava flows and thermal wonders at Yellowstone National Park. The North American plate and the continent on it moved across the hot spot while the spot remained stationary. The major outpouring of lava from the hot spot produced the Columbia River flood basalt layers of Washington State.

By 30 million years ago, the Farallon plate was being pushed by seafloor spreading away from the Pacific plate into a subduction zone at the edge of the North American plate. By 20 million years ago, the Farallon plate had largely been consumed under the North American plate, leaving the Juan de Fuca plate as the Farallon plate's northern remnant and the Cocos plate as its southern. Where the plate was totally consumed, movement between the Pacific plate and the North American plate caused slippage along a transform fault—the San Andreas.

As the Farallon plate sank into the subduction zone, mountains bristling with volcanoes

| 30 million years ago | 20 million years ago | 10 million years ago | Present |

were created. The Sierra Nevada was not the only range to be lifted as the Farallon plate said good-bye to the Earth's surface.

When the major portion of the Farallon plate stopped being subducted and pressure from the west lessened, upwelling of the hot asthenosphere led to uplift of the Basin Ranges province, of which the Sierra Nevada is a part. What is now the desert west of the United States broke into alternating linear mountains and valleys.

The Juan de Fuca remnant of the Farallon plate is disappearing, too, subducting in a sediment-filled trench between Vancouver Island and Cape Mendocino. Seafloor ridges formed at the spreading margin of the plate, and lava rises, spreads out, cools, and breaks along faults. Axial Volcano, where scientists found gold was being deposited, and some of the black smokers investigated by diving scientists lie on the Juan de Fuca plate.

Volcanoes, like Mount St. Helens, that lie along subduction zones often erupt explosively because the magma that feeds them is too stiff to allow volcanic gases to escape easily, causing pressure to rise. Finally, when the gas is too much for the volcano to contain, the pent-up pressure is released in a violent eruption.

Because the northern section of the Juan de Fuca plate is farther from the spreading center and therefore cooler and denser, it is sinking into the subduction zone faster than the southern section.

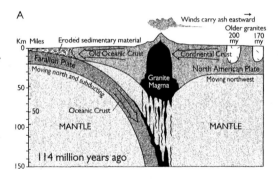

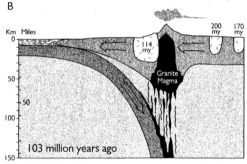

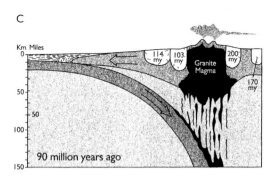

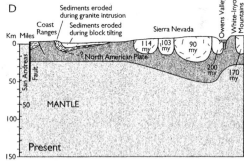

GRANITE, THE HEART OF THE MATTER

In these four diagrams, the dean of Sierran geologists, Paul C. Bateman, shows how the Farallon plate, in subducting, spurred the development of Sierran granite. The most widespread Sierran granites intruded into older rocks between about 85 and 114 million years ago. Hot magma, derived from partial melting of the mantle beneath the North American plate as water was released from the subducting Farallon plate, rose from the subduction zone and mixed with and melted lower crustal material, changing its chemistry. Pockets of granite (plutons) developed, spurted toward the surface, and consolidated at different times during the period of their formation. Some magma broke the surface in volcanic eruptions, but most cooled underground as granite.

MISPLACED PIECES

The edge of the continent is a very active place. Here, plates subduct or crash into one another; and here, too, smaller pieces of plates, sometimes having wandered from half a world away, crash into the continent and are fused to it, or dock. These pieces of oceanic or continental real estate, comprising not just the surface (the terrain) but also a slab of lithosphere, are referred to as terranes. Every continent has had out-of-place (exotic) pieces of terrane added to it. Western North America is a mosaic of patches accumulated ("accreted" is the technical term) through the ages. One large terrane attached itself to western North America in the late Devonian, some 380 million years ago, pushing almost to Utah. Another, the Sonoma terrane, docked in North America about 250 million years ago. The suture of the Sonoma (the place where the terrane attached) lies near Golconda, Nevada, at Nevada's Sonoma Range.

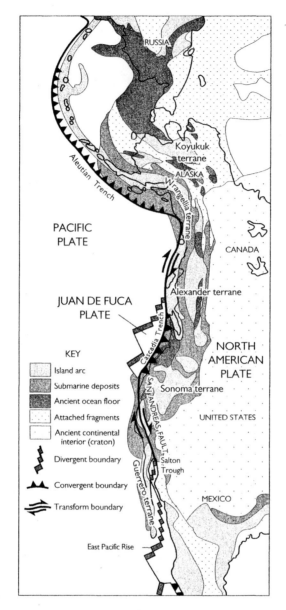

At the beginning of the Mesozoic Era (245 million years ago), there was still no vestige of the land that was to be California, but by the Jurassic two active trenches were off the California coast, one dipping east and one west. Both were destroyed by the arrival of the Smartville terrane, which docked in California in Jurassic times, creating the Mother Lode, and for the first time, land appeared in the Sierra Nevada. Another terrane—probably composed of many small pieces—was added later, creating the Coast Ranges.

Parts of southern California no doubt came to us courtesy of some distant clime, but where and when is not yet clear.

CHAPTER ELEVEN

Out of the Mines, into the World

Forty-niners who struck it rich, as well as those who found just a small amount of gold, faced a dilemma forty-eighters did not: crime. In the first year of the gold rush a miner could leave his gold in his tent, in his cabin, or at his claim, and no one would touch it. But with the hordes of forty-niners came criminals, and otherwise honest men who didn't succeed in the mines sometimes turned to crime in desperation. There was very little formal law, and what there was, was far away, so the miners acted as their own prosecutors, judges, and wardens, and those accused of crimes were punished at once. Rarely, in the early days, was anyone formally and legally convicted. Punishment ranged from cutting the ears off a "thief" to hanging. If an accused person was a foreigner (especially Mexican or Chinese) or an Indian, he was likely to get a speedier "trial" and a severer punishment. Almost all "criminals" were men. Only one woman was hanged at the mines, and she a Mexican.

But hanging and other punishments did not deter theft. Having laboriously dug up the gold, miners had to try to keep it—even by putting it back in the ground. They tried all sorts of clever ways to hide their gold until they could get it to San Francisco and send it east to their families on ships or spend it on a wild spree.

Some miners had their problem solved by a ferocious bandit named Joaquin Murieta, who relieved them of it—or so the legend goes. The facts are skimpy and dubious. In 1852 and 1853, after three years of harassment, and even murder by Yankee forty-niners, some Mexicans—and perhaps Californios, too—got tired of having the name of bandit without the game and began to prey on those who had driven them from the goldfields, those with whom they had been so lately at war. They organized into small groups that rustled cattle, robbed stores and saloons, and held up lone travelers for their gold.

In each robbery, it seemed, one "Joaquin" was the leader. By combining reports,

FIGURE 37. Capt. Harry Love.

one could count five Joaquins, all with different surnames. Prodded to "do something," in 1853 the California Legislature acted. The first proposal offered a $5,000 reward for "Joaquin," dead or alive, but one member pointed out that no one named "Joaquin" had been convicted of anything, and to offer a reward for a person who had never been brought to trial was not only immoral but might lead to the bush-whacking of any Mexican who could then be labeled "Joaquin."

The legislature compromised by hiring an ex-Texan, Capt. Harry Love, to raise a company of no more than twenty rangers to search the state for three months and capture the "company of robbers commanded by the five Joaquins," naming them as Joaquin Carrillo, Joaquin Valenzuela, Joaquin Bottilier, Joaquin Murieta, and Joaquin Ocomoreña. To this the governor added a $5,000 reward for any Joaquin, dead or alive, thereby sabotaging the legislature's more judicious intent.

Captain Love and his party ranged up and down California for two months, finding no Joaquins. At length they came upon a party of Mexicans sitting around a fire. Suddenly both groups were shooting, and in the foray the Mexican leader was killed. Another man, wounded, the rangers chased and shot. He was identified as

WILL BE
EXHIBITED
FOR ONE DAY ONLY!

AT THE STOCKTON HOUSE!
THIS DAY, AUG. 19, FROM 9 A. M., UNTIL 6, P. M.

THE HEAD
Of the renowned Bandit!

JOAQUIN!
—— AND THE ——
HAND OF THREE FINGERED JACK!
THE NOTORIOUS ROBBER AND MURDERER.

"JOAQUIN" and "THREE-FINGERED JACK" were captured by the State Rangers, under the command of Capt. Harry Love, at the Arroya Cantina, July 24th. No reasonable doubt can be entertained in regard to the identification of the head now on exhibition, as being that of the notorious robber, Joaquin Murietta, as it has been recognised by hundreds of persons who have formerly seen him.

FIGURE 38. Poster announcing exhibition of the head of Murieta and the hand of Three-Finger Jack. Posters like this appeared throughout California as the grisly artifacts were brought around to new audiences.

Manuel García, "Three-Finger Jack," wanted by the law. The rangers cut off his hand and preserved it in alcohol, then cut the head off the chief bandit and preserved it, too, in a large jar. For years the "head of Joaquin Murieta" and the severed hand of Three-Finger Jack were displayed around California. Most of the others escaped, except for two: one was drowned on the way to prison, the other lynched on reaching jail. Captain Love collected his salary and the governor's reward, even though no one could say for certain that the head he brought back was that of Joaquin Murieta, or any Joaquin at all, or for that matter, if the person whose head it was had had anything at all to do with any robbery anywhere. To the *Alta California*'s disgust, a grateful legislature voted Captain Love an additional $5,000.

From this confusing start, the writer Yellow Bird (John Rollin Ridge) concocted a tale of a Mexican Robin Hood who shared his loot with his Spanish-speaking friends that has become embedded in California tradition. As a boy, Yellow Bird, who was half Cherokee, had walked the seven-hundred-mile Trail of Tears. Because gold had been found on the Cherokee homeland in Georgia, and because whites coveted the land, the Cherokee Nation had been forced to walk from Georgia to a

FIGURE 39. Drawing of Joaquin Murieta,
from Yellow Bird's book.

new home in Oklahoma so that white gold miners could take the gold and the land.
The United States promised the Cherokees $9 million for the land, then charged
them $6 million to move them off it. On the long walk about a third of the Cherokees
died from starvation and exposure. When the relocation was complete, the United
States congratulated itself on its humane and generous action. So Yellow Bird knew,
firsthand, about bigotry, oppression, and greed. Ironically, oil was found in abundance on the new Cherokee land in Oklahoma after Yellow Bird's time.

In his story, which he titled *The Life and Adventures of Joaquin Murieta, the
Celebrated California Bandit*, Murieta was a "truly wonderful man," who looked
forward to intercourse with free and democratic Americans but instead found prejudice and persecution. He turned to outlawing when a group of marauding miners
ordered him to leave his claim. They beat him, then tied him hand and foot and
forced him to watch while they gang-raped his young mistress. Shortly after, he was
found riding a "stolen" horse, which his half-brother had lent him. The miners who
caught him would listen to no explanation. He was tied up and whipped, his
brother hanged without a trial. From then on Joaquin could think of nothing but

MURIETA'S GOLDEN LOOT

Since Joaquin is more legendary than real, locations where he was said to have buried his loot are of little value. This has not deterred countless treasure hunters from searching these and other sites for "Joaquin's treasure."

Alameda County	Caves near Brushy Peak, northeast of Livermore
Fresno County	Tres Piedras, near Coalinga
Los Angeles County	Immaculate Heart College, Hollywood
Mariposa County	A cave near Bagby
Monterey County	Los Laureles grade, between Monterey and Salinas
San Diego County	A cave east of Carrizo
San Joaquin County	Caves in Castle Rock, near Corral Hollow (near Tracy)
Shasta County	Volcanic caves in Lassen Volcanic National Park
Tuolumne County	"Murieta's Haunted House," near Tuolumne, razed in the 1920s
Ventura County	Red Mountain, near Ventura

revenge. He started by seeking out those who had whipped him, and one by one they met death.

In 1851 he organized a gang of Mexican bandits, among them Three-Finger Jack, a most vicious character, "utterly destitute of one merciful trait of humanity." To him was given the task of carrying out the most gruesome crimes. By the time Yellow Bird's blood-and-thunder story was well launched, he had assigned Joaquin more than two thousand followers. They roared up and down California, especially in the Mother Lode, robbing men and stores. From two miners on the San Joaquin River they took $20,000, according to Yellow Bird, leaving the miners—as well as some of their own henchmen—dead; at one point Joaquin sent $50,000 in gold to a partner in Sonora. If other legends are to be believed—not Yellow Bird's—Joaquin secreted gold in every county in the gold country and wherever else he happened to be.

Yellow Bird's narrative ends with the killing of Joaquin by Love's men, leaving no doubt in his tale that the head that had been circulating around the state was Joaquin's, and with the admonition "that there is nothing so dangerous in its consequences as *injustice to individuals* [his italics]—whether it arise from prejudice of color or any other source; that a wrong done to one man is a wrong to society and to the world."

The book was published in San Francisco in 1854. Yellow Bird, who expected to make money from his literary fiction, said that instead his publisher had vanished, leaving him to "whistle for his money." By 1857 his story was rewritten and pirated for the *Police Gazette*. Stolen Spanish editions, French editions, and a host of other pirated versions from many countries followed. Yellow Bird got nothing for them. Sometimes the names of the characters, particularly Joaquin's sweetheart, were changed, but not Joaquin's. The story line remained roughly the same. A four-act play, a new novel, articles in the *Saturday Evening Post* and the San Francisco *Call*, and story after story based loosely on Yellow Bird's work continued to be produced. One novel, *The Robin Hood of El Dorado*, by Walter Noble Burns, came out in 1932 (by this time Yellow Bird's work would have been long in the public domain anyway) and spurred a movie version. The saga is far from dead. Television has barely discovered it.

Without doubt, Mexicans were mistreated by the arrogant and prejudiced American miners. Although there is almost no grain of truth in the Joaquin story, some folk hero was desperately needed. "Since there wasn't a Murieta—at any rate, not much of a Murieta," wrote the late Joseph Henry Jackson, longtime editor of the *San Francisco Chronicle*, "it was necessary to invent one." Not just for the Mexicans and Californios—few of them probably even read the book. The legend of Joaquin became part of the fabric of California folklore, part of the romance of the early days so cherished by the Americans.

The problem of how to get the gold out of the mines and into the world was soon resolved by entrepreneurs who arrived on the scene. Express riders on horseback or foot (some even on skis), as well as mule and dog trains, braved wilderness, the elements, angry Indians, and bandits to carry mail and packages to the few post offices. They were soon joined by express companies run by men who knew the express business in the East: Alvin Adams, a Bostonian; John Butterfield of Utica, New York; and most famous of all, Henry "Stuttering" Wells, who owned an express business in Albany, New York, and William George Fargo, one of his messengers.

By the winter of 1851 Wells, Fargo and Company were in business. They would carry letters, packages, and miners' gold dust and bullion. Or they would buy the gold outright. They established offices in the main California towns and proceeded to make the Concord Coach stage famous. Sometimes the stage drivers were accompanied by shotgun messengers, sometimes they were alone. But they carried a locked box that held gold entrusted to Wells Fargo and Wells Fargo's own gold, occasionally as much as $100,000. It was this box that interested Black Bart.

Black Bart began his career in crime on a hot July 26, 1875, on Funk Hill, along a dusty road east of Copperopolis in the California Mother Lode. He was a grotesque and frightening sight when he stepped out of the bushes to halt the stage. He was enveloped in a huge linen duster, and on his head he wore a flour sack with

FIGURE 40. A Wells Fargo box, the type that Black Bart broke open to steal the gold, with an extra guard, "Jack on the box."

jagged cutouts revealing his piercing blue eyes. His shoes were covered with heavy boot socks. "Please throw down the box!" he commanded in a sepulchral voice, waving his shotgun at the driver. For emphasis, he called over his shoulder, "If he dares to shoot, give him a solid volley, boys!" The frightened driver thought he could see several barrels pointed at him from nearby manzanita bushes and hastened to kick down the strongbox. When a lady passenger tossed Bart her purse, he bowed, handed it back, and said in his deep bass, "I don't wish your money, madam, only [Wells Fargo] boxes." Black Bart (no one called him that yet) broke open the box with an ax, took the gold, and disappeared, as he was to do another 27 or 28 times throughout his eight-year reign as California's most feared bandit. When the driver went back to collect the broken box, he could still see the eight "boys" Bart had ordered to "give him a solid volley." They were sticks propped in the bushes.

For two years no one could put a name to the bandit. Then on August 3, 1877, he left the first of his literary efforts at the scene of the crime. It read:

> I've labored long and hard for bread
> For honor and for riches,
> But on my corns too long you've tred
> You fine-haired Sons of Bitches.

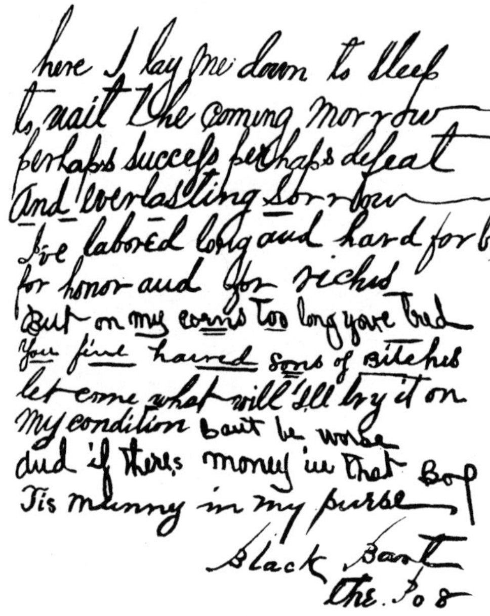

FIGURE 41. Poem left by Black Bart at the scene of one of his robberies.

He signed it "Black Bart, the Po8." Now he was identified; but it was to be another four years before he was captured.

Wells Fargo detective James B. Hume, who pursued him relentlessly all over California, built up a picture of his modus operandi. Bart found lonely spots on the stagecoach routes, preferably behind a concealing rock (one near Willits, close to U.S. Highway 101, is called Black Bart Rock); he carried a shotgun but never fired it (later, Hume found out it was never even loaded); he worked alone and was always on foot, most often wearing the same getup as in his first robbery. He always eluded his pursuers by muffling his tracks with the stockings he wore over his boots and by covering on foot as much as seventy-five miles at a stretch—far more than his trackers on horseback could credit.

He committed his last robbery on Sunday, November 3, 1883, at the same spot as his first one. The stage driver, Reason E. McConnell, was carrying more than $5,000 in gold coin, as well as dust and amalgam from the Patterson mine. At the Reynolds Ferry on the Stanislaus River, a young friend, nineteen-year-old Jimmy Rolleri, hitched a ride, saying he wanted to go hunting near Copperopolis with his new Henry rifle. Near the bottom of Funk Hill, Jimmy hopped off to see if he could scare up a rabbit while the coach toiled up the hill.

Just before the crest, a much-publicized figure, complete with sack mask, linen duster, and shotgun, stepped out of the rocks and bushes. This time, the deep voice

FIGURE 42. Black Bart Rock, off Highway 101 in the redwood country south of Willits. Behind this rock the highwayman lay in wait for his prey—a stagecoach.

FIGURE 43. A stagecoach of the type Black Bart loved to rob.

FIGURE 44. Portrait of Black Bart in his
city clothes as C. E. Bolton, a "mining man."

asked, "Who was that man who got off down below?" McConnell replied that it was just a friend, hunting stray cattle. Bart ordered the driver to get down from the seat so he could unfasten the box. McConnell said he couldn't—the stage would roll, as the brakes were weak.

Bart said, "The stage can't roll if you put rocks behind the wheel."

"Why don't you?" McConnell asked. Incredibly, Bart did. He then ordered McConnell to go farther up the road while he, Bart, broke open the box. McConnell, who had no gun, did as he was told. Bart began hammering at the box.

Meanwhile, Jimmy Rolleri was coming toward the stagecoach, wondering what was wrong. McConnell signaled him to circle the coach without being seen. Both men saw Bart straighten up and shoulder the heavy sack of gold. McConnell grabbed the rifle from Jimmy and shot at Bart. He missed. He fired again and missed. Jimmy took the gun back, saying, "I'll get him, and I won't kill him, either." He fired. Bart stumbled, dropping a handful of papers, but kept tight hold on the gold.

When lawmen reached the scene, they found a treasure trove of clues: a black derby hat, two paper bags with crackers and sugar from the Angels Camp grocery store, a pair of field glasses and leather case, a razor, a handkerchief filled with buckshot, a set of soiled linen shirt cuffs, and two empty flour sacks. Very soon they had a good description of the man—he had even stayed at Jimmy Rolleri's grandmother's hotel—but not the man.

It was not until they noticed a laundry mark, F.X.0.7, that they had a way of tracing Bart. In eight days they canvassed most of the ninety-one laundries in San Francisco, asking if the owners recognized the mark. Finally one did, and they were able to track Bart down. He proved to be a mild, dapper, well-spoken little man who called himself Charles E. Bolton (his real name was Boles), a mining man. He had deserted his family back East and although he wrote to them sporadically, never shared his spoils with them. Most of the gold he used to live well, but not lavishly. Bart soon confessed to the robberies, and eighteen days after his last robbery—justice was speedy in those days—he entered San Quentin, sentenced to six years.

Even when Wells Fargo or the miner himself managed to get the newly mined gold to San Francisco, there was no guarantee it would reach the families or com-

FIGURE 45. Cartoon suggesting that on release from prison, Bart would resume his larcenous ways. The lady is labeled "Wells Fargo." Bart has a belt reading "Black Bart." San Quentin prison is in the background. "Will he woo her again?" asks the cartoonist.

mercial markets it was meant for in the East. For one thing, professional gamblers acquired much of the gold the miners had toiled to obtain. Some took the gold back East, as at least one diarist noted on his return trip, but there is no record of where the rest went or how much the gamblers took and what they did with it. For another thing, the gold had to go by ship, and ships sometimes sank.

Compared to the hundreds of years that Spanish galleons traversed the Atlantic and Pacific oceans carrying silver and gold from the New World, the days of the ships carrying gold from the mines of California were brief. Even so, more than $300 million in gold went east through Panama in the first twenty years after the California rush began in earnest in 1849.

As it happened, the California gold rush came just as steamships made their first runs on the oceans of the world, so the ships that carried California gold ranged from elderly sailing vessels to the latest and newest steamers. Within a few months after the rush to California commenced, traffic began to flow eastward as well, as some of the luckier miners carried their gold back home.

Much of the gold that went east by sea in larger consignments was carried in the fast clipper ships that did not take passengers or, later, in Pacific Mail steamers. Of these ships, only a few were lost while carrying gold. The same cannot be said of those that carried passengers. Neither the sailing ships nor the steamers excelled in getting the passengers to their destinations alive, but the steamers that went to or from California had a worse mortality rate than the sailing ships, even counting the latter's difficult passage around the Horn. Although the steamers provided a much quicker journey, the passengers were crowded more closely together, which increased the danger of epidemic. Then, too, since one steamer carried them only halfway to their destination, the passengers were forced to make the hazardous journey through Panama or Nicaragua, where a variety of unfamiliar diseases—malaria, jaundice, dysentery, yellow fever—as well as the familiar but dangerous cholera, awaited them. Panama also held another familiar danger: robbers lurked (as Francis Drake had centuries before) to steal from the unwary or unprotected.

The *Tennessee,* wrecked in 1853 in Tennessee Cove, Marin County, was the first Pacific Mail steamer to be lost. Nine months later the *Winfield Scott,* a side-wheeler of the line, ran into Anacapa Island near Santa Barbara, California. The passengers and crew escaped, but the cargo sank with the ship. Although salvage had begun earlier, in 1965 divers discovered gold nuggets and pockets of gold near the remains of the ship and remined them from the bottom of the sea.

The Independent line, a competitor of the Pacific Mail, lost the *Union* in 1851 in Baja California. No lives were lost, and much of the gold was saved. The crew, later investigation showed, had celebrated Independence Day too freely. No one had been left on watch, and the helmsman had fallen asleep at the wheel.

FIGURE 46. The *Yankee Blade* as she lay crushed by rocks 135 miles south of Monterey Bay.

One of the most serious wrecks of the Independent line involved the *Yankee Blade*, a large, fast, paddle-wheel steamer, which crashed into the shore in a dense fog near Point Arguello, California, in 1854. The captain, Henry Randall, had been racing with the steamer *Sonora*, on a bet of $5,000. The *Yankee Blade* carried 819 passengers and 120 crew members. The undisciplined crew became confused, resulting in the loss of the first lifeboat and 17 of its 21 occupants. The captain jumped into a lifeboat, then deserted the ship and the passengers. About 300 of those shipwrecked reached the beach, where crewmen helped themselves to supplies sent ashore for all the victims, without regard for the needs of others. Some of the crew began to attack and rob the other survivors. Meanwhile, on board, crewmen had broken into the ship's liquor stores and were rioting. They tried to steal the gold still aboard her but could not. The rioting sailors murdered some of those who had not yet reached shore. Even though the body of a passenger washed ashore later bearing head wounds and with his pockets turned inside out, no one was charged with the murder. A small steamer, the *Goliath* (*Goliah*), saw the wrecked ship and managed to rescue the survivors, taking them to San Diego. All told, about 30 people lost their lives.

The ship's insurance company induced the U.S. Navy to accompany Captain Randall to the site of the *Yankee Blade*'s sinking to try to retrieve the gold. Two boxes were recovered, but Captain Randall reported that sea swells were too strong for further work. Nevertheless, two months later, reports say, he retired from the company and hired divers who brought up four boxes of gold that should have contained about $69,300. The divers were charged with stealing $34,000, the amount missing from the boxes, but were never brought to trial. Captain Randall, however, claimed a large portion as his share in the recovery.

According to John Potter in his *Treasure Diver's Guide*, all the gold was not raised in these attempts. A diver named Bill Ward claimed to have found the wreck in 1948, and another later group also said they had located her. Whether there is anything left to salvage is not clear.

One of the most sought-after ships carrying California gold was the Pacific Mail's *Golden Gate*, a 2,100-ton side-wheeler that made the run between San Francisco and Panama for more than a decade. After a calm and happy trip, on July 22, 1862, the ship caught fire about fifteen miles from Manzanillo, Mexico. Although crew and passengers worked diligently at putting out the fire, it spread rapidly. Many passengers, frightened by the heat and flames, leaped overboard. Some were swept into the churning paddle wheels; others were left behind and drowned. Virtually all of the passengers were soon struggling in the water, "drowning one another in ferocious embraces."

One survivor, Andre Chavanne, swam all night, only to find in the morning that he had been washed farther from shore than he had been when he started swimming. Eventually he was picked up, still swimming, by a passing Mexican schooner. When the survivors gathered on shore, 223 out of 338 on board were found to have died. All of the cargo, including $1.4 million in gold (at $20 an ounce) said to be on board, was lost.

Salvage began immediately, but no gold was reported recovered until 1900, when, according to Lt. Harry Rieseberg and A. A. Mikalov, writing in *Fell's Guide to Sunken Treasure Ships*, Duncan Johnston of Providence, Rhode Island, brought up $500,000. But Potter suggests that the only gold in the *Golden Gate* was "in her name."

Gold or not, the sinking of the *Golden Gate* made a deep impression on the people of California. In 1906 a song entitled "I Do Not Want to Be Drowned" was written by Frank Soulé and P. R. Nicholls and dedicated to the survivors of the wreck of the *Golden Gate*. George Holbrook Baker lithographed a handsome cover for the song. A copy is on exhibit in the Oakland Museum of California.

The sinking of the *Central America* in 1857 was one of the worst maritime casualties for the New York to Panama run, in both lives and gold lost. She was a side-wheel steamship, 272 feet long. On her last trip she carried three tons of gold from the California mines in bars and newly minted coins, as well as miners taking home their hard-won gold. To avoid the perils of an overland journey to the East or a long trip around the Horn, passengers and gold traveled by ship down the Pacific Coast to the Isthmus of Panama, where a recently constructed, comfortable railroad eliminated the fever-ridden overland hike to the Atlantic Ocean. On the Atlantic side, the *Central America* and others took them east.

The *Central America* was an experienced commuter. She had already made forty-three round-trips from New York to Panama. Her captain on this trip was Commander William Lewis Herndon, a career navy man, veteran of the Mexican-American War. He was a highly respected officer, and the ship considered one of the best in service. The *Central America* belonged to the United States Mail Steamship Company, a private firm. However, to be a mail carrier, the steamship had to be built under congressional regulations and be commanded by an officer of the U.S. Navy.

She began her fatal trip at the beginning of September 1857 in the midst of hurricane season. She carried 476 passengers and 102 crewmen, as well as gold. On Wednesday, September 9, six days after leaving Panama, a strong wind developed into a gale, forcing passengers into their cabins and making many of them so sick they could not eat. The next day the ship was struck by a major hurricane. Within a day she had taken on so much water that the boiler fires were put out, despite frantic bailing by the passengers and crew. At daylight on Saturday, the captain lowered the flag to half mast, upside down—the signal of distress. At 1:00 P.M., the brig *Marine* appeared and stood by to help. Captain Herndon quickly ordered the women and children on deck and sent members of the crew off in the lifeboats with them. The fifty-six-year-old stewardess, Lucy Dawson, a well-liked black woman, fell into the sea three times, being caught once between the lifeboat and the *Marine* when a huge wave drove her against the rescuing ship. She was quickly taken below to be cared for, but she was to die just as the rescuing ship reached Chesapeake Bay.

Captain Herndon steadfastly refused to allow any of the men to leave until the women and children were rescued, although before he issued the order, five men and three firemen jumped into a rescue boat, nearly swamping it. The women and children of the *Central America* were taken off safely (one girl even snatched up her canary), but most of the men had little chance. To keep men from swamping the lifeboats, the captain sent the chief engineer, George Ashby, in one boat to assure its return for the men. But when Ashby reached the rescue ship, the storm was so strong the lifeboats could no longer go back and forth—or at least Ashby could not get any of the crew to man them. Neither threats nor money would persuade them.

A small sailing ship, the *El Dorado*, tried to stand by to help the *Central America*, but the storm parted them. By 8:00 P.M. the *Central America* could no longer stay afloat. She gave three lurches and headed for the bottom, stern first. Men jumped into the sea, some with life preservers, some with hatches, some with doors or other parts of the ship.

In the middle of the night the crew on board a crippled Norwegian sailing ship,

TABLE 4. *Sunken Ships That May Have Carried California Gold*

Compared to the number of sunken Spanish galleons carrying New World silver and gold, the sunken ships carrying California gold are few. Here are some of the best-known ones.

Ship	Date	Remarks
Warren	1846	Military ship lost with 12 men in the Sacramento River. Since this was before the gold rush, the loss of gold was slight: $846.
Rosetta Joseph	1850	Australian vessel returning to Sydney with California gold rush passengers. Struck Elizabeth Reef, north of Lord Howe Island. Passengers rescued, but gold had to be jettisoned.
Winfield Scott	1852	Wrecked near Anacapa Island. Divers have searched the wreck since 1880. Site now under the jurisdiction of the U.S. National Park Service.
Santa Cecilia	1852	Wrecked off Catalina Island. Said to have carried $200,000 in gold and silver. (Some writers set the amount of gold at $2 million.)
Yankee Blade	1854	Sank off Point Arguello. Said to have on board $3 million in gold (worth $20 million at $800 gold).
Donna Maria	1854	Swedish ship, sank off Cape Mendocino, with—it is said—$40,000 in gold coin.
Central America	1857	See chapter 11.
Golden Gate	1862	Ship caught fire and sank off Manzanillo, Mexico. Only 81 of the 338 passengers survived. Gold said to have been worth $1.4 million, most of which has been salvaged.
Phantom	1862	American ship, sank off Hong Kong with an alleged $10 million in California gold on board.
George Sand	1863	German ship, sank near Hong Kong with—it is said—$13 million in California gold.
Princeza	1863	British ship, sank off South Moreton Island, Queensland, Australia, with U.S. gold aboard.
Ada Hancock	1863	Sank between Wilmington and Los Angeles, with 26 deaths. Wells Fargo gold worth $25,000 at the time was not recovered. Legend says pilfered gold, worth perhaps $100,000, was also on board.

continued ☞

Ship	Date	Remarks
Brother Jonathan	1865	A 220-foot-long wooden coastal steamer. Sank within an hour after striking St. George Reef, near Trinidad Head, while making a run between San Francisco and Victoria, B.C., with a loss of 166 lives. Rumor says she had $1 million in gold on board. Cargo included, among other items, mill machinery, mining machinery, camels, horses, and a Newfoundland dog. Gold ingots were found in 1930. In the 1990s Deep Sea Research of Diamond Bar located the wreck and prepared to salvage it. They were challenged by the State of California. In 1999 the courts ruled that the salvager would get the gold, the state the artifacts.
Golden City	1870	A 340-foot-long steamer, stranded in a fog off the tip of Magdalena Island, Baja California, Mexico, with $320,000 in gold and silver aboard. Some has been salvaged.
Sacramento	1872	Steamer went down off Point San Antonio, Baja California, Mexico. Said to have $2 million (at 1872 prices) in gold bullion and specie. Some has been salvaged.
Mollie Stevens	1875	Desert-based steamboat regularly carried silver and a little gold from Cerro Gordo mines across Owens Lake when it had water. Some of the wreck has been recovered.
Bremen	1883	Sank off Farallon Islands with an alleged $60,000 in coin on board.
City of Rio de Janeiro	1901	Struck Fort Point. One hundred twenty-nine people died. Rumor says she carried as much as $6 million.
H. J. Corcoran	1912	Collided with another ship in San Francisco Bay. Much of her gold, estimated between $100,000 and $500,000, has been salvaged.
Cuba	1923	Sank off San Miguel Island. Said to carry gold and silver bullion and specie.
San Juan	1929	Said to have sunk off Pigeon Point with gold and silver bullion aboard.
Columbia	1931	Sank off Point Tosca, Baja California, Mexico, with gold and silver on board. Much has been salvaged.

the *Ellen*, heard cries nearby in the water. As fast as possible, the *Ellen* picked up survivors, as many as could be found, and at great danger to the *Ellen* itself. Even so, they found only 49. Altogether, 425 people drowned.

Lives and gold were not the only losses in the *Central America*. The drawings, notes, and paintings so carefully made by forty-niner John Woodhouse Audubon (see chapter 4) had been entrusted to a friend and were lost when the ship sank. The only copy of a manuscript on the history of the Vigilantes in San Francisco, written by Leslie Wood and on its way to be published in New York, also was lost.

The gold shipment, valued at $1,219,189 in 1857, was headed for New York banks, and its loss shook the financial world. Besides this official gold, fresh from the California goldfields, individual passengers had to abandon carpet bags filled with their personal fortunes, in gold dust as well as coins and bars. Some passengers jumped overboard as the ship sank, fatally weighed down with heavy gold. Others abandoned their hard-won treasure. "The love of gold was forgotten in the anxiety and terror of the moment," said one survivor. "Many a man unbuckled his gold-stuffed belt and flung his hard-earned treasure upon the deck."

The disaster was front-page news for months, until it was crowded off by news of the impending Civil War. The gold—other than personal gold—was intended for various companies. Wells Fargo and the American Exchange Bank each expected about 20 percent of it. The shipment was insured for $1.6 million. If each male passenger carried an average of $3,000, as has been estimated, then the 400 men would have been carrying $1.2 million, making the gold lost nearly $2.5 million (125,000 ounces), at the official price of gold in 1857. The wreck of the *Central America*, taking such a large amount of gold to the bottom of the sea, helped turn the nation's economic depression into a panic. Excessive debt, experts said, caused the problem—especially the debt incurred from building railroads. Railroad companies went bankrupt, cotton mills stopped, ironworks were sold—the entire industrial complex felt the blow.

Because so many people were affected by the *Central America*'s loss, the public searched for a scapegoat—something or someone to blame for the disaster, the worst on the Panama run. They latched on to the owners, the United States Mail Steamship Company. A song, "Loss of the *Central America*," excoriating the company, became immensely popular.

But where lay the blame? Piecing together the story from various accounts, students of marine history have concluded that the ship was seaworthy when she left Panama and was following a route her officers knew well. At some point she developed mechanical trouble and lost power. When the two big paddle wheels did not turn, she could not be kept facing into the storm and she wallowed broadside in the waves, leaking through the shaft that powered the wheels. Although the men aboard

The *Central America* painted so fine
  Went down like a thousand of brick,
And all the old tubs that are now on the line
  Will follow her two at a lick.
'Twould be very fine were the owners aboard
  And sink where they never would rise;
'Twould any amount of amusement afford,
  And cancel a million of lies.

'Twould be very fine were the owners aboard
And sink where they never would rise;
'Twould any amount of amusement afford,
And cancel a million of lies.

These murdering villains will ne'er be forgot,
  As long as America stands;
Their bones should be left in the ocean to rot,
  And their souls be at Satan's commands.
They've murdered and swindled the people for years,
  And never will be satisfied
Till death puts an end to their earthly careers,
  Then may they with demons reside.

They've murdered and swindled the people for years,
And never will be satisfied
Till death puts an end to their earthly careers,
Then may they with demons reside.

bailed frantically for thirty hours without sleep, they did not win. It is likely that a valve was not turned which would have allowed steam pressure to get to the pumps so they could work. By the time anyone remembered about the valve, it was under extremely hot water. Whether or not the company was responsible, at the end of its government contract in 1859 the company ceased to exist, and the ship lay forgotten at the bottom of the sea except by historians and the treasure-hunting community.

In the twentieth century, Melvin A. Fisher's spectacular find of the Spanish galleons *Atocha* and *Santa Margarita* and many other marine salvage stories spurred ocean treasure hunters to begin searching for sunken ships all over the world, to the dismay of marine archaeologists. In 1985, a young oceanographic engineer, Thomas (Tommy) Thompson, from Columbus, Ohio, who once had worked as a diver for Mel Fisher, set his sights on the *Central America*.

The first problem he faced was, where exactly did the ship go down? No one was certain. One writer on marine disasters placed her in twenty-eight fathoms of water two hundred fifty miles southeast of Cape Hatteras, North Carolina; Lieutenant Rieseberg (who was always positive about everything) wrote she was about four miles off the east tip of Diamond Shoals, Cape Hatteras, in fourteen fathoms (eighty-four feet) of water. All these assumptions proved wrong.

Thompson operated his treasure hunt scientifically. He recruited his boyhood friend, journalist Barry Schatz, and his neighbor, geologist Bob Evans, as directors of the project. He began the actual hunt by studying everything he could find about the *Central America*—both primary and secondary documents. The men compiled a correlation chart twelve feet wide by twelve feet long, on which they plotted every fact they came across in books, newspapers, letters, and official documents. The vertical line represented time—when things happened—while on the horizontal line they plotted events. That way they could ascertain not only the progress of the ship but every event of her last hours.

They engaged an expert, Larry Stone, to build computer models of the data using the *Central America*'s last known coordinates as well as tides and currents. With the computer crammed with all this information, they could play out various scenarios of the sinking. Finally Stone was able to narrow the last resting place of the *Central America* to a 1,200-square-mile area, a section of the sea about the size of Rhode Island.

The first season, 1987, using their initial capital of $1.4 million, they spent forty days searching the seafloor, not in diving suits or scuba equipment, but in the darkened cabin of a leased boat, staring at monitors. The monitors showed sonograms (sound pictures) of the ocean floor, obtained by a side-scanning sonar.

During the winter of 1987–1988, Thompson raised another $3.6 million and built a remarkable submersible device of his own invention. He called it *Nemo* after the captain in Jules Verne's novel, *20,000 Leagues Under the Sea*. (The name Verne used for his submarine, *Nautilus*, was already in use by the U.S. Navy.) *Nemo* was six feet wide, nine feet high, and twelve feet long and had gadgets galore. It was equipped with powerful lights, television cameras, thrusters, and arms that could lift three hundred pounds or pick up a tiny coin.

In August *Nemo*'s television cameras sent back a picture of what was clearly a side-wheel at a depth of eight thousand feet—ten times the depth of any previous salvage. Much of the wooden structure of the ship had been eaten away, leaving a heap of crisscrossed timbers like, as *Life* magazine noted, "a collapsed barn." Then on October 20, 1988, *Nemo*'s cameras focused on two gold coins and a gold bar. A heavy storm hit before *Nemo* was safely aboard the mother ship, and the doughty device crashed to the deck; but it had gotten the coins and the bar.

The next year the crew could not work until September. When the repaired *Nemo* was lowered to the bottom, the monitors showed glimpses of round, yellowish objects. The crew turned on one of *Nemo*'s thrusters and blew the sand away. The ocean floor was covered with gold. That season *Nemo* brought up 2,600 gold coins and bars to be quickly and carefully cataloged. As bullion, it would be worth $10.5 million at 1988 prices for gold, but as collector's items the coins would bring much more. These were rare coins on the numismatic market. They were coined in the then-new San Francisco mint and had just been struck, so they were, when loaded, in mint condition. One coin recovered was listed at $15,000 in coin catalogs. One single bar of gold brought up from the deep weighed 754 ounces.

Nemo's cameras showed a shiny cluster biologists thought might be tube worms on a projecting beam, but a closer look revealed the beam to be covered with gold coins cemented together. The area was, Thompson said, "a garden of gold, a bridge of gold bars. . . . There were rivers of gold coins. . . . Bags that held gold dust were long gone, but the dust was stuck together. *Nemo* blew off silt, and a carpet of gold coins appeared." Besides gold and artifacts, the wreckage contained two invertebrates heretofore unknown to science and an unusual sponge.

Despite years of work and millions of dollars spent, Thompson's group and his investors did not get all of the treasure. Once Thompson found the wreck, which took eighty *Nemo* dives, thirty-nine insurance companies stepped up to claim the gold. They had, they said, paid off the claims for its loss and deserved to get the gold back. After a considerable legal battle, Judge K. K. Hall of the Fourth U.S. Circuit Court of Appeals noted that the salvors had expended "monumental" labor as well as money, that they had worked with great care and had even made new scientific discoveries. The insurance companies, in sharp contrast, had made no effort to find the ship in the past 131 years. The judge awarded them 10 percent (quite a lot considering the cost of the search) and quoted from Virgil: "To what cannot you compel the hearts of men, O cursed lust for gold!"

GOOD-BYE TO THE *CENTRAL AMERICA*

The *George Law,* launched in 1852, left on the first of many trips from New York to Central America on October 20, 1853. She made many round-trips before being renamed the *Central America* in June 1857. Until then, it was illegal to change navy ship names as it was considered bad luck. She had made one round-trip from New York to Aspinwall, Panama, as the *Central America* when bad luck did indeed strike and she sank to the bottom of the sea.

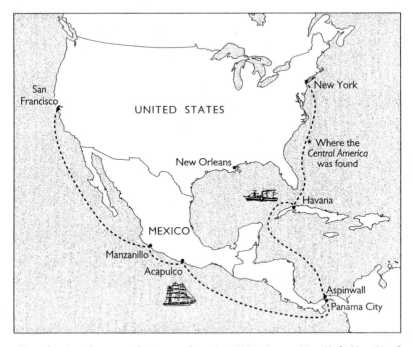

Map showing the route of steamers from San Francisco to New York City. Until 1987, no one knew exactly where the Central America *had gone down.*

Passengers attempt to bail out the leaking Central America.

Lowering the women and children into the lifeboats. To the credit of the men aboard the Central America, *all the women and children were saved. Only the stewardess, who was thrown violently against the rescue ship by the raging sea, was seriously injured. She died before reaching port.*

A huge wave engulfs the sinking Central America.

Passengers from the Central America *having hot tea aboard the brig* Marine *after rescue.*

Second Engineer John Tice and Fireman Alexander Grant pull passenger George Dawson into their boat.

After floating two days alone on a plank, Tice spotted one of the lifeboats of the *Central America*. Although he was a strong swimmer, he was exhausted by the time he reached it, and it took him three or four hours to climb aboard. He drifted alone for two more days. Meanwhile, about fifteen minutes before the *Central America* sank, Grant had joined with several others in hastily building a raft. The ten men aboard the raft had to lie down with their feet in the water, holding their heads up. Even so, the weight of those on the raft kept it submerged about a foot, causing them to swallow large quantities of salt water.

Dawson had also been working on the raft but did not get on it in time. He reached for a passing plank, but another passenger grabbed it. When the ship went down, he was drawn down, too, but when he surfaced, he found himself near a life preserver. He captured three pieces of board and used them to aid him. He was within a hundred feet of the rescuing ship *Ellen*, but no one heard his cries or could see him in the dark. When it was light, Dawson saw Grant and the others on the raft and swam to them, but he dared not get on for fear of swamping the makeshift craft. He stayed nearby, on his planks, holding to a rope on the raft. (Grant and Dawson were experienced at shipwreck. Grant had been rescued after two vessels sank beneath him; a third time he was stuck on a reef in the Bahamas, surrounded by sharks, but was rescued, along with Dawson, by men salvaging a wrecked ship.)

On Monday four men died on the raft, and that night four more died. Dawson joined the survivors on the raft. They passed other survivors, holding to planks and buoys. Gradually the other starving men on the raft died and dropped off the raft, or lost their perilous hold and sank into the sea. On Thursday, the fifth day after the shipwreck, Grant spotted a small boat and, tying a life preserver around himself, attempted to swim toward it. Dawson stayed on the raft. The boat proved to be the lifeboat Tice had salvaged, and Tice pulled him aboard. The two then made for the raft, where Dawson, the only remaining survivor, was still

Sailors from the Mary *haul up the emaciated survivors.*

on board. They pulled him in as well. On the eighth day it rained, the first time they had had fresh water since the ship sank. That day, too, they saw a sail, but it vanished without seeing them. On the ninth day, the bark *Mary* spotted them and threw a rope, but the three skeletal men were too weak and near death to be able to hold it. A sailor jumped down and made a rope sling to hold them and they were carefully hoisted on board.

CHAPTER TWELVE

Lost and Gone Forever

All California gold did not make it to the world's markets, not just because it was sunk in ships, but because the miners themselves put it back in the ground and could not, because of forgetfulness or death, return for it. Heinrich Lienhard, who had been in California since 1846, went off to the mines. He wrote of seeing one miner stop about fifty or sixty yards away and begin digging. Soon the miner pulled out a bottle containing a large amount of gold he had buried earlier. Lienhard followed the miner's example and buried his own gold in the ground, as did many another lucky miner.

Some miners of the nineteenth century, returning to San Francisco from the rich goldfields, hid their gold in pokes in stumps of cut redwood trees near Larkspur in Marin County. Some of the trees were larger and finer than any preserved today, even in nearby Muir Woods National Monument. The cut redwoods, very resistant to decay, remained as stumps for many years but finally succumbed to time. Sprouts from the gigantic trees grew up around the edges of the stump and today are large trees themselves. The location of an old stump can be identified by the "fairy ring" of trees surrounding it. Now and then, pockets of gold dust or nuggets have been found within the rings, hidden by long-dead miners.

California has buried treasure stories, whose will-o'-the-wisp lights countless treasure hunters have followed, but it is not as rich in buried treasure legends as many other states. California has no heritage of pirate lore. Except for Drake, the one or two pirates who haunted California shores were two centuries too late to be part of the golden age of piracy. They gathered little gold and probably buried none of it. California has not been the site of large-scale warfare, so tales of buried wartime treasure—household valuables hastily concealed during the Civil War, for example—are not part of its heritage. Nor does California have buildings old enough to house old ghosts.

But California was founded on gold, and gold has been the focus of the state's chief folklore staple: lost mines. Lost mine stories do not begin with "Once upon a time . . . ," but perhaps they should. Most lost mines never were working mines. They were what the Spanish called *minas,* which could mean "mine" but more often meant "prospect," or "showing" or "occurrence." The U.S. Southwest is rife with lost "mines." Some were said to be real, working mines covered up and lost. Some were said to have been covered up by the Jesuits when they were expelled from the New World in 1769; some were hidden by Indians after killing or driving off the white men working them. Still others were hidden by Indians who rebelled against Spanish masters. In New Mexico an American Indian revolt in 1680 drove the Spanish back into Mexico for a time. While they were gone, it is said, the Indians hid the mines so they would no longer have to work them.

Most California lost mines are of another type, also common throughout the Southwest: "mines" that could, perhaps, have become real mines if the finder could have developed them. They exist only in campfire tales and an occasional fragment of gold-rich rock. Stories about these lost mines have a definite shape. First, they are told as true. Second, someone has found a rich deposit but did not or could not take the time to claim it legally. Third, the finder cannot find it again, despite extensive searching. Either he has forgotten where he was or some natural event (fire, flood, landslide, animals—even humans) has covered it up or changed the landscape so the territory is unrecognizable. The critical point is that the mine has been searched for and not found. Not *yet* found. Such tales appeal to our desire for adventure, and per-haps to our cupidity, too. We yearn for a great quest, like seeking the Holy Grail. Sinclair Drago, in his book *Lost Bonanzas,* wrote: "When you are dealing with lost mines, one rule takes precedence over all others: if you believe it, it's so."

In 1977 the folklorist Byrd Howell Granger published a study of tales of lost mines and treasures in Arizona. She divided their motifs into three periods: Spanish (before 1847), Early American (1847–1900), and Modern (after 1900). The Early American period, which includes the California gold rush, produced twice the num-ber of tales. Although she wrote about Arizona, without doubt the bulk of California tales would fall in that time period as well. Very few California tales date back to Spanish days, and almost no lost mine tales have surfaced since 1900.

A great many mines have been lost in California, if the number can be measured by the multitude of books and stories about them. Most are gold mines. In 1977, also, Thomas Probert published a bibliography, *Lost Mines and Buried Treasure of the West.* In it he lists 322 lost mines in California. Lost mine excitements rise and fall, like interest in UFOs. A high point in recent years was reached in the 1950s and 1960s.

People who seek lost mines are a special type of prospector, going where they think they are more assured of a big find, as someone before them had already found and lost gold. In 1869, when lost mine stories were in flower, J. Ross Browne, himself a mining man, wrote this of prospectors, and it is especially true of hunters of lost mines:

> The prospector is a man of imagination. He is a poet—though not generally aware of the fact. Ragged and unshaved, he owns millions, yet seldom has two dimes to jingle in his pocket—for his wealth lies in the undeveloped wilds. The spirit of unrest burns in his blood. He scorns work, but will endure any amount of hardship in his endless search for "rich leads." There is no desert too barren, no tribe of Indians too hostile, no climate too rigorous for his researches. . . . Hunger, thirst, chilling snows, and scorching sands seem to give him new life and inspiration. It matters nothing that he discovered "a good thing"—a nest of ledges [*ledge* is an old-time word for *vein*], worth say a million apiece—this is well enough, but he wants something better; and after a day or two spent in "locating his claims" [i.e., putting stakes in the ground to claim them legally] he is off again—nobody knows where—often with scarcely provision enough to last him back to the settlements. He travels on mule back, when he happens to own a mule; on foot, when he must; with company, when any offers; without, when there is none; any way to be driving ahead, discovering new regions and locating claims. He locates so many claims that he forgets where his possessions are located. If he discovered a ledge of pure silver, six feet thick, he would die in a week if he had to work it on his own account. His industry runs in another direction. Variety is the spice of his existence, the motive-power of his life.

Four North American lost mines are famous the world over: the Lost Adams, Breyfogle's Lost Ledge, the Lost Dutchman, and the Lost PegLeg Smith. Of these, the Adams is probably on the border between Arizona and New Mexico (recently a searcher claimed to have found it); the Lost Dutchman is in the Superstition Mountains of Arizona; and the other two are in the deserts of southern California.

The better known, more confusing, and less likely of the two is the Lost PegLeg Smith mine. To begin with, there was more than one PegLeg Smith. Of course, Smith is a common name, and often chosen by forty-niners who didn't want to give their real names for their own reasons. As for PegLeg—accidents were common in those days, particularly in the untamed West; doctors were scarce, hospitals scarcer. In Probert's bibliography, the Lost PegLeg Smith mine has 238 entries, plus numerous short articles in seventeen newspapers. In the years since 1975, the closing date for Probert's bibliography, doubtless many more have been added, even though no new information has come to light.

One PegLeg Smith was a well-known trapper, a friend of Kit Carson and other legendary mountain men. He was born Thomas L. Smith on October 10, 1801, in Kentucky. His father was an Irish immigrant who with his wife raised a family of nine daughters and four sons. Thomas (he wasn't PegLeg then) got a minimal amount of

schooling. Philip A. Bailey, in his book *Golden Mirages*, wrote, "After two years atten-
dance he was tolerably acquainted with the first three letters of the alphabet; but as
eighteen months more of school brought him only as far as the letter K, for which he
never seemed able to find any use, he quit and went to work on his father's farm."
When he was ten, he returned to school and became a good student, apparently getting to the end of the alphabet.

It was said of Thomas that he would not tell a black lie. You may believe that if
you wish, but his career thereafter gave him great scope to do so. He was a gambler,
a brawler, and a wanderer. His wanderings took him into the lands of the Choctaw
and Chickasaw, where he stayed to learn their life and habits. Wandering with the
Indians, he met Antoine Rubidoux, an early western explorer and fur trapper, whose
tales convinced Smith that he had found his life's work.

For a while Smith trapped with the Indians; then he threw his lot in with other
white fur traders, probably because he would get to see a larger piece of the country.
When one of his party was killed by Indians, Smith went to recover the body and
was hit in the leg by an arrow. He tried to induce his friends to cut his leg off; when
none would, he operated on himself. Although the other trappers expected him to
bleed to death, they nonetheless carried him on a litter strung between two horses
for one hundred fifty miles to a Ute Indian village, where the women poulticed the
wound and he survived. He whittled a wooden leg for himself and from then on was
"PegLeg Smith."

The year 1829 had been good for trapping, so Smith and fellow trapper
Maurice LeDuc had a large load to take to market for the group. No one has yet dis-
covered which market they took it to—Taos or Santa Fe on the Spanish Trail, or
Los Angeles, following Jedediah Strong Smith's route of 1826, or down the
Colorado to its junction with the Gila and then west to the California coast. Judging
by what Smith said later, he probably went down the Gila and across the Colorado
Desert to the coast.

The Colorado Desert is an arid, hot region just west of the Colorado River. Once
Smith and LeDuc left the river, water became exceedingly scarce. Large reaches of
shifting sand dunes and mountains with only desert shrubs made it one of the most
fearsome deserts the forty-niners had to cross on any route. It is a low region,
bounded by faulted mountains. In centuries past it held freshwater lakes, which
dried, then filled again. During the days of the gold rush, it was quite dry. Today the
Salton Sea, formed by the flooding Colorado River in 1904–1905, occupies the center of the basin.

Smith and LeDuc soon discovered they had far too little water, and if they were
to get across the feared desert they would need fresh supplies. Smith climbed to the
top of one of three small buttes to scour the vista for spots of green. He saw none. He

FIGURE 47. PegLeg Smith.

sat down to rest and think, but the place he chose was too full of small stones to be comfortable. He pushed a couple aside, then picked up a particularly large one to toss away. It was very heavy. He cracked it against another rock and saw, under the black desert coating, that it was yellow, much like copper. Perhaps, he thought, he could use it to make bullets. He put several pebbles in his pocket. The next morning he and LeDuc found a spring of cool water, enough to get them to Los Angeles. His task completed, he began a circuit of the cantinas, where he showed his pebbles to his drinking buddies, who pointed out they were solid gold.

The Pueblo of Los Angeles was a small adobe country village then, but it had enough temptation to suit Smith. His escapades were soon the talk of the town, and he was asked to leave. He did, accompanied, it was said, by four hundred horses, unaccompanied by their owners. He continued to trap, headquartering in Santa Fe, until the bottom fell out of the beaver market when silk hats became more popular. He returned to his second profession, horse rustling. But the authorities and ranchers kept their eyes on him, and this, too, began to wear thin.

After the Mexican-American War ended and California became U.S. territory, and after Marshall's trumpeted gold discovery, Smith decided to go back to the desert to find the source of his nuggets. He took a small party with him but deserted them, and no one found gold. He gave it another try, with no success, then settled down to talking about it in Los Angeles and, in his last years, in San Francisco. He died in October 1866 without having located his fabulous mine.

Not much is known of the next PegLeg Smith. He is said to have appeared in the Colorado Desert in the 1850s, and was still going strong ten years after trapper Smith died. This PegLeg Smith turned up at Warren's Ranch in San Diego County telling a tale of black gold in the desert. Which Smith he was is not clear. Leland Wallace, writing in *Lost Mines and Hidden Treasure*, tells of a James "PegLeg" Smith who knew the location of black gold. This PegLeg Smith said he was prospecting with an Indian guide in 1859 when he found a spot where coal black stones lay strewn about the ground. They were gold, he realized. He asked his Indian companion to take him to their source, but the Indian refused, saying he would die—the death fumes would get him. The fumes came from a steaming crater, the Indian said, and when members of his tribe went to the bottom, they never returned. The fumes were the breath of the gods, protecting their gold. White men who tried to enter the crater also lost their lives. The way in was plainly marked by bleached bones of animals and men, lying beside empty canteens. This Smith died in 1865 but not of arsenic poisoning, which may be what the fumes were. Others who have searched have never managed to bring back the riches of either PegLeg Smith, if they are not one and the same.

There is even a third PegLeg Smith, though probably without a mine. A bandit who held up the stage from Coyote Wells and had a wooden leg told his victims they had been robbed by "PegLeg Smith."

The controversy over the identity of PegLeg Smith of the lost mine has raged since the mine was supposedly discovered. Eugene Conrotto, in his book *Desert Bonanzas*, said Smith was a forty-niner, which does not fit Thomas Smith. He also wrote, "Some say PegLeg Smith was a fall-down drunk who had quickly learned that the best way to get free drinks was to tell his patrons what they wanted to hear: a crazy tale about the desert and three hills and black gold."

In 1876, an Indian woman, ill from exposure in the desert, was befriended by some railroad workers. Grateful, she gave them some heavy black rocks and disappeared. Aha, thought many lost mine seekers when they saw the rocks, she knows where the Lost PegLeg Smith mine is. Since then many searchers have looked for the source of the stones, but none have found it.

In 1940 a prospector claimed to have found PegLeg's mine but was disputed by others. In the pages of *Desert Magazine* that year, various writers and writers-to-the-editor entered the PegLeg mine controversy. One claimed that there were not one, not two, but three PegLeg Smiths (not counting the bandit): John O., Thomas, and Lazarus, each of whom had found a mine, but in a different place. If this is true, it brings the total number of "PegLeg Smiths" to five. As the discussion continued, various other claims and "clues" about the Lost PegLeg were printed, culminating in another claim that PegLeg Smith (one of him, at least) was an "artistic old liar."

More people have searched for the Lost PegLeg Smith mine, noted Sinclair

Drago, than for any other, probably because its purported location is so close to Los Angeles. But lost mine seekers come from everywhere. The roster of those who searched for the elusive PegLeg Smith mine is long. Adolph Ruth, who lost his life hunting for the Lost Dutchman in Arizona, had looked for the PegLeg Smith. Leland Lovelace, in his book *Lost Mines and Hidden Treasure,* even suggests that Judge Joseph Crater, a supreme court justice in New York State who disappeared on August 6, 1930, without leaving a trace and was declared legally dead in July 1937, actually deserted his prestigious position, as well as his wife and family, and came West to look for the PegLeg Smith mine. Several people, Lovelace says, recognized his picture and identified him as the "city type" prospector who was roaming the desert.

In the decades since the first "discovery" of the PegLeg Smith mine, party after party has gone out searching for it. Each has had adventures that have been added to the PegLeg Smith tale, confusing it even further. Some of the "PegLeggers" even found gold, though no one concedes that the Lost PegLeg has been found. One old prospector, who had spent two years searching for the PegLeg, was asked, "What'll you do if you find it?" "Cover it up and look for another," he replied.

The PegLeg Smith mine (or mines), if the stories are even remotely true, was not a mine at all but merely a hope engendered by the finding of gold-bearing rocks. This is so also of Breyfogle's Lost Ledge. Both share a characteristic Granger found to be a common motif of lost mines: the finder could never find the spot again, in spite of having taken careful note of landmarks. The two stories do not, however, have the deathbed map and revelation common in many lost mine stories. Both Smith and Breyfogle talked freely of their finds throughout their lives.

Just as there were many PegLeg Smiths, there were many Breyfogles tangled in the tale of the lost Breyfogle ledge. Harold Weight, publisher of *Desert Magazine,* said there were seven Breyfogles who came to California from Ohio in the early days. Among them was Charles C. Breyfogle, the focus of the legend. In addition, there was another Charles Breyfogle, a cousin, and another cousin, William, who had a business in San Francisco. Of these, cousin Charles was the most successful, going home around the Horn with $20,000 in gold. Later, Jacob, another of Charles C. Breyfogle's brothers, came to California and became the most persistent searcher for the lost Breyfogle mine.

There are innumerable versions of the Breyfogle tale. One writer says there are 1,001, and it does seem like it. In Probert's bibliography there are sixty-nine articles and books on the lost Breyfogle ledge, plus articles in sixteen newspapers. That's just up to 1975.

Charles C. Breyfogle was in his thirties when he made the trip to California. He spent several years placering in the diggings but never struck it rich. From 1854 to

1857 he was county assessor of Alameda County, and from 1857 to 1859, its treasurer. He probably lived in Oakland, the county seat. Breyfogle ceased being Alameda County treasurer when he was convicted of embezzling $6,511 from the county treasury and went to jail. In 1861 he was pardoned by Governor Leland Stanford because he had been wrongly convicted and the guilty party had been identified.

Released from jail, he hurried to Virginia City, where he may have worked in the mines. In 1862 he followed the lure of gold and silver to Austin, Nevada, when the Reese River Mining District burst into life. He moved a few miles south to the new town of Geneva, where he managed a "commodious stone hotel." Geneva has since faded from view.

Breyfogle's big adventure began at this time. This much seems certain, but from there the story diverges according to the teller. The late J. Frank Dobie got his information from a man who knew a man who knew Breyfogle quite well—in fact, the assayer who studied his samples and who spent many weeks searching for Breyfogle's mine. Dobie wrote that Breyfogle and two others were in Los Angeles when they heard of the Reese River excitement. According to this version of Breyfogle's travels, the three men set off on foot to go from Los Angeles to Austin, electing to take the short route through Death Valley. The forty-niners were not afraid of Death Valley because they did not know about it. Some of those in one party headed for the goldfields lost their lives in the shocking sink. By Breyfogle's time, it was well known and should have been well feared.

Established as a national monument in 1933, Death Valley was upgraded to a national park in 1994. Most of it is in California, but a small piece reaches into Nevada. The park encompasses 3,400,000 acres. Of this, 352,125 acres are below sea level. The lowest point in the Western Hemisphere is near Death Valley's Badwater, 282 feet below sea level. Badwater also holds the record for the hottest North American shaded temperature: 134°F.

Besides being hot in summer, Death Valley has very little drinking water. Its average annual rainfall is 1.66 inches; the highest annual rainfall on record is 4.5 inches, and there have been years when no rain fell at all. Most water on the floor of the valley is salty, but there are a few tiny freshwater streams that flow, and then sink into the sand.

Death Valley is a graben, a tract of land sunk between two faults. The faults bounding Death Valley have lifted the Panamint Range to the west (and perhaps also the valley has sunk) to heights of over 11,000 feet, high enough to intercept any moisture coming from the ocean. On the east the Black, Funeral, and Grapevine mountains seal the desert in. Whatever route Breyfogle's party took, they were not likely to find much water.

The Mojave Desert was difficult enough, but when the party tackled the steep

Panamints, they really began to worry. Finding a water hole along an Indian trail, they camped by it. Space was too limited beside the water for all three of them, so Breyfogle selected a flat spot some six hundred feet away. During the night Indians attacked and killed Breyfogle's two companions. A frightened Breyfogle grabbed his boots and ran, over rocks, over thorns, through the inky blackness, downhill toward Death Valley. When he could run no farther, he found himself on the edge of Death Valley itself, alone, without food or water. His feet were so cut, bruised, and swollen that he could no longer get his boots on, but he kept them.

Another version of this much of the story comes to us through Harold Weight, who had access to the Breyfogle family papers and who had sought the lost Breyfogle mine himself. According to his version, which he got from a man who got it from a man who went with Breyfogle to look for his lost mine, Breyfogle had been told of a rich ledge of gold-bearing quartz by a forty-niner. The forty-niner even gave him a sample of the ore and a map to its source.

Weight's version said that three men stopped at Geneva, probably at Breyfogle's hotel, and then, burdened with supplies, headed south. Breyfogle, concluding they knew something that he didn't about the lost Gunsight silver mine, which many people were then seeking, elected to follow, unknown to the men. They pushed their way to Ash Meadows, east of Death Valley. There Breyfogle joined the group, only to find they were Southerners headed for the Old Spanish Trail so they could get to Texas to join the Confederates. Now Breyfogle was alone—one would think. But somehow he joined up with two other men who had come from Los Angeles. The three camped together, and here the two stories also join.

When we left Breyfogle in the Dobie version, he was running though the desert in his bare feet, carrying his boots. All versions agree on this. He had no canteen, no food, no weapons. Barefoot, ragged, thirsty, and scared, he managed to get to Coyote Holes, a watering place so named because coyotes, who know where in the desert to find water, had dug the holes. But the water was bad—though not as bad as at Salt Springs (also sometimes called Coyote Holes), where a mixture of Glauber's and Epsom salts in the water had killed thirsty men. Breyfogle did get sick but plunged on, still carrying his boots, which he had filled with the bitter water.

He thought he crossed Death Valley and climbed the Funerals, eating anything he could lay his hands on—roots, lizards, mesquite beans, toads. At last he spotted a flash of green and headed toward it. As he hobbled along on his sore and bleeding feet, his eye caught a glint of gold. He picked up a few samples and went on toward the spot of green, which proved to be a mesquite tree. He gorged himself on mesquite beans and rested, he never knew how long, and then headed again toward what he hoped would be water, food, and people.

Somehow he made his way, over two hundred miles, to Big Smoky Valley, where a rancher was dumbfounded to see footprints of a man's bare feet, and then the man. Dobie wrote, "Breyfogle . . . was all but naked. His pants were in shreds, the shreds coming only to his knees, while the tattered remains of a shirt did little more than cover the shoulders. His black hair and beard were long and matted. . . . He was heavy boned, thick through the breast, stood all of six feet high, and under normal conditions weighed around two hundred pounds. He was strikingly bow-legged, and . . . had enormous feet. . . . He [was] a cadaverous giant parched and seared as if by the fires of hell. He was still carrying his shoes. In one of them was stuffed a bandanna tied around some specimens of ore." The ore he had brought out, it is said, was unbelievably rich. One piece he left with his cousin William in San Francisco contained eighteen ounces of pure gold.

Breyfogle spent the rest of his life searching for his "lost mine," but he never found it. He left with his cousin a copy of a rough map he drew, and copies have been circulating since. However, since *he* couldn't relocate the source of the gold, the map is not likely to be of much use. Many mining people and writers are convinced of the essential truth of Breyfogle's story. Hundreds have searched for Breyfogle's Lost Ledge, and in the process some have lost their lives; but they did open up the whole desert area to mining, and it has proven rich. Mining man George Hearst, father of publisher William Randolph Hearst, sent two men into the field for two years to search for the lost Breyfogle, but they never found it.

Two questions are critical: What exactly is everybody looking for, and has it been found?

According to Dobie, Breyfogle first picked up some grayish white float with gold glittering in it, then tossed it aside when he found the vein itself: pink feldspar even richer in gold than the float. Writers since Breyfogle's time have said the samples were reddish brown, decomposed quartz, half gold; rose pink quartz with free-milling brown spots; dirty brown quartz; blood red quartz with gold the size of wheat grains; rich yellow carbonate; pure yellow carbonate full of black silver sulfides and gold; pink quartz; and simply brown, red, or gray. The assayer who knew Breyfogle and saw his ore said it was reddish, a kind of porphyry.

Many have claimed the Breyfogle has already been found—it was the Chispa or the Johnnie in Death Valley, or it was the Amargosa at the southern tip of Death Valley; it was Gold Mountain north of Lost Valley; the Keane Wonder in the Funeral Range; Chloride Cliff on the crest of the Funerals; California Hill in the Amargosa Desert; the National Bank mine at Rhyolite, Nevada; the Jumbo mine at Goldfield, Nevada. Most of these have been identified as the Breyfogle on the basis of the similarity of their ore to Breyfogle's samples. Since no piece now exists that can definitely be proven to be Breyfogle's, such identifications are doubtful.

In 1951 Weight, basing his judgment on the statement of the assayer that it was a

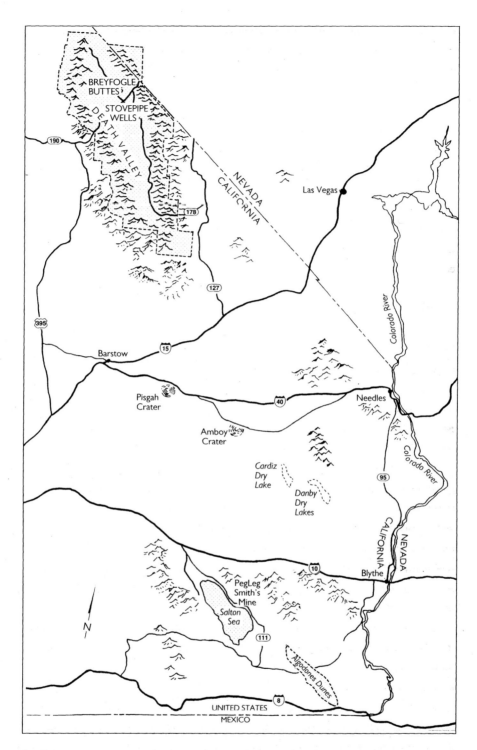

MAP 8. The desert country of southern California. Somewhere here are the reputed sites of Breyfogle's and PegLeg Smith's lost mines. Breyfogle Buttes are located in Death Valley northeast of Stovepipe Wells.

kind of porphyry, identified Round Mountain, Nevada, as Breyfogle's Lost Ledge—not exactly in Death Valley, but not far from Big Smoky Valley. Round Mountain has been rich, producing more than $10 million in gold when gold was $35 an ounce.

When President Hoover signed the bill establishing Death Valley National Monument in 1933, the law allowed mining and prospecting within its boundaries. For years it was one of six exceptions to a "no mining" rule in the national park system. Hoover, himself a gold miner, no doubt knew the story of the lost Breyfogle and was reluctant to dash prospectors' dreams. In 1976 Congress passed legislation removing Death Valley National Monument from mineral entry—now no one can stake a mining claim inside the monument. Mines and claims already there would be allowed provided the owners record their claims with the Secretary of the Interior. Now that Death Valley is a national park, the same rules apply. So if Breyfogle's Lost Ledge truly exists, and truly is in Death Valley, it must remain lost, and a dream.

CHAPTER THIRTEEN

Mining Gold for Fun
and Maybe Profit

California's gold rushes are far from over. In the 1930s, when the Great Depression hit, at least 200,000 people flocked to California streams and beaches, hoping to scratch out a living. In 1930 there was one would-be miner for every ten men in California. As many as 100 men per mile hunted for gold along the California creeks in 1932–1933. Some did find gold: the U.S. Mint reported that it bought gold from 12,422 small-scale California miners in 1937. Most miners just made a little extra to help make ends meet, but now and then a lucky miner found a richer pay streak or a nugget. The average weekly earnings of small-scale placer miners in California in the three-year period 1935–1937 was about $3.50. Not quite enough to live on, even when a family could manage on a dollar a day, but it was a lifesaver for those whose jobs were seasonal or nonexistent.

These depression era miners were using the same equipment the forty-niners had used—pans, rockers, long toms. But eighty years of mining had exhausted most of the easily won gold, and much of what they found was too fine for them to save—almost too fine to see.

Although most would-be miners tried California's streams and rivers, knowing they had been rich in the past, some mined the sands of the seashore. The ocean beaches in Santa Barbara County, for example, contain fine grains of gold and platinum in thin layers (lenses) of black sand. The sand is black because it consists of fine particles of heavy, dark minerals. The deposits extend from Point Arguello north to the Santa Maria River, and were especially rich at "Surf-Point Sal," now on the Vandenberg Air Force Base. In 1889, the year of the highest recorded beach harvest, miners took out $41,000 in gold and platinum. (Gold at that time was about $20 an ounce.)

Ocean Beach, in the city of San Francisco, was another of California's beaches to

FIGURE 48. Beach mining in the 1930s, Humboldt County.

yield a small amount of gold to placer miners. From 1938 to 1960 it produced about $13,000 in gold (at $35 an ounce). Most of the gold came from the beach south of Fleischaker Zoo. The black sand on beaches from Santa Cruz to Pajaro were worked also during the Great Depression, but not much gold was recovered. Miners had tried the beaches near Crescent City as early as 1850, but with little luck. Gold had been accumulating there in small quantities, probably being carried down the Smith and Klamath rivers.

Except for the fabulously rich beach at Nome, Alaska, the best-known and most productive western American beach is Gold Bluff near the mouth of the Klamath River in California and Oregon, where a series of gold-bearing black sand lenses extends for about ten miles. Miners have worked these beaches on and off since 1852. The high production point was 1888, when they took out a million dollars in gold and platinum from the California portion. Behind the beach are gold-bearing terraces and bench gravels, which, when broken up by storms, are washed onto the beach. From there the surf washes the gold in and out, winnowing it and eventually depositing it in black sand layers. Enterprising miners tried to copy the back-and-forth winnowing action of ocean waves to help recover gold by constructing surf washers, a special type of long tom, but the machines were never successful enough to warrant manufacturing.

World War II put a damper on gold mining of all kinds. Wartime work was available for everyone, so eking out a living by panning gold was not worth the effort. But two pieces of equipment designed for war proved to be invaluable in the postwar search for gold: "frogmen" suits and mine detectors. With this new gear a whole new breed of miner entered the scene: the recreational gold miner.

Diving for gold was not new. DeGroot had tried it in 1849, and the Spanish had used divers to salvage the wrecks of their ships since the sixteenth century. But the hold-your-breath type of diving the Spanish persuaded the Indians to do gave little time for underwater exploration or recovery. After DeGroot's abortive efforts, Chinese, Hawaiian, and South American miners probably tried diving in California's rivers, but there is no record of their success. Beginning in 1851, divers clad in deep-sea diving suits, "subaqueous armor," brought up sand and gravel to process for gold. The San Joaquin Diving Bell Mining Company was one of the most successful of these efforts.

The new scuba outfits, developed during World War II, spurred interest in diving, and soon there were diving clubs all over the world. It did not take long for someone to think of using scuba to dive for gold and someone to encourage others to do so. In the late 1950s that person emerged. His name was Melvin A. Fisher. He was a veteran of World War II and had tried a number of different occupations, ending up helping on his father's California chicken ranch.

At the age of ten Fisher had nearly drowned himself in Lake Michigan diving in a helmet of his own making. As an adult, after scuba was invented, he became so enamored of scuba diving that he was at it every spare minute. But having to go here and there for equipment and compressed air was time-consuming and annoying, so he opened a minimal dive shop at one end of a shed on his father's chicken ranch and then started a new, independent business in Redondo Beach, the first dive shop in the world. He gave courses in diving, produced television shows, and invented equipment for diving and exploring old wrecks.

All this brought in money, but treasure hunting cost even more. Fisher began taking hopefuls to the California gold country to pan or dive for gold. One weekend he took five hundred families to the Sierran rivers. He wrote an enticing booklet, *Mel's Gold Finding Tips*, and invented and sold an underwater vacuum dredge that has become a major piece of equipment for diving miners.

Newspapers of the late 1950s were full of stories of "skilled deep sea divers" (meaning scuba divers) bringing up California nuggets. One youthful group, working in twenty feet of water in the North Fork of the Yuba River, found $900 worth of gold (at $35 an ounce) in two days. But Fisher wanted more than rivers to search. He had his eyes on the gold resting in and near sunken Spanish galleons in the ocean. He dived on ships here and there, then set his sights on the nine or ten sunken ships of the twenty-eight-ship Spanish fleet of 1622 that met a hurricane off the Florida Keys. For fifteen long years he searched the floor of the Gulf of Mexico near Florida,

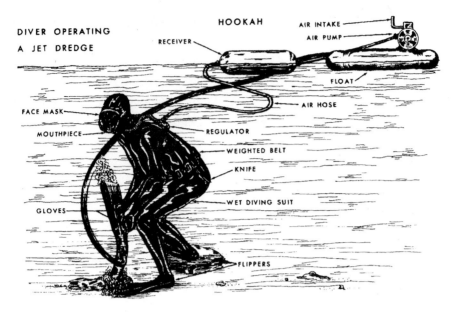

FIGURE 49. Equipment for a modern-day underwater gold miner.

encouraging his crew and divers with the ringing call, "Today's the day!" He used the latest equipment—some of which he invented—and careful research, even hiring an historian to help him. Finally it *was* the day. In June 1971 he located the galleon *Atocha*, carrying forty-seven tons of registered silver and gold, as well as a great deal of contraband, all worth an estimated $400 million. Then in 1980 he found her sister ship, the *Santa Margarita*, also heavily laden. He had dived into the pages of history.

Because of Mel Fisher's flamboyant salesmanship back in the 1950s and 1960s, long before his discovery of the *Atocha* hit the front pages, California streams were teeming with would-be gold miners, using new equipment especially developed for underwater mining. The winter of 1964–1965 brought disastrous storms to California, yet they were a blessing for recreational gold miners. During the storms a dam broke in the Sierra Nevada, and the rushing water uprooted great trees, bounced huge boulders like they were tennis balls, destroyed houses, swept away bridges, *and* carried with it new gold from the mountains. One group of divers working in the Alleghany River took out nearly two hundred ounces of gold.

Although underwater prospectors can get along with only a face mask, a snorkel, and a gold pan, most soon progressed to complete scuba outfits, perhaps with suction dredges, pumps, compressors, and gasoline motors, as well as various types of gold recovery equipment. Elaborate outfits can run to more than $10,000.

A minimum outfit, according to experienced divers, should consist of a close-fitting diving suit, made of rubber (as DeGroot's was), gloves, often with a freely moving thumb and forefinger, fins if the diver plans to move about, boots if he or she does not, and a weighted belt. The weights should be able to be discarded in an emergency.

A miner working in shallow water may need only a snorkel, a tube that protrudes from the water to give the diver air. In deeper water, instead of DeGroot's bellows, modern divers use scuba, which consists of a mouthpiece, an air regulator, and an air supply. The miner can either carry a high-pressure cylinder on his or her back (true scuba) or be connected by hose to an air compressor on the surface. Divers who use this latter arrangement call it a hookah.

Another item needed underwater is a crevice tool. This can be a knife, a large spoon, a screwdriver, or a crowbar. A trowel, tweezers, and a "gold sniffer"—essentially a large syringe—are also helpful. Once above water, the miner can use an eyedropper for picking up bits of gold.

For prospecting and cleanup in or near water, modern-day prospectors still use a gold pan, but gold pans have changed in recent years. No doubt one can still use a frying pan, as the forty-niners did, and one can still buy the old standby, the flat-bottomed, cold-rolled steel pan, ranging in diameter from twelve to sixteen inches, or the conical steel batea, built like a Chinese wok. But modern prospectors and miners prefer the new blue or green plastic pans, which show the gold more easily and have ridges and other gold-trapping features.

By panning up a river or creek and noting where the largest number of colors—glints of gold—are, one can pinpoint likely places for mining. Even on land, by panning carefully along streams and up slopes one may be able to pinpoint a gold-bearing pocket on the hillside. Jack London explained this method well in his famous short story "All Gold Canyon."

As of this writing the record for hand panning was set in the 27th World Gold Panning Championships on April 16, 1989, in Dahlonega, Georgia. Don Roberts of California panned eight planted gold nuggets in 7.55 seconds. The women's record was set in 1983 at Knott's Berry Farm, Buena Park, California, by Susan Bryeans, also of California, when she recovered the planted nuggets in 10.03 seconds.

For use underwater, a modern-day miner might invest in a suction or jet dredge, similar to that invented by Fisher. These are not the giants used on land that process thousands of yards of gravel a day but are portable, handheld or hand-guided tools. The suction dredge, from four to eight feet long, is built like a pipe and curved at one end and weighs up to twenty pounds. A jet dredge is usually made of galvanized metal, with a stainless steel intake mouthpiece. By feeding water under pressure through the hose from a pump on the surface, a vacuum is created that sucks in gravel from the streambed and blows it out the discharge end.

As recreational gold mining increased in popularity, more and more small "personal" floating dredges made their appearance. In California in 1979 the state issued permits for 5,215 dredges; in 1980, when the price of gold hit a high point, it issued 12,773.

Miners working underwater remove the gravel on top (the overburden) from a gold-bearing lens by sending the overburden through the pipe, then over a series of riffles to catch any gold that has come up with it. When the miner has uncovered the gold-bearing lens, she or he uses one of the various crevice tools to pry out the elusive metal, then "sniffs" it up with the gold sniffer, which some miners make from a grease gun. If the area is nuggety, a hopeful miner lashes a small bag to his or her belt to contain the nuggets picked from the gold pocket. Once the miner has taken the gold-bearing gravel out of the water, he or she will recover the gold in much the same way the forty-niners did: with rockers or sluice boxes, either floating or on land. In the desert miners often use air-blown techniques similar to those used by Sonoran miners in 1849 to concentrate the gold.

What the miner accumulates is black sand containing heavy minerals, including gold. It is important to clean the sluices as soon as they get full, or the gold might wash over them. At the end of the day the black sand can be further concentrated by using the gold pan, or even amalgamated with mercury right in the pan. For this one can use copper or brass pans, to which the mercury adheres.

During the concentrating stage other pieces of equipment are useful: tweezers, eyedropper, a magnet to take the heavy, magnetic minerals out of the sand, and a geologist's magnifying hand lens (ten power is a good all-around magnification) to see what is in the sand. At this point pocket scales or balances to weigh the gold are handy, and, after the gold is extracted, it is nice to have neat glass vials to store the gold.

The other significant piece of equipment World War II contributed to recreational gold mining, the mine (metal) detector, is used on dry land, particularly in the desert. These electronic devices have been adapted by treasure hunters and gold miners to seek gold, lost coins, or other metallic treasure. The machines operate on the principle of electromagnetic induction. A coil-type antenna generates an electromagnetic field that can induce a secondary field around any nearby electrical conductor. Another antenna measures the strength of the secondary field and displays it as a flashing light, a moving needle, or sound. By the 1960s instruments manufactured for treasure hunting could detect gold nuggets smaller than a dime, as well as dimes themselves.

That metal detectors really work is attested by the discovery of the nugget "The Hand of Faith," found in Australia in 1980 and weighing 875 troy ounces. Wayne and Doris Leicht, prospecting in California's Mojave Desert in 1977, found a nugget weighing 156 troy ounces. It was put on exhibit at the Los Angeles County Museum Hall of Gems and Minerals.

Recreational gold mining accounted for a good percentage of the gold mined in

FIGURE 50. Probing the California desert with a metal detector. Metal detectors can locate gold nuggets as well as coins, jewelry, can lids, and other buried objects. The 875-ounce Hand of Faith, the largest nugget found in the twentieth century, was found near Melbourne, Victoria, Australia, using a metal detector. It was sold for $1 million for display at the Golden Nugget Hotel in Las Vegas, Nevada.

California until the 1970s, when the price of gold increased. But many recreational miners are so delighted with their finds that they keep the gold or have it made into jewelry, so much of it is never entered in the official records. The $35-an-ounce price that held from 1934 to the 1970s was discouraging, not so much for recreational miners, who were interested in exercise and adventure, but for professional miners, who could not afford to work their mines. In 1960 at a meeting of the Western Mining Council, composed of professional miners, the members admired some of the new equipment used by recreational gold miners and came up with a plan to put the country—or at least the State of California—back on the gold standard via the back door. They suggested that the California legislature authorize the striking of one million commemorative gold medals, each to contain one ounce of gold, 990 fine. It was to be an octagonal medal, similar to coins minted in the gold rush, with California's great seal on one side and an engraving depicting the discovery of gold on the other. In addition, a million smaller, similar medals containing half an ounce of gold were to be struck, and another million with a quarter of an ounce of gold. The State would sell the large medal for $60, the smaller ones for $30 and $15, thereby making considerable profit and putting gold miners to work. Since these medals were to be used as money, it would raise the price of gold and put California on the gold standard at one stroke.

An interesting idea, but the State did not take them up on it. That is, not for two decades. In 1981 California Assembly Bill 676 proposed that the State mint medallions from California gold to compete with South African Krugerrands and Mexican gold pesos. But when the U.S. government ceased controlling the price of gold for its citizens, the complexion of gold mining changed throughout the world. In the marketplace the price of goods is usually determined by the cost of production, barring government interference. Not so for gold. One cannot produce gold on demand, or increase it indefinitely. Mines cannot always be found, or when found, worked, or when worked, made to yield gold at a profit. It is neither the cost of production nor the usefulness of gold that determines its value.

What exactly is the "price" of gold? The best way to determine the price would be to measure what it will buy. But because the price of goods varies the world over, that is not always possible. In some places, such as Peru before the conquest, gold could not be used to buy anything; it all belonged to the ruler. Another way is to compare it to the price of silver, so one can see how many silver dollars (or pounds sterling) an ounce of gold will buy. This has worked for comparing prices until recent years. The United States no longer makes silver dollars, and even its so-called silver coins—dimes, quarters, half-dollars—are no longer silver. Nowadays the price of gold is quoted in American dollars. Silver itself is not nearly as valuable, compared to gold, as it once was. Its price in 1995 was about $5 per ounce. Gold was almost $400, giving a ratio of 80:1.

Throughout history, the relative worth of gold and silver has fluctuated. In ancient times silver was sometimes more valued than gold, so that in ancient Arabia, for example, one unit of silver would buy 10 units of gold (1:10). In 1792 Alexander Hamilton priced the American dollar at 24 ¾ grains of gold (not quite 1/20 of an ounce, making its price $19.393939) and set the United States on the gold standard. Between the end of the American Revolutionary War in 1783 and 1823, the United States had accumulated between $15 million and $20 million in gold, bought at about $15 an ounce. Much of this gold went to England after the end of the War of 1812. To again accumulate gold for coinage, the United States raised its buying price to $16 in 1837 and built up a reserve of $250 million. During the Civil War most of this gold was sold to England for $16 an ounce. (Gold has changed hands most often during and after wars.) In 1934, after the onset of the Great Depression, President Franklin Roosevelt raised the price of gold from $20.67 to $35 an ounce but abandoned the principle that an American paper dollar would be redeemed for its value in gold, although the paper "silver certificate" dollar could still be redeemed for silver as late as the 1960s.

Roosevelt's purpose was to stimulate the economy and help the United States out of the depression. U.S. government–authorized gold buyers went house to house buying gold coins, as they were no longer legal tender. The law also made it illegal for private people to hold gold—it was considered hoarding, and inimical to recovery from the depression—except for jewelry and industrial purposes, such as dentistry. They bought other gold as well. If you had a gold chain you could part with, the buyer would weigh it and give you paper money for it—money that would buy pork chops at ten cents a pound or oranges at a penny apiece. And raising gold's price did spur gold mining.

In 1944 a foreign-exchange gold standard was adopted to regulate international trade, and currencies of many countries were valued in terms of the U.S. dollar. In theory, the United States would redeem its paper money for gold on the international market, but few countries demanded it, since the dollar at that time was "good as gold."

In the 1950s, in an ill-fated attempt to change the world's thinking about gold—to wean it away from gold as a medium of exchange—and to set gold's worldwide value at $35, the United States spearheaded the London Gold Pool. This was designed to counteract the accusation that the United States was flooding the world with paper money with nothing to back it up and to suppress the price of gold, still fixed at $35 in the United States. If the international price rose above $35, the countries in the pool agreed to sell off their gold stocks until the price dropped.

Soon the government reserve stocks of the members of the pool—the United States, the United Kingdom, France, Switzerland, Belgium, Italy, the Netherlands, and West Germany—were being bled to the tune of $991 million of gold reserves, perhaps partly by Swiss banks and people. The French, too, gleefully began to buy rather than sell, increasing their reserves by $601 million, and, in a slow burst of honesty, pulled out of the pool. The United States soon lost $3.2 *billion* in gold. By 1968 one-fifth of its gold reserves were gone, and President Lyndon Johnson asked the Bank of England to close the pool.

The U.S. law was changed so that gold producers could sell their gold not only to authorized gold buyers but also to anyone who had a legitimate use for it, such as making jewelry. The U.S. Mint no longer bought gold on the private market or sold it to private individuals. The holding ("hoarding") of gold by ordinary people (except as jewelry or collections) was still prohibited.

In 1971, to prevent further leakage of gold, President Richard Nixon raised the price from $35 to $38 an ounce, thus lowering the value of the dollar. Within fourteen months he again raised it, to $42.22. This was still less than gold was selling for internationally. Before 1971, when gold in foreign markets was bringing as much as $100 an ounce, American miners were required to sell their gold for $35. In California, for example, an official ore buyers inspector was a member of the State Division of Mines staff. His job was to inspect the records of the mines, to make certain that the gold they recovered went to government-authorized gold buyers or the mint, and to inspect the records of the gold buyers to see that they also reflected only domestic sales or sales to the mint. It was the job of the U.S. Secret Service—an agency of the Treasury Department—to see that no gold was smuggled *out* of the country.

The Nixon administration's raising of the price of gold did not stem the demand for gold in exchange for paper, so government regulation of the price of gold in the United States was abandoned, and in 1974 President Gerald Ford repealed the sanctions against U.S. citizens owning gold or selling it to anyone they wished. Gold had become a commodity and was now listed in the New York commodities exchange.

As everyone expected, the price rose rapidly, reaching a high of $850 in 1980. Gold and gold mines became attractive investments on the stock market, and people who feared continued inflation invested in gold bars and often became "midnight gardeners," burying them. (To speak of "the" price of gold is somewhat misleading. Since gold has been on the open market, the price has been what the seller is willing to sell for, and the buyer willing to pay. Although prices are fairly close in world markets, there is usually a range. For example, on Friday, January 16, 1998, gold sold for $288.05 an ounce in Hong Kong, $290 in London, $287.53 in Paris, $287.64 in Frankfurt, and $289.30 in Zurich. In the United States the New York Republic National Bank quoted $285.30.)

The rising price of gold in the 1970s caused the gold mining industry to put on a burst of speed. Recreational miners continued to probe the riverbeds, delighted with the new price of gold but not depending on it. Between 1978 and 1980 the Gold Prospectors Association of America, a group of recreational gold miners, doubled its membership to 53,000. By 1996 the organization had nearly 70,000 members. Its head in 1980, George "Buzzard" Massie, claimed to have found more than his own weight in gold in California rivers. More than 16,000 mining claims were recorded in California in 1988, most of them for gold, and by January 1989 the total number on record was more than 150,000. By 1994 there were so many recreational gold miners that the U.S. Bureau of Mines, which keeps statistics on mining in the nation, gave up trying to keep track of recreational and other small-scale gold placer miners and no longer tried to tabulate their production.

CHAPTER FOURTEEN

The Corporate Gold Rush and Its Disreputable Offspring

Today's corporate miners are not grizzled prospectors with burro and pan but men in business suits armed with computers and earth movers. What made their entry on the gold stage possible was not only a surge in the price of gold, but new techniques of mining and refining that reduced costs.

Gold began to be mined not only from newly discovered deposits but also from mines that had been worked on and off for more than a century. Many nearly derelict mines sprang to new life. In the Mother Lode, the Carson Hill mine and the old Harvard mine right on the gleaming white quartz vein known as the Mother Lode vein had a resurgence. Although the Mother Lode vein, in places tens of feet wide, is a prominent landmark, it is not itself rich, but parallel veins close to it are. Ore from the Harvard mine and five others operated by the same company were concentrated in Jamestown in the largest flotation mill in the United States. The mill had formerly been at a copper mine in Arizona and was hauled to Jamestown.

The Harvard was estimated to contain 15.8 million short tons of ore of an average grade of 0.073 ounce per ton when it reopened. The other five mines owned by the same company had total reserves of 17 million short tons of an average grade of 0.06 ounce per ton. Altogether, that was more than 2 million ounces of gold in the ground in a mine passersby had long thought mined out and abandoned.

These were not the only underground mines to be reopened. The Sixteen-to-One mine and others in the Alleghany district, mines in the historic Grass Valley district (notably the Idaho-Maryland), and even some drift mines were cleared for working. But most mines, especially new ones, were open air ("open pit"). Dredging, shut down in 1967 because the cost of operating exceeded the value of the gold won, began again, especially in the Yuba Goldfield north of Sacramento.

Underground mines, dredging, and small-scale placer mining accounted for much of the gold production in the 1970s, but by 1988, when California's annual gold production exceeded $320 million, most of the gold came from fifteen large open-pit mines. By 1995 California was second in the nation in gold production, exceeded only by Nevada.

The most productive of California's revitalized mines was not in the Sierran gold country at all but in the Coast Ranges in Napa, Lake, and Yolo counties north of San Francisco, in an area long mined, not for gold, but for mercury. The gold at this "new" mine (it had actually been a mercury mine) was too fine to see with the naked eye, but because of the mercury mining, it was already known that fine gold was scattered through the rocks. The gold was first mentioned in print in the 41st Report of the California State Mineralogist, published in 1945, but since the quantity of gold was only five parts per million, it was not then of commercial interest. Using this report and other careful library research, followed by detailed mapping and core drilling, Homestake Mining Company, for many years the leading U.S. gold producer from its Homestake mine in South Dakota, announced that the new mine contained more than one million ounces of gold. The turncoat mine was named the McLaughlin in honor of the geologist Donald McLaughlin, longtime board chairman of the company.

The project quickly ran into opposition from nearby residents and environmental groups. Perhaps they were alerted by a sign said to have been in the mine superintendent's office at Homestake that read, "Remember the golden rule: he who owns the gold, makes the rules."

The environmental fight for the McLaughlin was not easy for the company. They had to obtain 327 different permits before one bar of gold could be poured. As Raymond E. Krauss, environmental manager for Homestake Mining Company, wrote, "Each [of the counties of Napa, Lake, and Yolo] is empowered to exercise independent land use authority and requires separate permitting procedures including extensive environmental review with public participation. In addition, the project is subject to the authority of three different Air Quality Management Districts, two State Department of Fish and Game Regions, both a Regional Water Quality Control Board and a State Water Resources Board and the Federal Bureau of Land Management. . . . Northern California is the birthplace of the Sierra Club and the home of much of the American environmental movement. Certainly no project of the scale of the McLaughlin Mine could expect to escape the intense scrutiny of the environmental community."

With this in mind, Homestake took an aggressive environmental stance—that is, they struck first. They sought out regulators, environmentalists, and community leaders to show them what the company planned to do and to get their questions and suggestions. Homestake gave slide shows, invited environmental groups to visit,

FIGURE 51. Plant of the McLaughlin mine.

threw barbecues for neighboring ranchers. Before the permitting process was over, Homestake was sending newsletters to seven thousand interested people.

The Sierra Club, often the most vigorously opposed to mining (and often with good reason), was invited to inspect and consider the project. After some study groups and soul searching, the Sierra Club, Krauss wrote, "concluded that gold was indeed a necessary and desirable commodity in their lives and that to oppose the McLaughlin Mine was to in effect endorse the production of the resource in a manner that might have less desirable environmental and social consequences. At a public hearing the Club officially took the position that they had conducted an extensive review and concluded that they would not oppose the project."

Among the many considerations the Homestake had to take into account were the possibility of encountering a fault that would threaten nearby dams; the maintenance of good surface air and groundwater quality; protection of rare plants; protection of wildlife and their habitat, including fish and particularly rare and endangered species; checking for archaeological and historical resources; and reducing noise levels. All of this was carefully monitored. The problems were—happily for the company—compounded when the ore deposit proved to be much larger than expected.

According to the company's plan, when mining is complete, the company will make the mine into an environmental field station, which will have a library of data from the twenty or more years of extensive monitoring unmatched elsewhere. The station will be available for use by educational institutions and the public. In the

FIGURE 52. Main pit of the McLaughlin mine. The pit was being filled in 1998.

meantime, until it has completed its mining operations, Homestake plans to use the surrounding 7,500 acres it owns for the environmental research station.

The mine pit will be fenced, the upper benches restored (the company saved the topsoil) and revegetated. The water reservoir built by Homestake for mining use will remain for wetland habitat. Grasses will be reseeded, and native plants will be replaced. All of this is guaranteed by a trust should the company default on its plans.

Altogether, Homestake spent $284 million to get the mine in operation. Of this less than 2 percent—about $5 million—was for environmental studies and permitting costs. Since the mine then made money at the rate of $10,000 an *hour*, it was cheap at the price. The McLaughlin poured its first gold bar on March 4, 1985, and was expected then to have a life of twenty years.

Not only did the McLaughlin become a large mine, it was also a new type of gold mine. It is the remnant of a hot spring that had been active between half a million and two million years ago, a spring similar to Steamboat Springs, near Carson City, Nevada, where gold is now being precipitated from hot spring waters. Bacteria and algae live in the Steamboat Springs waters. The same species are fossilized at McLaughlin.

The richest ore at McLaughlin is beneath a capping of silica sinter, a deposit left by the hot spring where it bubbled out of the ground long ago. "At least five times," wrote John Burnett in *California Geology*, "during this formation process, violent underground episodes of steam explosions occurred which fractured and reoriented the rock all the way to the surface. The mine is located on five (and possibly more)

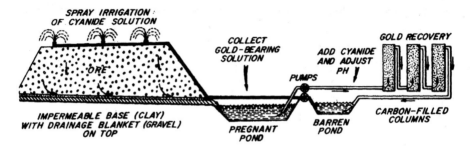

SPRAY IRRIGATION OF CYANIDE SOLUTION

ORE

IMPERMEABLE BASE (CLAY) WITH DRAINAGE BLANKET (GRAVEL) ON TOP

COLLECT GOLD-BEARING SOLUTION

PREGNANT POND

PUMPS

ADD CYANIDE AND ADJUST PH

BARREN POND

GOLD RECOVERY

CARBON-FILLED COLUMNS

FIGURE 53. How heap leaching works. Ore is placed on an impervious pad, which may be clay or some other impermeable material. A dilute solution of sodium cyanide is spread over the heap, often by sprinklers. The solution trickles through the ore, dissolving the gold and silver. The pregnant solution containing the precious metals drains from the heap and goes to a large, plastic-lined pond. From there it is pumped through tanks containing activated charcoal, which adsorbs the gold and silver on its surface. The gold-bearing charcoal is chemically stripped of its gold and silver and the strip solution treated in an electrowinning cell, where the gold and silver is plated by electrolysis on steel wool. The wool, in turn, is melted in a furnace, and a doré bar (a bar of mixed gold and silver) produced. It, in turn, is smelted, resulting in a bar of nearly pure gold. The barren cyanide solution, from which the gold has been taken, is pumped back to a holding basin for reuse.

shallow craters, or *maars,* caused by contact of the hot magma and groundwater. Within and below the maars, fracturing provided new open spaces which allowed more metal-rich minerals to be deposited. This deposition gradually clogged and restricted the hot water from reaching the surface and eventually led to another explosive episode."

The McLaughlin inspired the search for other hot spring deposits in the western United States, resulting in the discovery of gold deposits at Hasbrouck Mountain, Hog Ranch, and Buckhorn in Nevada, Thunder Mountain in Idaho, and Quartz Mountain in Oregon. Other old mercury deposits may be new McLaughlins, and hot spring areas such as at Steamboat Springs and active volcanoes like Mendeleev in the Kurile Islands, are probably forming McLaughlins for mining a few million years from now.

In California, nearly all the gold output for the year 1986—400,000 ounces— came from five large mines using a new refining technique called heap leaching. Heap leaching certainly saves money, but it is poisonous if not carefully controlled, and the initial expenditure can be huge. At the McLaughlin mine the cost of installing the heap leaching equipment was $250 million. Except for small-scale placer mining, the modern gold rush is not for everyone.

Heap leaching is a method of treating low-grade gold ore by piling it into an outdoor heap, then sprinkling a cyanide solution over it. Within a few weeks the cyanide will have dissolved the gold and run down a sloping, impermeable pad into sluices. If a stray nugget were to end up in the heap leaching pile, the outside of it would dissolve in the chloride and the rest would be tossed into the waste rock pile, but nuggets are virtually unknown in the McLaughlin.

The pad on which the ore is leached must be impermeable to prevent the solution from leaking into the groundwater, carrying not only the gold but poison as well. If the leach pad is not impermeable, disaster can result. In 1991 a leak in the Summitville, Colorado, leach pad was reported to have killed all life in the Alamosa River for seventeen miles downstream, and some probably seeped into the Rio Grande. Pads have been made of concrete, asphalt, clay, and plastic sheeting.

Dissolved gold from the so-called pregnant solution is sent to the mill, where it is recovered on activated carbon, often made from coconut shells, or, at some mines, on zinc dust. When all the gold has been taken out, the "barren" solution goes to a tank where more cyanide is added to bring it to the right concentration for reuse. The gold, now on carbon or zinc, is recovered by electrolysis on steel wool, which is sent through an electric furnace to produce doré bars, a mixture of gold and silver (because gold almost always is mixed with a certain amount of silver), that are then sent to the smelter.

The process can be fairly quick because the McLaughlin gold is fine, but in California mines where nuggets once abounded, heap leaching is more cautiously applied. The old Carson Hill mine in Calaveras County, first opened in 1850, was reopened in the 1980s. (The largest nugget ever found in North America—2,340 ounces—came from the Carson Hill mine in 1854.) It took about three months for 60 percent of the gold to be leached but at least eighteen months to be sure all coarse gold had been dissolved. Heap leaching can take years. At Nevada's Cortez and Gold Acres mines, it took seven and a half years to leach gold from reworked tailing piled in 117,000-ton heaps stacked twenty feet high.

Heap leaching is not as effective as some other techniques—often getting only 50 to 70 percent of the gold—but it is far less expensive. It was used for many years on copper ore and has allowed many gold mines to operate that otherwise could not, as it, coupled with the recovery of gold from the leach fluid on charcoal, has cut the overall cost of mining 30 to 44 percent, according to the U.S. Bureau of Mines.

In most mines where heap leaching is used, cyanide is sprayed over the ore, but if the climate is cold and spray pipes will freeze, the ore is sent to a leaching pond. In some places drip irrigation is used instead of spraying. Between half a pound and two pounds of sodium cyanide are required per ton of solution. Aeration is important because it supplies oxygen, which promotes solution of the gold and prevents the production of volatile and poisonous hydrogen cyanide (HCN). Cyanide is a poison, of course, which has caused much concern among environmentalists. Thus, the long and fierce battle between environmentalists and mining interests, which began with the hydraulic mining fight of the nineteenth century, continues today.

Today's mining companies are taking a different view of the fight. Here is what T. P. Philip, then president of Newmont Gold Company, one of the largest gold-mining companies in the world and the largest in the United States after its merger with Santa Fe Gold in 1997, had to say in 1990:

> Environmental issues are not only real . . . they are correctly applied as to principle in most cases involving mining.
>
> I know this is heresy! However, if we approach the problem from the position that all environmental issues are wrong and that all so-called environmentalists are wrong, we're never going to survive.
>
> We are not operating in the third tier of the Himalayas. We're operating in a communications fishbowl today. Not only can [television] point its slanted cameras at us, anyone can find us and put us on the six-o'clock news around the globe.
>
> Even though we have clear title, in a larger sense, the land we operate on is still environmentalists' land as well as ours. The waters on our lands are their waters as well as ours. And the future is theirs as well as ours.

Other modern miners have taken Philip's words to heart. At an elevation of 4,500 feet in the eastern Mojave Desert, at the southern end of the Castle Mountains, lies the Castle Mountains gold deposit in the Hart Mountain mining district. When the deposit was first discovered in 1907, it was fabulously rich, carrying as much as eleven ounces of gold per ton. At $100 an ounce, each ton would be worth $1,100; at $500, each ton would be worth $5,500. As time progressed, miners struck a vein carrying 500 ounces of gold per ton. At $100 an ounce, it would be worth $50,000 per ton; at $500, $250,000 per ton. However, the average grade of ore through the mine's first incarnation was between one and two ounces per ton—still rich ore.

The town of Hart grew quickly around the mines. At its peak Hart had four hundred tent and wooden buildings, six saloons, and a newspaper, but no church or school. "Gunplay and litigation have broken out," commented a mining magazine of the time. The rich ore soon petered out, and within three years the town had only forty people. During the Great Depression, one of the mines reopened but produced little gold.

The Castle Mountains are a small range at the end of Lanfair Valley, San Bernardino County, that extends into Nevada. The basement rocks of the range are Precambrian, overlain by 13- to 22-million-year-old Tertiary volcanic rocks. Geologists who have studied the area think that Lanfair Valley may be a large volcanic caldera (a crater formed by the collapse of a volcanic cone) in which ore was deposited about 15 million years ago. The gold deposits are in volcanic rocks. About 13 million years ago, the ore-carrying volcanic rocks were covered by more volcanic rocks. In some places this covering and more recent gravel layers completely mask the ore deposits. Grains and masses of gold were mined in the early days, and a few large pieces were unintentionally left for today's miners, but most of the gold in the ore mined now is too small to see with the naked eye.

When the mine opened in 1991, the mining company expected to produce 8,000 tons of ore per day, or 2.8 million tons per year. The ore was expected to last through the year 2000. Only 115 acres of the Castle Mountains mine is on the patented private land of the old mine. The rest—2,620 acres—is public land, administered by the U.S. Bureau of Land Management.

Scars on the desert are very visible and can last for centuries. Therefore, in 1990, when Castle Mountains mine gained approval from the San Bernardino County Planning Commission for its reclamation plan after lengthy public hearings, newspapers all over the country carried the story, because support for the plan came not only from the mining company but also from San Bernardino County, the Mined-Land Reclamation Project, the U.S. Bureau of Land Management, and the Sierra Club Legal Defense Fund (which also represented the Wilderness Society and the Natural Resources Defense Council). The plan was hailed by environmentalists as a precedent-setting model for future reclamation planning. In 1991 the Castle Mountains Venture, managed by Viceroy Gold Corporation, was awarded the Excellence in Reclamation Award by the California Mining Association.

Mines do dig up the landscape, and the Castle Mountains mine was to be an open-pit mine, with cuts clearly visible. And the mine would use heap-leach recovery methods. Many heap-leach systems use open storage ponds, attractive and poisonous to wildlife. Viceroy installed sealed steel vats.

As the ore was mined, the cuts were revegetated with native plants, and tortoise fences were erected to keep the endangered desert tortoise (*Gopherus agassizii*) from wandering in front of trucks or being poisoned. While the tortoise fence was being built, biologists searched the area daily for tortoises. Mine employees were told to report any tortoise they saw so that a tortoise-handling expert could deal with it. To help further in saving the lives of desert tortoises, Viceroy purchased the Walking Box Ranch, established by film stars Clara Bow and Rex Bell in the 1930s. The ranch is prime tortoise habitat. Viceroy gave the Nature Conservancy an option to buy the ranch at half what Viceroy paid for it, to make a desert tortoise preserve.

Viceroy went yet another mile. Beginning in the 1920s, clay was mined (not by Viceroy) from land to the west of the gold deposits. Two large open pits worked the clay, one of which engulfed what was left of the town of Hart. The clay went to make "sanitary ware"—toilets and basins—and tile. The white quarry scars were visible for miles. Viceroy's reclamation plan includes restoring the clay pits, terracing and then planting them with native vegetation. The company had to obtain permits to move

THE DESERT TORTOISE

The tortoise of the Mojave Desert, *Gopherus agassizii,* is the largest member of the turtle order in North America. A typical desert tortoise is about a foot long (220 millimeters), with a carapace about six inches (150 millimeters) deep. The top of the carapace of a desert tortoise is brown, with an attractive geometric arrangement of growth rings. Males can easily be told from females: the male's carapace is deeper, and the female's carapace ends in a little flange like a tiny skirt.

Desert tortoises' hind legs are long and thick, like miniature elephant legs. Their flattened forefeet have a permanent bend at the elbow and end in long claws. They are called gopher tortoises (from which comes their scientific name) because of this arrangement of their front feet, so admirably suited for digging.

Tortoises tend to congregate in roomy dens when they hibernate during the cold weather. They come out again in spring, when the weather is warm and plants (their chief food) are green and tender. A tortoise may dig a small burrow to hide in when the desert sun is hot or water is scarce.

Where once there were herds of desert tortoises in southern California, Utah, and Arizona, human construction in their homeland, capture of babies for sale (no longer allowed), and highway and off-road disasters (motorcyclists have been seen deliberately and cruelly running over tortoises) have reduced their numbers to the point that *Gopherus agassizii* is now classed as an endangered species.

Turtles as a group are very long lived, and have been long lived in the geologic sense, dating back, nearly unchanged, to the Triassic (245 million years ago). The land tortoise, of which *Gopherus agassizii* is a member, may have originated in North America, as more than fifty species lived here during the early Cenozoic (60 million years ago). Most of them became extinct during the last 5 million years, leaving only three species in all of North America. Bones of fossil *Gopherus agassizii* were entombed in the tar pits of southern California. ✕

native plants. To get the plants to grow, Viceroy had to conserve all the soil in the area.

State, county, and federal officials as well as members of university faculties have made periodic inspections to ensure that all was proceeding according to this imaginative, generous, and thoughtful plan. To be certain that it would not cut and run, the company posted bond large enough so that if for some reason they didn't carry the plan through, someone else could.

All gold mines did not fare so well in the environmental fight. Residents of San Juan Ridge, California, objected so strenuously to a renewal of mining that they succeeded in stopping it, and residents of Banner Ridge, Nevada City, in the heart of the old gold-mining district, were up in arms over the possibility that mines would be working under their houses.

Corporate gold mining took another setback in the late 1990s. The price of gold fell below $300 an ounce in January 1998, for the first time in twelve and a half years. On January 12 the price was only $280—about a third of what it had been in 1980. Worldwide, mines whose costs were greater than the price cut back or shut down. Some mining companies declared bankruptcy, and many reduced their workforces or halted operations altogether, leaving only a skeleton crew to protect the mine until the price should rise again.

Within the new corporate gold rush a mini-rush of a different kind developed. Newspapers called it the "Fool's Gold Rush." Spurred by the high price of gold in the 1980s, crooks of all kinds began "boiler room" operations, in which slick-tongued salesmen urged investors to buy shares in gold mines, or even a gold mine of their own. Citing fabulous returns at mines like the Carlin in Nevada and California's McLaughlin, they spoke glibly of the wonderful assays they could show and the marvels of the heap-leach method. The shares they sold were often to nonexistent or nonproductive mines, and the actual gold mines investors got for their money, although they may have existed, were either too expensive to mine or impossible to get permits to operate. Many investors who thought they could do it themselves had no idea of how to mine or how to handle the mountains of paperwork.

Mark Twain once said, "A mine is a hole in the ground with a liar at the top," but in some known gold-mining areas, "dirt mines" not even boasting a hole in the ground were touted by crooks. This was a wonderful scam, because it cost the crook next to nothing. Find a wild piece of public land, stake a claim, record it at the county seat, rent a bulldozer, and push around some dirt. Take a picture, cook up a fake assay, and telephone your "marks." A pretty prospectus helps, showing the rich dirt you've moved, the great assay, and how much gold real mines like McLaughlin are getting out of the ground, but it isn't strictly necessary. People will—and did—buy over the phone, without seeing the "mine."

Newspapers reported that one salesman, selling investors worthless dirt in an inactive Utah mine for $6,250 each, used the phones in the Wyoming prison in which he was an inmate to solicit business from people in Wyoming and Minnesota. When discovered, he was moved to solitary confinement. Promoters of another dirt scam gave prospective investors such a high value for the gold and silver in their dirt that it would have qualified as the richest deposit on the face of the Earth. A test of the dirt showed that there was more gold in seawater, yet people in forty-one states contributed a total of $2.5 million to the swindlers' pockets.

Another scam, this one harmless, took place in southern California, where three men told reporters they had found nuggets of gold while on a hiking trip near Sierra Madre, California. Newspaper photographs showed a beaming prospector, Herb Robbins, with a pan full of gold, which he said was worth $799.26. The men staked claims in the national forest, where, they said, they had found the gold. Within days, the men confessed they were actors promoting a play, "The Treasure of the Sierra Madre," and that the gold find was a publicity stunt cooked up with jeweler's gold to promote the play. (The Sierra Madre of Mexico, where the book, play, and movie were set, are considered by some to be an extension of California's Sierra Nevada range. The Mexican Sierra Madre were very rich in gold and silver.)

Finding gold—or saying you have—is a great way to generate publicity. Within a few months after the Sierra Madre find, Herb Robbins was again active in touting "The Treasure of the Sierra Madre"—this time in San Anselmo, California, again according to newspaper reports. He and Charles Hubbard, who was making scenery for the play and had experience in mining, staked gold claims in San Francisco Bay—or tried to. They dropped cans filled with cement to mark their claims and recorded them at the recorder's office in Marin and San Francisco counties. After that they ran into difficulty figuring out just who was in charge of San Francisco Bay. They argued that through the years, nature had dumped a lot of gold in the bay and that the not very efficient mining methods of early days let a lot more gold find its way down the rivers into the bay. "Think of it as a big bathtub full of gold," Robbins told a newspaper reporter. There probably is a lot of gold in the bay, but getting it out is a daunting prospect. Whether or not Robbins and Hubbard could figure that problem out, Robins hit on a good way to propel his acting career.

"The Treasure of the Sierra Madre" cheated no one, but thousands were cheated by real confidence men. At the height of the Fool's Gold Rush in the mid-1980s, more than one hundred fifty gold-mining scams were in progress around the country. Swindlers moved from state to state, making it difficult for the law to catch up. Finally Jack Hiatt, then director of the Securities Division of the Regulation and Licensing Department in New Mexico, put out a call to other states to cooperate in shutting down the scams and, if possible, in prosecuting the scammers. The result was Project Goldbrick, which eventually included the securities agencies of sixteen states, the Securities and Exchange Commission, the Internal Revenue Service, the Federal Bureau of Investigation, the Postal Inspection Service, and the Council of Better Business Bureaus.

Newspaper reports said one of the companies involved in dirt schemes was located in Burbank, California. Lawmen arrested three men and charged them with grand theft and selling unregistered securities, but the law ran into a snag when the California courts ruled in a similar case, that of William M. Moreland, who had promised investors that he would process twenty ounces of gold for every person who paid him $5,000 for 133 tons of dirt. He was not, the court ruled, offering securities, merely dirt. After this ruling, twenty out of the twenty-two charges were dropped against the men involved in the Burbank firm. Despite this setback, Operation Goldbrick persisted, and by 1990 had managed effectively to quench the fire in the boiler rooms, routing out most of the con men.

A case in New Mexico climaxed the effort. A former California businessman, Maurice E. "Ed" Barbara, Sr., well known in the San Francisco Bay area for his flamboyant television commercials, was tried for racketeering, fraud, and other misdeeds in 1988. Barbara was the power behind Dynapac, a company the prosecution described as a "shell corporation" set up to house Barbara's confidence games. In 1984 Dynapac got control of the Golden Gulch mine near Truth or Consequences, a small town in southern New Mexico, and issued reports that calculated reserves at nearly a billion dollars, showed glowing assay reports, estimated revenues at $7.8 million in gold *per month,* and stated that ore was being produced for $50 an ounce. Money from investors poured in. For more than a year the stock issued by the company was touted as a good buy, lifting its price to as much as $8 a share. Using the price of the shares as leverage, Barbara bought a country club near Las Cruces in late 1985.

Barbara showed potential investors pyramids that gleamed like the sun. Copper pyramids, it is true, but he told investors they were pure gold. He even had the local police escort people to the mine, where the gold-struck investors were given a VIP hard-hat tour. But geologists and engineers at the New Mexico Bureau of Mines and Geology had reservations. To be sure, there was gold in the area, but not nearly as much as the company was claiming. Then David Fingado, who had been the original on-site assayer for the mine, told Cable News Network that prospective stock purchasers were being given inaccurate information about the mine's potential. A week before the interview was broadcast, Fingado died in a one-car accident. Fingado's uncle, Donald Fingado, took a sample of the ore concentrates from the mine to the New Mexico Bureau of Mines and Geology, which found only small amounts of gold. Then geologists from the bureau examined samples of the ore

WHOSE GOLD?

American forty-niners were certain they knew whose gold it was. California now belonged to the United States and they were U.S. citizens; therefore, it was their gold. It was this mindset that caused so much tension with foreign miners. The whole of California, as far as the miners were concerned, was open land. Never mind the native tribes whose ancestral territory it was, never mind the Californios who held some paper from the king of Spain or rulers in Mexico—what had that to do with citizens of the United States?

The miners themselves developed rules regarding mining claims that became the prototype of U.S. mining law. Colonel Mason and other military authorities simply let the miners be, so mining proceeded as the miners wished. When California became a state, that attitude continued with the new political leaders and became embedded in the state's political stance. As can be seen by the hydraulic mining controversy (see chapter 7), anything that adversely affected mining was unconscionable to the legislature. All through the rich years, the millions of dollars' worth of gold taken out provided not one penny for state or federal coffers.

Horace Greeley, editor of the New York *Tribune*, after seeing California in 1859, found the mining laws astonishing:

> I believe, too, that the time is at hand when some modification of the present mining laws will be demanded and conceded. Hitherto, the operators with pick and pan have been masters of the state, and have ruled it, like other aristocracies, with a sharp eye to their own supposed interests. To dig up a man's fenced garden, or dig down his house, in quest of gold, is the legal privilege of any miner who does not even pretend to have any rights in the premises but such as the presumed existence of gold thereon gives him. Of course, the law contemplates payment for damages sustained; but suppose the digger is pecuniarily irresponsible, and digs down your house without finding any more gold than he spends in the quest, what are you to do about it? Such laws, I trust, cannot stand. I am sure they should not.

It is still true today that "mineral rights" and "surface rights" are often separate. You can purchase property for building a house and find you have only surface rights—that any mineral deposits on and under your land belong to someone else. This has been most troublesome in oil-producing areas, but is also confusing in gold-mining country. The town of Placerville is said to be honeycombed below the surface with old gold-mining shafts and tunnels. Who owns these old workings is largely in doubt, but if a miner could show title to one of the old mines he could easily be digging beneath a restaurant, a school, or even the city hall.

The federal government took no action to regulate mining until after the Civil War, when the price of that disaster had to be paid. The result was the Mineral

continued ☞

Location Act of 1872, commonly called the 1872 Mining Law. Its ostensible purpose was to regulate mining claims. This would encourage mining and stimulate the economy, legislators reasoned, but part of its purpose was to give the veterans of the Civil War something to do—a type of Civil War "G.I. Bill." If lawmakers also had in mind revenue for the government, it failed.

The 1872 Mining Law is, as of this writing, still the basic law. It has been modified several times, the most important revisions being the Mineral Leasing Act of 1920, which allowed for leasing—not claiming—of government land containing such minerals as oil and gas, and the Common Varieties Act of 1955, which made many "common" minerals (such as salt and sand and gravel) subject to lease, not claim. Metals, including gold, have been left as claimable. All one has to do to claim and mine a gold deposit is to fulfill three conditions: (1) discover a valuable mineral on open public land; (2) locate the claim and mark and record it; (3) diligently develop the claim into an operating mine. The law specifies the size of placer, lode, and mill site claims and how a claim must be staked.

In the days of the forty-niners and now, claims were and are staked on public land. Although it is possible to buy property without mineral rights, particularly in old mining towns where mining companies may sell houses and land but retain mineral rights, it would be difficult to stake a claim nowadays on someone's private property, even if the owner did not possess the mineral rights, although it could be done, as Greeley noted.

Almost all claims are staked on public land, generally federal land. In the United States the stewardship of the 724 million acres of public lands is chiefly in the hands of the Bureau of Land Management, which controls 42 percent of the unreserved public lands; the U.S. Forest Service in the Department of Agriculture, which watches over 30 percent; the U.S. Fish and Wildlife Service, 15 percent; and the National Park Service, 13 percent. There are other federal holdings that are reserved and not locatable, such as military holdings and lands belonging to various Native American tribes. But at least 72 percent of federal "public" land is open to mining and prospecting. As of 1977, the National Parks are no longer open, although early laws permitted mining and prospecting in six parks: Death Valley, California and Nevada (then a national monument); Glacier Bay, Alaska (also then a national monument); Crater Lake, Oregon; Organ Pipe Cactus National Monument, Arizona; Mount Denali, Alaska (then Mount McKinley National Park); and Coronado National Memorial, Arizona.

After turning a claim into a working mine, the owner can apply for a patent, which, if granted, makes his claim and mine his own private property, which he can do with as he pleases, including building housing developments.

In recent years there has been much agitation to change the 1872 mining law. Those desiring change point out that the government does not receive revenue for gold or other metals mined on public lands and that such mining is disruptive of the environment, destroys the beauty of the landscape, and sacrifices wildlife. They maintain that "public" land belongs to all citizens and that allowing private individuals to benefit from it—even to own it—with virtually no recompense is a form of legalized stealing. They point to abuses in the law: to land developers who took out mining claims that they transformed into housing developments. In some cases, even foreign mining companies, having developed a working mine in the United States via the mineral claims route, were then able to patent the land and pay roughly $5 an acre for land that produced millions.

Those who prefer to keep the mining law as it is point out the high cost of developing a claim into a mine. They view public lands as available to anyone, not reserved for everyone. They see the 1872 law as a fundamental freedom, part of our heritage, a cornerstone of the American Dream.

Although claims are "free" on public land, to reduce fraud and make mining easier to control, stewardship agencies of the federal government have issued regulations that must be met in order to ensure that a claim owner truly intends to mine and to keep that mine from causing "significant disturbance of the surface resources." The U.S. Forest Service, empowered by an act passed in 1897 that allowed the Secretary of Agriculture to regulate the use of national forests, now requires a mining plan from would-be mining operators. Even so, the federal government has no control over who locates a mining claim, what and how much is mined, to whom it is sold, or the price obtained.

In addition to federal regulations, the State of California, through its Surface Mining and Reclamation Act of 1975, has inventoried its mineral lands so that planning agencies will be able to make intelligent plans for land use. The act also provides for reclamation of mined lands. The purpose of the act was not only to prevent mining companies from leaving unsightly or dangerous messes in the landscape but also to protect mineral deposits from encroaching urbanization. In the Los Angeles, San Diego, and San Francisco Bay metropolitan regions, for example, sand and gravel (aggregate) resources that could have served the state for thousands of years were so built over that only a few decades of resources remain. The Mother Lode gold belt in the Sierra Nevada, too, is facing urbanization, even though it is still a significant gold resource. A basic principle should be, in the words of Theodore Roosevelt, "The nation behaves well if it treats the natural resources as assets which it must turn over to the next generation, and not impaired in value." ✕

given to them by the company. These samples contained more gold, but the bureau was suspicious of the gold's origin. Some was amalgamated and some looked like gold filings, not like newly mined gold. The Securities and Exchange Commission, in charge of stock dealings, and the New Mexico Attorney General's office began looking into Dynapac. Ed Barbara, his wife, and others were arrested and brought to trial.

"Barbara was a big, burly, charming guy," Rafaelita Bachicha, foreperson of the jury at his trial, said. "He dressed nicely, and was able to convince people they, too, could have the better things of life—clothes, cars, country clubs—just like he had without having to work for them." His charisma did not keep him from being convicted and sentenced to nineteen and a half years in prison. His wife, found guilty in a later trial, was sentenced to nine months. Because she had not signed documents, as Barbara had, and because she told the jury she was very ill, her sentence was lighter. Others involved in the company, including the geologist who helped fake the assay report, got lighter sentences at separate trials. But before Barbara could be sent to jail, he disappeared, and his lawyer and wife claimed he was dying. The next year documents were presented to the court to prove that Barbara had died of cancer in Florida, but the documents included a death certificate made out for "Norm Peterson" and signed by a doctor not present at the time of death. The body was cremated—thus, as Judge Art Encinias commented, sending the best evidence they had "up in smoke."

Barbara, if he was not "Norm Peterson," has never been found. Even a television program about him failed to turn up his whereabouts. Perhaps he is alive, well, and living high on his ill-gotten gains.

CHAPTER FIFTEEN

What Good Is Gold?

After the forty-niners got the gold out of the ground, they still were short of money. Shopkeepers and gamblers would take nuggets and gold dust—marking it down for questionable purity and their trouble—but the U.S. government would accept only cash. This meant that anything brought into California—even the miners' clean shirts, which they sometimes had laundered in Hawaii—had to be cleared through the Custom House and duty paid for it in coin. Custom duties collected in this way were the government's chief source of taxes from California. The SS *California*, a three-masted, armed sailing ship, was sent to California to be certain the miners paid duties. So scarce were coins that miners were known to trade an ounce of gold for a silver dollar. Gold could be sent to the U.S. Mint in Philadelphia—with luck and a good ship—to be minted into coin, but that did not solve the miners' shortage in California.

Private mints seemed to be the answer, so Col. R. B. Mason, then military governor of California, gave permission on July 21, 1848, for private individuals to make "grain gold into convenient monetary shape to serve as substitute for gold and silver coins." However, because of its doubtful legality, Mason's proclamation was rescinded two weeks later. Private coinage began anyway, with or without government approval.

Some California gold coins may even have been issued in 1848, but the first coin we have certain record of was a $5 gold piece minted at Benicia City on May 31, 1849 (although it carried a San Francisco imprint), by the firm of Norris, Gregg (also spelled Grieg and Grigg), and Norris, who had brought their minting equipment from New York. Later they issued coins from San Francisco. (In 1996 a Norris, Gregg, and Norris $5 gold piece was priced in the numismatic market at $1,200 to $10,000, depending on its condition.)

FIGURE 54. Returned Californians waiting at the Philadelphia mint. Since no mints existed in California before the middle of 1849, forty-eighters and forty-niners who "made their pile" early and returned back East took their gold to the mint to have it made into coin.

In March 1849, one day before leaving office, President Polk signed legislation authorizing a $1 and a $20 gold coin, the latter called a "double eagle" because it was worth twice as much as the common $10 gold coin, the golden eagle. Sample double eagles were struck at the U.S. Mint in Philadelphia in 1849, but it was not until 1850 that the coins were deemed satisfactory and began circulating. Only one 1849 double eagle is known to exist, and it is in the Smithsonian Institution. One reason for minting $20 gold pieces was to convert California gold to coin as rapidly as possible, so perhaps even this double eagle, minted in the East, is California gold.

On September 30, 1850, Congress authorized private coinage, and soon about twenty mints were operating in San Francisco, Sacramento, Stockton, Lone Pine (which produced only silver coins), and, perhaps, Mount Ophir. Some of the coiners had operated in Georgia and North Carolina during the gold rush there, and brought their equipment with them. The various mints produced coins in denominations of twenty-five cents, fifty cents, $1, $5, $10, $20, $25, and $50. Some mints also issued gold bars.

The Pacific Company is credited with producing the first octagonal gold coin— a $50 gold piece bearing the date 1849. Just who the Pacific Company was is not known, nor is it certain where the coins were minted.

Legend says the mint at Mount Ophir in the Mother Lode, said to have been erected by John Moffat, who came from the Georgia goldfields, was California's first mint and was also noted for its eight-sided gold coins. But the Mount Ophir mint was not built until 1850—if at all. No coins from the Mount Ophir mint are listed in numismatic catalogs. In fact, some libraries, numismatic societies, and coin collectors insist that this mint never existed, although a rock ruin near State Highway 49 bore the sign, "Mt. Ophir Mint."

The late Erwin G. Gudde, in his *California Gold Camps,* wrote that he made a search through the records of the Merced Mining Company (which operated the Mount Ophir mine), of which Moffat was a director, and found no mention of the mint, nor did he locate any other contemporary record of it. The numismatist Donald Kagin, in his book *Private Gold Coins and Patterns of the United States,* agreed: "The author has found no acceptable reference to confirm such a mint."

However, the 14th Report of the State Mineralogist (1893) contains a photograph said to show the ruins of the mint—the same stones marked recently by the sign. Other later publications also show photographs of the few stones that mark what tradition calls the Mount Ophir mint. Kagin wrote that Moffat and Company ingots, in values of $9.45 to $28.28, were probably the first gold specie made of local gold to pass as money in California. It may be that Moffat's minting efforts in San Francisco and his mining efforts near Mount Ophir have become confused through the years.

A Mother Lode legend says that in the 1850s a Mariposa county tax collector, Joseph Marre, was caught in a cloudburst. He was carrying a bullhide bag containing three hundred $50 octagonal gold coins to be deposited in the county treasury at Mariposa. He drowned while crossing a swollen creek. His body and his horse, which had not drowned, were recovered the next day, but the gold coins were not in the horse's saddlebags. Mother Lode residents speculated that Marre hid the money for safekeeping before attempting the creek. If that is true—if a passerby did not discover a gold-laden horse and relieve it of its gold, leaving the saddlebags in place— then somewhere there is a fortune in gold coins hidden.

This is the story the way it is usually told. Assuming it is true, it leaves questions. If the tax collector had just gathered the taxes, they would surely be in gold dust, nuggets, and possibly small coin. It is not believable that every taxpayer gave him a $50 gold piece. Therefore, he must have come, not from collecting taxes, but from a mint, where he had had the taxes made into coin. Did he go all the way to Stockton or Sacramento or San Francisco? If so, it was a long horseback ride. The story makes more sense if there really was a mint at Mount Ophir, just a few miles from Mariposa. Of course, the story and the mint may be a fiction; but there may be a grain of truth in both.

The price on the collectors' market for a gold piece from the Mount Ophir mint—if it existed—could conceivably be more than $20,000; but if one found a treasure trove of three hundred and they were thrown on the market all at once, it would lower the price of the coins. Each coin would have contained two and a half ounces of gold, making its bullion value—the value of the gold alone—$250 when gold is $100 a troy ounce; $2,000 when gold is $800.

The gold ingots issued by Moffat and Company bring high prices on the numismatic market. The $9.45 ingot is so rare it has no price. In fact, a price is given for only one bar: a Moffat and Company $16 ingot: $14,000. In 1996 Moffat and Company's round $5 and $10 gold pieces were priced at $400 to $4,500 for the $5 coin and $850 to $6,250 for the $10 one, depending on its condition.

In 1851 John Moffat was appointed United States Assayer in San Francisco by President Zachary Taylor, but he soon left to work for the San Joaquin Diving Bell Mining Company, located on the San Joaquin River, which used diving bells to bring up sand and gravel from the river to process for gold. Moffat sold the minting company at the end of 1851 to Curtis, Perry, and Ward, which continued to coin money. Moffat and Company officially disbanded early in 1852. The new owners contracted with the government to serve as the United States Assay Office of Gold. They issued $50 octagonal gold pieces (which may have contributed to the Mount Ophir legend), now priced as high as $20,000, as well as $10 and $20 gold coins.

Many of the privately minted coins resembled official U.S. coins, but some did not. The mint masters used almost one hundred different designs. A liberty head with stars, together with the date, mint, and place of minting on the obverse and an eagle holding a shield on the reverse was common. (The obverse of a coin shows the place of manufacture and the principal design.) Some coins, however, like the octagonal gold piece issued by the U.S. Assay Office, had the eagle together with the place of manufacture on the obverse and the liberty head and stars on the reverse. One $10 gold coin shows a horseman throwing a lasso in the center with "1850" under the horse. Coin collectors know it as the Vaquero coin.

In 1852 Congress repealed the 1850 act that allowed private mints to make public coinage. (Today many private mints exist in the United States, but they make commemorative coins, medals, and the like.) In 1854 a branch of the U.S. Mint was established in San Francisco. The mint accepted privately minted coins as well as newly mined gold, melting down the coins to make official U.S. coins. This is one reason privately minted California coins command high prices on the numismatic market.

The tiny California gold coins, called fractional coins because their value was less than a dollar, were round or octagonal, made of local California gold. According to Michael Locke, a specialist in California fractional coins, no one knows if they actually circulated or were simply kept as souvenirs. Because there was a desperate need for small change, they may well have passed from hand to hand. For many years coin collectors were not certain the fractional coins really existed, but when some were recovered from the wreck of the *Winfield Scott,* their reality was proved.

The $50 octagonal gold pieces, officially called ingots, but nicknamed "slugs" or "five eagles," astonished easterners when they saw them. Congress had thought that there would never be a need for a coin larger than $10. This is what the *Daily Alta California* of February 21, 1851, said of the octagonal coins:

> The new fifty-dollar gold piece, manufactured under the Act of Congress appointing a United States Assay Office in California, and made under the supervision of the United States Assayer, was issued by Moffat & Co. yesterday.
>
> The coin is peculiar, containing only one face, an eagle in the centre, around which are the words "UNITED STATES OF AMERICA." Just over the eagle is stamped "50 DOLLS." The other face is ornamented with a kind of work technically called engine-turning, being a number of radii extending from the common centre, in which is stamped, in small figures, "50." Around the edge is stamped the name of the United States Assayer. We trust our readers may learn the character of this new coin by ocular demonstration.

Since most of the gold mined and minted in California in the early days was sent to the Philadelphia mint and from there to the markets of the world, few of us today have had "ocular demonstration" of a $50 gold slug. That may change soon, however, as the treasure found on the *Central America* and other sunken ships carrying Calfornia gold comes on the market.

Most nations of the world no longer use the gold standard for commerce, so few of us see gold coins in day-to-day transactions. However, because gold is said to have intrinsic value, some say we should return to the gold standard to "keep the government honest," so that it does not print more paper money than it has gold to back it up, whether that gold exists as coins circulating in the marketplace or as bars hidden away. Yet the United States and most other Western nations maintain a supply of gold, generally in bars, for international use. America's gold bars are stored in vaults in Fort Knox, Kentucky, West Point, New York, the U.S. Assay Offices in New York and San Francisco, the Denver and Philadelphia mints, and the Federal Reserve Bank of New York. True, these gold reserves are not for private circulation, but they nevertheless represent money.

Gold serves as a barometer of the economic health of nations. The price of gold rises when inflation hits; it drops when the economy is stable. Wars inflate the price of gold; peace deflates it. Bad times are good times for gold.

The common argument that gold has intrinsic value and therefore serves as a standard of value for all other goods is, Rep. Henry S. Reuss declared, "merely mystical." Later he called it "nonsensical." He expressed his views in the 1982 report issued by the Commission on the Role of Gold in the Domestic and International Monetary Systems, of which he was a member. One of the possibilities the commission considered but then rejected was a complete return to the gold standard.

Congressman Reuss was partly right. The *American Heritage Dictionary* defines *intrinsic* as "of or pertaining to the essential nature of a thing; inherent." Although we use the phrase "intrinsic value" frequently, it is somewhat misleading. *Intrinsic* refers to the essential nature of something, while when we add the word *value* we mean its value to humans. Gold's essential nature is totally independent of what we think of it, how we value it.

Nevertheless, gold does have value to humans because it is useful. Some of its uses are wise, some foolish and ostentatious; some necessary, some vain. The uses for limestone total more than seven hundred. Homely limestone is far more useful to humans (has more "intrinsic value") than noble gold.

The amount of gold used each year until nations stopped using gold for currency was about evenly divided between coinage and jewelry. Nowadays a fairly small amount goes into monetary storage. Most of it goes for jewelry and industrial purposes.

Gold, once mined, is with us forever. Very little is lost in use. Even buried gold does not lose its luster and can be recovered or discovered and used again. The gold in your wedding ring may have been brought from the mysterious land of Punt by the Egyptian queen Hatshepsut in the fifteenth century B.C. and later may have graced Cleopatra's finger. The gold mined in California during the days of the forty-niners is still in the marketplace—perhaps as some of the gold bars buried in the vaults of Fort Knox. The gold being mined today in California meets the same fate: it is added to the world's stock of gold where it will recirculate as long as humans value gold.

A survey in the United States showed that 75 percent of Americans thought of jewelry when they heard the word *gold*. For millennia humans have been using gold for jewelry and decoration. The oldest gold treasure found as yet came from southwestern Bulgaria; archaeologists unearthed more than two thousand gold artifacts—necklaces, bracelets, gold-covered ax handles—all dating to 4600–4200 B.C.

So for at least six thousand years goldsmiths have been making jewelry. Until the twentieth century, all of it was handmade by master craftsmen. Today most jewelry is designed by master artisans but mass produced by machine. One of the largest factories, Gori and Zucchi in Italy, consumes as much as sixty metric tons (nearly 2 million troy ounces) yearly. Their jewelry is sold wholesale by the pound.

Italy is the largest gold jewelry producer, the United States the biggest consumer. Americans like 14-karat yellow gold jewelry, which, because it is only three-fourths gold and one-fourth alloying metals, is hard enough to wear well, whereas pure gold is not. White gold can be gold plus nickel and zinc as alloying materials, or more expensively, silver, platinum, or palladium. Palladium is more expensive even than gold, but it is also less popular, partly because it gives a muddy color. Silver, the most common alloying element, allows gold to retain its gold shine and gives a soft, yellowish hue. Green gold contains cadmium and zinc; red gold has copper. Blue or violet gold contains iron; black gold contains bismuth. These odd gold colors are most often used by goldsmiths in special designs, as few people would purchase blue or black gold for itself.

The use of gold for industrial purposes has been growing. Medicine is one of these industrial purposes, and has been for thousands of years. Ancient medical practice in Mesopotamia prescribed gold as amulets to ward off disease; in China, potable gold made by alchemical means allegedly conferred long, perhaps eternal, life. Hippocrates, a Greek physician of the fifth century B.C., used gold wire to stitch a broken jaw; Pliny the Elder, a naturalist of the first century, reported in his *Natural History* that gold would remove sties in the eyes. Long before stainless steel was invented, some ancient physicians used gold scalpels and gold probes. The sixteenth-century Danish astronomer Tycho Brahe wore a nose made partly of gold after he lost his own nose in a duel.

Gold, said twelfth-century physicians, was an antidote to poisons, cured heart problems, prevented vomiting and loose bowels (as well as bowel stoppage), reduced fever, and cured palsy. In the nineteenth century, and for some time before, gold was reputed to be a cure for alcoholism, and although it never seemed to have worked well, or at all, legend still persists that a slug of gold will abolish the desire for a slug of hooch. Even as late as the early nineteenth century, gold was used in the United States as a cure for syphilis and snakebite. In Eastern countries, powdered gold is held in high esteem as an aphrodisiac.

Gold is still used in modern medicine, though more sparingly. It has been part of the pharmacopeia for rheumatoid arthritis, though less is used than formerly as recent studies have cast doubt on gold's value for the purpose. Gold instruments are still used in surgery and for acupuncture. Radioactive gold (Au-198) is sometimes given to patients suffering from leukemia and malignant lymphoma. It also serves as a diagnostic tool for liver scans and bone marrow tumors.

Tiny gold particles, each about 20-millionths of an inch across, are used as markers in electron microscopy in science and medicine. Body temperature can now be measured from thermal energy radiated from the eardrum by inserting a small gold-lined pipe into the ear cavity. The gold reflects heat from the eardrum and does not lose heat to the measuring device.

According to the Gold Institute, the laboratory coupling of gold particles with DNA has produced new microscopic structures that open new avenues of research and treatment in biochemistry, genetics, and medicine. The gold-DNA combination can help to create new biological structures on a nanometer scale (one-billionth of a meter) that may be a valuable tool for quick detection of bacteria, viruses, and other disease-causing microorganisms. This technique may, in the future, be used in electronics, allowing parts to be reduced to the molecular level. According to Chad Mirkin, co-researcher in the project, the spherical gold particles, only thirteen nanometers in diameter, are ruby red when suspended in water and maintain their color when attached to certain strands of DNA. But when that combination of gold and DNA joins with a second strand of complementary DNA, the gold particles clump, changing the color of the solution to purple; then as particles settle, the color fades to pinkish gray. The color change allows quick, colormetric diagnosis. Although such uses may help fight disease, they will not deplete the world's supply of gold by very much, as they require nanoscopic quantities.

Today gold is used less often in the Western world for tooth replacement, not only because of its high price, but because less obvious replacements can now be made of porcelain and other substances that, like gold, do not react with body fluids. Only those who want gold teeth need have them. Even so, dentistry used, worldwide, 2.1 million troy ounces (almost 70 tons) of gold in 1995. Of this, 310,000 ounces were put into teeth in the United States.

Gold has many uses, or proposed uses, in the kitchen. A good frying pan should heat evenly and impart no taste; therefore, the columnist L. M. Boyd suggested, gold would be the best. (It might be difficult to hold the heavy pan while one dished out the contents.) Although gold is soluble only with difficulty, the addition of gold to food has been increasing in popularity. The Swiss Gold coffee filter, made to fit most coffee makers, is a 24-karat gold-plated reusable filter claimed by its manufacturer to give coffee a richer taste.

In 1988 the *Free China Journal* reported that in Japan an old Chinese custom of adding gold to food to clear poisons from the system and to stimulate beauty has gained popularity. One Japanese restaurant alone sprinkled eight kilograms of gold yearly on the food it served. Gold for food should be 23 or 24 karat, according to a newspaper interview with Marty Horowitz, partner in Gold Leaf Framemakers of Santa Fe, New Mexico. Gold less pure contains too much copper and silver. Horowitz celebrated his fortieth birthday in November 1989 by gilding his birthday cake.

FIGURE 55. Large optics diamond turning machine at Lawrence Livermore National Laboratory. Gold was used to coat telescope mirrors to give more precise images.

A recipe for chocolate truffles uses three pounds of semisweet chocolate, a cup and a half of crème fraîche, five tablespoons of unsalted butter, three tablespoons of cognac, half a tablespoon of vegetable shortening, and twelve three-inch-square sheets of 23-karat gold leaf. The truffles are decorated with the gold leaf before being served.

Fortunately, gold does not have to be eaten to be enjoyed. A new toothpaste on the market in 1997 lists gold as one of its ingredients, although its purpose is not stated. Monarchs the world over have favored gold tableware. Aztec nobles of Mexico served chocolate in gold cups to one another. At a White House banquet in October 1997, hosted by President Bill Clinton to honor the Chinese president Jiang Zemin, tables were swathed in gold damask and set with Eisenhower gold charger plates. On the menu were Yukon Gold potatoes.

Earthly gold, whatever its origin in the universe, is now hurtling through space. Because gold does not react with its environment (unless it is near cyanide or one of the halogens), it can be relied on to maintain its integrity. And because it has excellent electrical conductivity and does not tarnish, gold makes superb electrical switches, contacts, and connectors. The *Galileo* spacecraft, which explored Jupiter in 1995, has gold-plated molybdenum wire mesh for its textilelike antennas because the wires must maintain good contact to send the clearest possible information back

FIGURE 56. *Galileo* spacecraft. *Galileo* explored Jupiter in 1995 and sent fascinating information back to Earth through its gold-plated molybdenum wire mesh antennas. Gold, which has superior electrical conductivity, was used in many places in the spacecraft.

to Earth. *Galileo* is a dual-spin satellite—that is, the main part of the craft spins while the antenna continues to point toward Earth. Electrical connections composed of gold-coated wire brushes are attached to one part of the satellite and brush against gold-covered grooves in the other. They obtain electrical current from solar arrays.

Because gold has a large atomic size, tiny hydrogen atoms do not flow through it. Gold coatings on the impeller of the space shuttle fuel pumps prevent hydrogen fuel from passing into the impellers themselves. If the gold were not there, the hydrogen would quickly make the impellers brittle, and they would shatter long before the 113 tons of hydrogen fuel used to blast the satellite into orbit is used up.

The temperature in the space shuttle nozzle is a blazing 3,300°C (6,666°F)—far above the 1,400°C (2,500°F) melting point of the metals in its lining. To keep the nozzle from melting, the liquid hydrogen is carried through four miles of tubing brazed to the lining of the nozzle. The braze is a 35 percent gold alloy, used because it is the most tenacious and long-lasting alloy. And because ordinary lubricants evaporate in the vacuum of outer space, durable gold is used to lubricate gears and slip rings.

Gold, which can reflect infrared rays better than any other metal, was used in the space shuttle to keep the engine's heat from melting its walls, and in the *Magellan* space orbiter to keep the electronic components from overheating in the direct rays of the sun. Even commercial and military aircraft use gold in their windshields and windows to reflect the intense solar radiation away from pilot and passenger when flying, and to clear frost off the windows on the ground. To prevent electromagnetic interference, gold is used to coat boxes containing electronic equipment on military and commercial aircraft. When the spacecraft *Pioneer* left the ground in 1972, it sported a gold anodized aluminum plaque on its side. The late astronomer Carl Sagan and his colleague, Frank Drake, together with Sagan's former wife, Linda, an artist, created the plaque, which shows a nude male and female, a reproduction of the solar system, and other clues designed to help inhabitants of other worlds to pinpoint *Pioneer*'s earthly origin. Eventually *Pioneer*'s feeble signal ceased being heard, so the spacecraft was officially retired in March 1997, having traveled 6.2 billion miles. Retired or not, it has now sped past the solar system, carrying earthly gold with it.

The Mars landing of NASA's *Pathfinder* on July 4, 1997, was made possible by a gold shield protecting it and gold electronics controlling the landing. Even the intrepid little roving vehicle *Sojourner*, which the world watched nosing its way around Martian rocks, used gold electronics to make a detailed report of the planet's chemical composition and send 3-D photographs back to NASA scientists.

Even peering into space uses gold. The twin Keck telescopes on Mauna Loa, Hawaii, made at the University of California, Santa Cruz, each use a twenty-one-inch gold-coated secondary mirror to gather the reflection of infrared radiation from outer space. The new mirrors give images two or three times more precise than earlier telescopes gave.

The superior electrical conductivity of gold makes it vital to the electronics industry for switch contacts, connectors, and circuits. In the late 1970s one of the geologists at the Menlo Park regional office of the U.S. Geological Survey in California's Silicon Valley tested the sludge at the local sewage plant and found it to contain considerable gold, washed into the sewers when electronics firms cleaned up. It was richer "ore" than Nevada's Comstock Lode had boasted. Soon there were several offers to mine the sewage, and electronics companies put in gold traps.

Altogether, the electronics industry—not just computers, but telephones, audio equipment, camcorders, and other instruments—consumed, worldwide, 6.1 million troy ounces of gold in 1994. The U.S. share was 1.5 million.

Architects, too, have found uses for gold. Because gold is so malleable, one ounce can be beaten into a sheet that will cover one hundred square feet. The Denver, Colorado, capitol is coated with gold leaf, the first coat, twenty-five ounces, donated in 1906 by the gold mining industry of Cripple Creek. The Oregon capitol boasts a statue, "Pioneer," on top, which is covered in gold leaf. Gold leaf, properly applied, will last outdoors for more than twenty-five years without retouching; inside, indefinitely. The California capitol also has a gold dome, but it was done by brush gold plating, an electroplating technique that uses an electrified paintbrush. The same method can be used to plate statues.

To conserve energy, gold is used in windows on Earth as well as in space. The gold helps block heat from the sun while admitting light. Air-conditioning costs are reduced, as is glare. The Mirage Hotel in Las Vegas, Nevada, is glazed with 350,000 square feet of gold-coated glass. Developers of a new office complex in Dallas, Texas, credit gold reflective glass with saving 31,400 kilowatts of energy on an average summer day—enough to light homes in fifty city blocks every night for a week. In winter gold reflects internal heat back into the structure, thus retaining warmth. In Toronto, Ontario, the new headquarters of the Royal Bank of Canada has more than a million square feet of gold glass. The 27,000 windows used 2,500 troy ounces of gold.

Depending on how it is done, one ounce of gold will coat between 400 and 1,000 square feet of glass. Gold glass is two to three times more costly than noninsulating glass, but the cost is quickly recovered as gold glass is the most energy-efficient glass on the market. Gold is also used for color in stained-glass windows.

Inside buildings, gold-plated plumbing fixtures have come into vogue. They remain lustrous as long as harsh abrasives and chemicals are not used, and are a necessity in hot tubs, where other fixtures rapidly deteriorate.

Gold has many scientific uses. It can enhance fingerprints. Tiny particles of gold 100 millionths of an inch in diameter are attracted to the protein in fingerprints, making them more easily photographed. The method works on plastic, glass, and metal. In one case, the Secret Service detected prints on black adhesive tape used to wrap a bomb. In another scientific use, a "gene gun" shoots gold pellets so tiny they penetrate a cell without damaging it, giving scientists the opportunity to alter gene structures—to improve wheat, for example. The internal cavities of lasers, which have many scientific, medical, and commercial uses, are coated with gold to reflect and concentrate a powerful burst of light energy.

Athletes "go for the gold" in the Olympics and other sporting events; actors and actresses vie for Oscars, Emmys, Tonys, and other golden awards. All manner of

FIGURE 57. Mirage Hotel, Las Vegas, Nevada. The thousands of windows in the hotel are glazed with gold-coated glass.

contests involve gold medals and trophies. Most of these are not solid gold, merely gold plated, but the winning of one is a golden event.

World-class flautists Jean-Pierre Rampal and James Galway both have gold flutes, and in 1996 the Hohner Company issued a gold harmonica in celebration of the hundredth anniversary of its Marine Band model. Ian Fleming used a gold-plated typewriter to create his best-sellers. Anyone can order another writing instrument, a solid gold fountain pen encrusted with 4,810 diamonds for a mere $120,000. The pen, called the Meisterstück Solitaire Royal, is manufactured by Montblanc. Mont Blanc, the mountain, is 4,810 meters (15,780 feet) high, hence the number of diamonds.

Possibly the most beautiful and valuable piece of gold artwork in the world is Tutankhamen's beaten gold bust. Tutankhamen was buried in gold coffins, one inside the other; Alexander the Great was also buried in a gold coffin. Alexander's coffin has disappeared, but Tutankhamen's may still be seen. An ordinary person, provided his or her relatives have the money, can also be interred in a sarcophagus of polished gold decorated with a replica of King Tut's mask—several of these expensive caskets have been sold. At the National Funeral Directors Association trade show in Oakland, California, in October 1997, one firm exhibited what it called "the world's smallest casket" in 18-karat gold.

A solid gold bathtub, appraised at $5 million, was said to belong to a high-ranking official in a former Nigerian government. When he took it to his vacation home in England, the insurers would not insure the tub. They suggested it be left in a bank, not a common place to take a bath. It would take resourceful thieves to steal a heavy gold bathtub. A Japanese hotel, according to Ripley's "Believe It or Not," has a 22-karat, 313-pound gold tub for its guests' pleasure. It is not in the bank. In 1989 Japanese department stores offered numerous gold items for sale, including gold golf clubs and a gold refrigerator.

Throughout history gold has been used lavishly in sacred buildings and for other religious purposes. For example, in Peru the holy temples were sheeted with gold, as was Solomon's temple in ancient Israel. The six-story sacred stupa of the Great Fifth (the fifth Dalai Lama), built in the seventeenth century, was constructed of sandalwood covered with more than eight thousand pounds of gold. It was one of eight golden stupas that were the tombs of Dalai Lamas in the Tibetan capital of Lhasa. The sacred object of highest monetary value is the fifteenth-century gold Buddha in a temple in Bangkok, Thailand. It is ten feet tall and weighs about six tons (175,000 troy ounces). At $100 an ounce, the gold would be worth $17.5 million; at $800, $140 million. The Buddha is covered with plaster, and the gold beneath the plaster was not discovered until 1954.

Gold opened up the West, beckoning all who wanted adventure, riches, or a better life. It propelled California directly into statehood, bypassing the slow steps other states had to take. Gold made California a place of legend, where all could hope for wealth and glamor.

Like the Sirens of old, gold sings a seductive song, enticing us weak humans even to our deaths. Gold charms us into thinking that with it we are safe from the vicissitudes of life. Some say it weaves a magic spell that mere humans cannot break. It gleams and glistens, blinding our eyes to its dark side, to it as the author of immeasurable human misery, yet we continue to follow after it. It is fireproof, yet it fuels our desires. It is indestructible, yet it can destroy the lives of its seekers.

To the miner, gold is a livelihood; to the prospector, a vision; to the investor, profit; to the goldsmith, a metal of promise and a thing of beauty. To the alchemist, it was a route to everlasting life. To the newlywed, it is a symbol of eternity; to the dispossessed, security; to the homeless, asylum.

Yet gold itself is none of these. It is merely a metal, like tin, or lead, or iron. Gold, though it may be a maker of kings and a seducer of saints, is neither friend nor enemy. It is the reflector of our dreams.

Appendix

TABLE A1. *Properties of Gold*		
Chemical properties	**Crystallography**	**Mineralogy**
Chemical symbol: Au	*Crystal system:* Cubic	*Hardness:* 2.5–3
Atomic number: 79	*Strongest diffraction lines:*	*Cleavage:* None
Atomic weight: 196.9665	2.355 (100)	*Crystal habit:* Crystals octa-
Group in periodic table: IB	2.039 (52)	hedral, dodecahedral, or
Density at 20°C (68°F): 18.88;	1.230 (36)	cubic. Commonly dendritic,
at 0°C: 19.297 (measured),	*Lattice constant:* $a = 4.0781$	arborescent, reticulated, or
19.309 (calculated)	*Optical constant:* $N = 0.366$	spongy. Also occurs as massive
Boiling point: 3,080°C (5,576°F)	(sodium)	nuggets, flattened grains, or
Melting point: 1,064°C		scales. Sometimes twinned
(1,948°F)		on {111} faces.
Valence: 1–3		*Color:* Yellow, also silver-white
Radioactive isotopes: mass num-		to reddish owing to
bers 186–196 and 198–203		impurities. Opaque. Metallic.
		Streak golden yellow.
		Fracture: Hackly. Malleable and
		ductile.
		Occurrence: Found in hydro-
		thermal veins, associated with
		pyrite and other sulfides; also
		in conglomerate, and in placer
		deposits throughout the
		world.

Name	Found at	Date	Weight (*troy oz.*)	Remarks
Carson Hill mass	Carson Hill, Tuolumne County	1854	2,340	54" x 5½". Taken from lode mine, not placer. Valued at $43,534 at the time. (California's largest gold mass)
Monumental gold mass	Monumental mine, Sierra Buttes, Sierra City	1869	1,893 (?)	
Monumental gold mass	Monumental mine, Sierra Buttes, Sierra City	1860	1,596	Lode gold mass. Was on exhibit at Woodward's Gardens in old San Francisco for many years
Bonanza mass	Bonanza mine, Sonora	1850	1,500	Mass of gold in lode, not placer
Golden Destiny	Camp Corona, Tuolumne County	1853	1,248 (incl. matrix)	Oliver Martin discovered while digging grave for partner. Gold in quartz.
Rainbow mass	Alleghany, Sierra County	1870	1,200	Mass of gold in lode. Not placer
McClellan	Mokelumne Hill	1852	1,200	Placer nugget (California's largest nugget)
French Gulch	French Gulch, Tuolumne County	18—	1,176	Quartz boulder in placer
Monumental quartz mass	Monumental mine, Sierra County	1869	1,140	Found in vein
Wood's Creek	Sonora district, Tuolumne County	1848 (?)	900	
Sonora	Big Bonanza mine, Sonora	1890	800	Found in quartz vein. Not a placer nugget
Weaverville	Weaverville, Trinity County	1891	800	Placer nugget
Siamese Twin	French Ravine, Sierra County	1854	784	Two nuggets, one 604, one 160 oz. connected by ligament of gold
Cook	Alleghany, Sierra County	1855	780	Placer nugget
—	Jamestown	—	720	
Diltz	Diltz mine, Mariposa County	1934	685	Lode gold mass. Broke knee of miner who helped discover it
Willard	Magalia ancient river channel of the Feather River	1858	648	Placer nugget
—	Knapp's Ranch, Columbia district, Tuolumne County	1850s	600	
Watermelon Seed	Melones, Calaveras County	1853	590	Many placer nuggets of watermelon seed shape found; town named for them

continued ☞

Name	Found at	Date	Weight (*troy oz.*)	Remarks
—	French Ravine, Sierra County	1855	532	
—	French Ravine, Sierra County	1855	426	
Pilot Hill	Eldorado County	1867	426	
—	Sullivan Creek, Columbia district, Tuolumne County	1849	408	
Gold Hill	Gold Hill, near Columbia, Tuolumne County	1849	360 or 380	
Holden Chipsa nugget	Sonora district, Tuolumne County	1850s	336	
Summitville mass	Summitville, Rio Grande County, Colorado	1908	316	A large "gold boulder" weighing 81.43 pounds. On display at Denver Museum, Natural History
—	Mokelumne River, Amador County	1848	300	
—	Downieville, Sierra County	1850	300	
Carolina	North Carolina	1803 (?)	300 (?)	North Carolina's largest (?)
Wheeler Mountain	Osceola, Nevada	1870	288	Nevada's largest. Another nugget found in 1877 said to weigh 408 oz.
Polar Star	Dutch Flat district, Placer County	1876	288	Mass of gold in quartz, but mostly gold
Hornblower	Boulder Field, Alaska	1897	About 285	Alaska's largest gold mass. Said to be worth $5,700. Found in quartz mass
—	Columbia district, Tuolumne County	1853	283	Mass of gold in quartz, but mostly gold
—	Little Mule Creek, Trinity County	1870	277	In two nuggets
Minnesota	Alleghany district, Sierra County	1850s (?)	266	
French (Spring Gulch)	Near Columbia, Tuolumne County	1850s	250 (?)	Next day the finder, a Frenchman, went insane, sent to asylum at Stockton. French consul sold nugget, sent money to his family in France
—	Michigan Bluff, Placer County	1864	226	

continued ☞

Name	Found at	Date	Weight (*troy oz.*)	Remarks
Fricot	Grit claim, Spanish Dry Diggings, Eldorado County	1865	204.1	Cluster of gold crystals shown at Paris World's Fair
—	Remington Hill	1855	186	
Ruby	Ruby mine, Sierra County	1891	183	Found in mine 300' below surface
Anvil Creek	Near Nome, Alaska	—	182	Largest Alaskan placer nugget
Snow Gulch	Snow Gulch, on Little Blackfoot River, Montana	1873	176	Montana's largest. Placer nugget found in tough, yellow clay 12' above bedrock
—	Live Yankee Claim, Alleghany district, Sierra County	1854 – 1862	170	Twelve nuggets, largest 170 ounces, smallest 30 ounces
Hanging Lamp	Kittitas County, Washington	—	168	Washington's largest
Breckenridge	Breckenridge, Colorado	—	156	Colorado's largest placer nugget
Sunnyside	Sunnyside mine, near Johnsville, Plumas County	1921	150 (?)	Placer gold in an old channel
—	Smith's Flat, Sierra County	1864	140	
Columbia	Columbia, Tuolumne County	1902	133	
North Carolina	Crawford, North Carolina	1895	120	North Carolina's largest
Dilman	Mojave Desert, San Bernardino County	1877	108	From desert placer diggings
—	Remington Hill, Nevada County	1869 (?)	107	
—	Little Grizzly Diggings, Sierra County	1869	107	
Tom's Baby	Farncomb Hill, near Breckenridge, Colorado	1887	102	Said to have weighed 160 oz. before breaking. Newspaper reports gave weight of larger piece at 136 oz. On display at Denver Museum, Natural History
—	Oregon claim, Alleghany district, Sierra County	1856 – 1862	100	Largest of several nuggets weighed 100 oz.
—	Crawford, North Carolina	1895	96	
—	Hope claim, Alleghany district, Sierra County	—	94	
—	Campo Seco, Calaveras County	1854	93	

continued ☞

Name	Found at	Date	Weight (*troy oz.*)	Remarks
—	French Ravine, Sierra County	1860	93	
Horse's Hoof	Eldorado Creek, Yukon Territory, Canada	1900	84	Canada's largest. True nugget. Resembled horse's hoof
—	Plumas County	1881	81	
—	Smith's Flat, Sierra County	1861	80	
Snow Creek	British Columbia, Canada	1877	77	
Jerseyman	San Jacinto Mountains, San Bernardino County	1894	70	From desert mountains
—	Lowell Hill, Nevada County	1865	58	
La Paz	Yuma, Arizona	—	57	Arizona's largest. Placer nugget
—	Hudson Gulch near Coloma	—	54	
—	Ruby mine, Alleghany district, Sierra County	1930s, 1940s	52	Several nuggets, largest 52 oz.
Miser's Face	Swaub, Washington	—	51	
Gaarden gold mass	German Ridge mine, Angels Camp	1933	50	Won prize at California State Fair in 1933
Lykkegaard	Atlin, British Columbia, Canada	1936	42	In ancient river channel
McDowell	McDowell Gulch, Oregon	1904	25 (?)	Oregon's largest
Penn Hill	Bulgar placer, Park County, Colorado	1937	11.95	Colorado's largest nugget. Found at 12,500 feet. Said to be North American nugget found at highest elevation. On display at Denver Museum, Natural History

Note: All locations cited are in California, unless otherwise indicated. Nuggets and gold masses are listed separately, although miners often did not differentiate. Nuggets are lumps of gold from placer deposits, worn by streams. Masses are chunks of gold, often directly from a vein, that are untouched by erosion. They are often mixed with quartz. No doubt many nuggets and masses have been left out. The ones listed, particularly those dating from the days of the forty-niners, may be mostly hearsay; but certainly many were found and sold for their gold without being cataloged at all, even by the lucky finder. More recent finds have been carefully cataloged and weighed, and their authenticity vouched for.

TABLE A3. *Some Gold Conversions*

1 troy ounce =
  20 pennyweight
  480 grains
  31.1 grams
  1.1 ounces avoirdupois
1 troy pound =
  5,760 grains
  373.24 grams
  12 troy ounces
  0.82 pounds avoirdupois
  0.37 kilogram

1 metric ton (plural: tonnes) =
  1,000,000 grams
  32,154 troy ounces
1 avoirdupois ounce =
  28.35 grams
  0.91 troy ounce
1 avoirdupois ton (short ton; 2,000 pounds) =
  29,170 troy ounces (about 1 cubic foot of gold)

Note: 1 cubic foot of gold is worth $3 million at $100 gold; $24 million at $800 gold.

TABLE A4. *California Gold Production (values in dollars)*

Year	Troy ounces	Value at that time	Value when gold is $100 an ounce	Value when gold is $800 an ounce
1848	11,866	$245,301	$1,186,600	$9,492,800
1849	491,072	10,151,060	49,107,200	392,857,600
1850	1,996,586	41,273,106	199,658,600	1,597,268,800
1851	3,673,512	75,938,232	367,351,200	2,938,809,600
1852	3,932,631	81,294,700	393,263,100	3,146,104,800
1853	3,270,803	67,613,487	327,080,300	2,616,642,400
1854	3,358,867	69,433,931	335,886,700	2,687,093,600
1855	2,684,106	55,485,345	268,410,600	2,147,284,800
1856	2,782,018	57,509,411	278,201,800	2,225,614,400
1857	2,110,513	43,628,172	211,051,300	1,688,410,400
1858	2,253,846	46,591,140	225,384,600	1,803,076,800
1859	2,217,829	45,846,599	221,782,900	1,774,263,200
1860	2,133,104	45,846,599	213,310,400	1,706,483,200
1861	2,026,187	41,884,995	202,618,700	1,620,949,600
1862	1,879,595	38,854,668	187,959,500	1,503,676,000
1863	1,136,897	23,501,736	113,689,700	909,517,600
1864	1,164,455	24,071,423	116,445,500	931,564,000
1865	867,405	17,930,858	86,740,500	693,924,000
1866	828,367	17,123,867	82,836,700	662,693,600
1867	883,591	18,265,452	88,359,100	706,872,800
1868	849,265	17,555,867	84,926,500	679,412,000
1869	881,830	18,229,044	88,183,000	705,464,000
1870	844,537	17,458,133	84,453,700	675,629,600
1871	845,493	17,477,885	84,549,300	676,394,400
1872	748,951	15,482,194	74,895,100	599,160,800
1873	726,554	15,019,210	72,655,400	581,243,200
1874	835,186	17,264,836	83,518,600	668,148,800
1875	816,377	16,876,009	81,637,700	653,101,600
1876	755,169	15,610,723	75,516,900	604,135,200
1877	798,249	16,501,268	79,824,900	638,599,200
1878	911,343	18,839,141	91,134,300	729,074,400
1879	949,439	19,626,654	94,943,900	759,551,200
1880	968,986	20,030,761	96,898,600	775,188,800
1881	929,920	19,223,155	92,992,000	743,936,000
1882	829,458	17,146,416	82,945,800	663,566,400
1883	1,176,329	24,316,873	117,632,900	941,063,200
1884	657,900	13,600,000	65,790,000	526,320,000
1885	612,478	12,661,044	61,247,800	489,982,400

continued ☞

Year	Troy ounces	Value at that time	Value when gold is $100 an ounce	Value when gold is $800 an ounce
1886	711,911	14,716,506	71,191,100	569,528,800
1887	657,349	13,388,614	65,734,900	525,879,200
1888	616,000	12,751,000	61,600,000	492,800,000
1889	542,425	11,212,913	54,242,500	433,940,000
1890	595,486	12,309,793	59,548,600	476,388,800
1891	615,759	12,728,869	61,575,900	492,607,200
1892	608,166	12,571,900	60,816,600	486,532,800
1893	606,564	12,538,780	60,656,400	485,251,200
1894	670,636	13,863,282	67,063,600	536,508,800
1895	741,798	15,334,317	74,179,800	593,438,400
1896	831,158	17,181,562	83,115,800	664,926,400
1897	767,779	15,871,401	76,777,900	614,223,200
1898	769,476	15,906,478	76,947,600	615,580,800
1899	741,881	15,336,031	74,188,100	593,504,800
1900	767,390	15,863,355	76,739,000	613,912,000
1901	821,845	16,989,044	82,184,500	657,476,000
1902	818,037	16,910,320	81,803,700	654,429,600
1903	788,544	16,300,653	78,854,400	630,835,200
1904	901,484	18,633,676	90,148,400	721,187,200
1905	914,217	18,898,545	91,421,700	731,373,600
1906	906,182	18,732,452	90,618,200	724,945,600
1907	809,214	16,727,928	80,921,400	647,371,200
1908	907,590	18,761,559	90,759,000	726,072,000
1909	979,007	20,237,870	97,900,700	783,205,600
1910	953,734	19,715,440	95,373,400	762,987,200
1911	954,870	19,738,908	95,487,000	763,896,000
1912	953,540	19,713,478	95,354,000	762,832,000
1913	987,187	20,406,958	98,718,700	789,749,600
1914	999,113	20,653,496	99,911,300	799,290,400
1915	1,085,646	22,442,296	108,564,600	868,516,800
1916	1,035,745	21,410,741	103,574,500	828,596,000
1917	971,733	20,087,504	97,173,300	777,386,400
1918	799,588	16,528,953	79,958,800	639,670,400
1919	807,667	16,695,955	80,766,700	646,133,600
1920	692,297	14,311,043	69,229,700	553,837,600
1921	759,721	15,704,822	75,972,100	607,776,800
1922	709,678	14,670,346	70,967,800	567,742,400
1923	647,210	13,379,012	64,721,000	517,768,000
1924	636,140	13,150,175	63,614,000	508,912,000

continued ☞

Year	Troy ounces	Value at that time	Value when gold is $100 an ounce	Value when gold is $800 an ounce
1925	632,035	13,065,330	63,203,500	505,628,000
1926	576,789	11,923,481	57,678,900	461,431,200
1927	564,586	11,671,018	56,458,600	451,668,800
1928	521,740	10,785,315	52,174,000	417,392,000
1929	412,479	8,526,703	41,247,900	329,983,200
1930	457,200	9,451,162	45,720,000	365,760,000
1931	523,135	10,814,162	52,313,500	418,508,000
1932	569,167	11,765,726	56,916,700	455,333,600
1933	613,579	15,683,075	61,357,900	490,863,200
1934	719,064	25,131,284	71,906,400	575,251,200
1935	890,430	31,165,050	89,043,000	712,344,000
1936	1,077,442	37,710,470	107,744,200	861,953,600
1937	1,174,578	41,110,230	117,457,800	939,662,400
1938	1,311,129	45,889,515	131,112,900	1,048,903,200
1939	1,435,264	50,234,240	143,526,400	1,148,211,200
1940	1,455,671	50,948,585	145,567,100	1,164,536,800
1941	1,408,793	49,307,755	140,879,300	1,127,034,400
1942	847,997	29,679,895	84,799,700	678,397,600
1943	148,328	5,191,480	14,832,800	118,662,400
1944	117,373	4,108,055	11,737,300	93,898,400
1945	147,938	5,177,830	14,793,800	118,350,400
1946	356,824	12,488,840	35,682,400	285,459,200
1947	431,415	15,099,525	43,141,500	345,132,000
1948	428,473	14,751,555	42,847,300	342,778,400
1949	417,231	14,603,085	41,723,100	333,784,800
1950	412,118	14,424,130	41,211,800	329,694,400
1951	339,738	11,890,620	33,973,800	271,790,400
1952	258,176	9,036,160	25,817,600	206,540,800
1953	234,591	8,210,685	23,459,100	187,672,800
1954	237,888	8,326,010	23,788,800	190,310,400
1955	251,737	8,810,795	25,173,700	201,389,600
1956	193,816	6,783,560	19,381,600	155,052,800
1957	170,885	5,890,975	17,088,500	136,708,000
1958	185,400	6,489,000	18,540,000	148,320,000
1959	146,141	5,114,935	14,614,100	116,912,800
1960	123,713	4,329,955	12,371,300	98,970,400
1961	97,648	3,417,680	9,764,800	78,118,400
1962	106,278	3,719,520	10,627,800	85,022,400
1963	86,867	3,040,345	8,686,700	69,493,600

continued ☞

Year	Troy ounces	Value at that time	Value when gold is $100 an ounce	Value when gold is $800 an ounce
1964	71,028	2,485,980	7,102,800	56,822,400
1965	62,885	2,220,975	6,288,500	50,308,000
1966	64,764	2,266,740	6,476,400	51,811,200
1967	40,570	1,420,000	4,057,000	32,456,000
1968	15,682	616,000	1,568,200	12,545,600
1969	7,950	335,000	795,000	6,360,000
1970	4,999	200,000	499,900	3,999,200
1971	2,966	122,000	296,600	2,372,800
1972	3,974	233,000	397,400	3,179,200
1973	3,647	357,000	364,700	2,917,600
1974	5,049	807,000	504,900	4,039,200
1975	9,606	1,551,000	960,600	7,684,800
1976	10,392	1,302,000	1,039,200	8,313,600
1977	5,704	846,000	570,400	4,563,200
1978	7,480	1,448,000	748,000	5,984,000
1979	3,195	982,000	319,500	2,556,000
1980	3,651	2,236,000	365,100	2,920,800
1981	6,271	2,882,000	627,100	5,016,800
1982	10,547	3,965,000	1,054,700	8,437,600
1983	38,443	16,300,000	3,844,300	30,754,400
1984	85,858	30,965,000	8,585,800	68,686,400
1985	223,097	72,507,000	22,309,700	178,477,600
1986	425,617	156,729,000	42,561,700	340,493,600
1987	602,605	269,937,000	60,260,500	482,084,000
1988	721,527	316,246,000	72,152,700	577,221,600
1989	1,051,310	366,595,000	105,131,000	84,248,000
1990	951,887	368,300,000	102,882,000	823,056,000
1991	977,511	355,125,000	97,751,100	782,008,800
1992	1,071,750	369,797,000	107,175,000	857,400,048
1993	977,511	369,797,000	97,751,100	782,008,800
1994	967,700	372,000,000	96,770,000	774,160,000
1995	842,300	326,000,000	84,230,000	673,840,000
1996	835,900	326,000,000	83,590,000	668,720,000
Total	116,121,513	$6,143,265,492	$11,619,844,600	$89,132,831,027

Note: Early-day figures are estimates, and figures since 1970 may not have accounted for all production by recreational miners. The U.S. Bureau of Mines ceased trying to keep track of small-scale placer mine production in 1994, so recent figures reflect only major mines. To figure the value for any year in terms of today's prices, multiply the $100 value by the factor for the daily gold price. For example, if the price quoted is $400, multiply the $100 value by 4; if $380, multiply by 3.8. The $800 price is shown for comparison. In the 1980s, gold sold for as much as $850 a troy ounce.

Here is a sampling of places to go to see gold and the remains of the search for it. Since California is truly a "golden" state, this list by no means exhausts the possibilities. There is much more to see in California—many more mines, many more sites, many more museums.

Throughout the Sierran and Klamath gold country, as well as in the southern deserts, the effects of gold mining may be seen in lonely head frames, tailing piles, and rusty machinery. Piles of rock along rivers attest to dredge mining; the pits of old hydraulic mines still dot the mountain landscape. But more poignant than these are the towns that once held gold rushers and miners: the relics of hundreds of mining camps, some deserted, others blossoming into modern bustling towns, dot the California countryside from Mexico to Oregon, from the Pacific to Nevada. Only a few of these are listed here, but coming upon them, like the remains of roofless mining buildings on the John Muir Trail, or the white walls near the crest of a Sierran pass, all that remains of a once-hopeful mining town, is like finding treasure in seashore sand.

Most museums in California have some gold connection, exhibiting gold or gold-mining equipment or belongings of those who sought gold. In some mining towns, historic houses, special exhibits, and small museums are sponsored by local historical societies and other groups. A few are listed here, but most county and city museums have exhibits related to gold. Almost all state and national parks in California have gold mines or gold relics.

California is a major player in the gold-mining industry of today. Besides seeing the gold-mining memorabilia of yesteryear, one can visit operating mines (with permission), some of which have even installed self-guided trails.

What	Where	What's There
Amador City hotel and museum	Amador City	Gold relics
Amador County Museum	Jackson 225 Church St.	Working model of Kennedy mine
Angels Camp	Angels Camp	Began as early mining town; some old buildings remain
Angels Camp Museum	Angels Camp 753 S. Main St.	Early mining equipment, wagons, minerals. Carriage house with horse-drawn vehicles from gold rush days
Anza Borrego Desert State Park Visitor Center	Anza Borrego Desert State Park	Geology, mineral, fossil exhibits
B. C. Baker Memorial Museum	Coalinga 297 W. Elm Ave.	Artifacts on mining, fossils, minerals
Bidwell Mansion State Historic Park	Chico 525 The Esplanade	John Bidwell's mansion
Big Basin Redwoods State Park, Natural History Museum	Boulder Creek 21600 Big Basin Way	Natural history and geology of Santa Cruz Mountains

continued

What	Where	What's There
Bodie State Historic Park	Bodie, 20 miles southeast of Bridgeport via U.S. Highway 395 and State Highway 270	170 buildings from gold-mining times. Museum in park
Bradford Street Park	Sonora Bradford Street at State Highway 49	Mining equipment from gold rush times: arrastra, stamp mill, Pelton wheel
Calaveras County Historical Museum and Archives	San Andreas 30 N. Main St.	Gold mementos and mining artifacts
California Academy of Sciences	San Francisco Golden Gate Park	Hall of gems and minerals
California Historical Society	San Francisco, near Moscone Center	Manuscripts, maps, documents, exhibits
California Living Museum	Bakersfield 14000 Alfred Harrell Highway	Fossil, geologic exhibits
California State Capitol	Sacramento	Gold-covered dome
California State Library	Sacramento 914 Capitol Mall	Files of early-day newspapers and manuscripts; exhibits
California State Mining and Mineral Museum	Mariposa Mariposa County Fairgrounds	Gold in nuggets, crystals, and replicas; gems and minerals; model of stamp mill, walk-through replica of mine. (Formerly in Ferry Building, San Francisco)
Castle Mountains gold mine	Along Nevada border north of Needles	Operating mine
Chapman's Gem and Mineral Museum	Fortuna 4 miles off U.S. Highway 101	Fossils, gems, minerals, petrified wood
Cherokee	Cherokee (ghost town) On Cherokee Road, Butte County, 12 miles north of Oroville off Highway 70	Scars of hydraulic mine; relics of mining days in small museum
Chico Museum	Chico 2d and Salem Sts.	Artifacts; Chinese temple
Chinese Historical Society of America	San Francisco 650 Commercial St.	Exhibits on role of Chinese in settling the West
Coloma	*See Marshall Gold Discovery State Historic Park*	
Columbia State Historic Park	Columbia	Town restored to appearance in gold rush days. Gold mine tours, gold panning. Outdoor exhibit has hydraulic monitor, shows bedrock after auriferous gravels were washed away

continued ☞

What	Where	What's There
Coulterville	Highway 49, Mariposa County	Gold rush buildings, relics
Crocker Art Museum	Sacramento	19th-century collection of paintings, prints, artwork
Death Valley National Park	Death Valley Furnace Creek Visitor Center	Geology and natural history of Death Valley
Diablo Valley College Museum	Pleasant Hill 321 Golf Club Rd.	Mineral exhibit
Discovery Center	Fresno 1944 N. Winery Ave.	Natural history museum
Discovery Museum	Sacramento 101 I St.	Mother Lode gold collection
Downieville Museum	Downieville Main St.	Operating miniature model of stamp mill; collection of horse snowshoes
Eagle Gold Mine	Julian (west of Anza-Borrego State Park) Eagle Mining Company North end of C St.	Guided tour through gold mine
Eastern California Museum	Independence 155 Grant St.	Restored blacksmith shop, assay office; antique mining equipment
El Dorado County Historical Museum	Placerville 100 Placerville Dr. in El Dorado County Fairgrounds	Mining equipment; exhibits of gold rush days
Empire Mine State Historic Park	Grass Valley 10791 E. Empire St.	One of California's richest mines, produced 6 million ounces of gold. Mine has 367 miles of workings and is over 11,000 feet deep on incline; absolute depth well below sea level. Owner's "cottage," well-kept gardens, blacksmith shop, machine shop restored. Stamp mills, cyanide plants. Hikes through buildings, mines
Folsom	Folsom	Mining town of the 1860s
Forest Hill Divide Museum	Foresthill 24501 Harrison St. in Leroy Batts Memorial Park	Gold rush history of Forest Hill and Iowa Hill divides
Gold Bluffs	*See Redwood National Park*	
Gold Bug Mine	Placerville From U.S. Highway 50, take Bedford Ave. for 1 mile	City-owned gold mine open to visitors
Gold Country Fair	Auburn	Early September

continued ☞

What	Where	What's There
Gold Country Museum	Auburn 1273 High St., on fairgrounds	Stamp mill, other mining equipment; saloon of gold rush days; visitors can pan for gold in creek. Nearby Bernard museum has restored Victorian house, exhibits of coopering, blacksmithing
Gold Discovery Site	*See Marshall Gold Discovery State Historic Park*	
Gold Nugget Museum	Paradise 502 Pearson Rd.	Mining artifacts
Grass Valley	Gold-mining town (a gold rush town, but not a ghost town)	Richest gold-mining town in California. Empire Mine State Historic Park and North Star Mining Museum in or near town
Greenhorn Park	Yreka South off Greenhorn Road	Restored miners' cabin, mining equipment
Griffith Park	Los Angeles West of I-25 between Los Feliz Blvd. and State Highway 134	Largest municipal park and urban wilderness area in the world. Named for Griffith J. Griffith, who made a fortune in gold-mining speculation
High-Desert Nature Museum	Twentynine Palms Community Center Complex	Displays of petrified wood, gems, minerals
Hornitos and Indian Gulch	West of Mariposa	Pre–gold rush community used by early prospectors; Hornitos ("little ovens") is built of adobe around a central quadrangle
Huntington Library, Art Collection and Botanical Gardens	San Marino 1151 Oxford Rd.	Library houses many manuscripts of gold rush days
J. J. "Jake" Jackson Memorial Museum	Weaverville	Paymaster mine stamp mill, a steam-powered, 2-stamp mill
Jackson	Historic mining town	On the Mother Lode; headframes of many rich gold mines nearby
Jackson Wheels	Jackson Gate East of Jackson	Four huge wooden wheels erected in early 20th century took tailing from Kennedy gold mine to dump away from creek; now part of a historical exhibit that includes the remaining mine buildings
Jurupa Mountains Cultural Center	Riverside 7621 Granite Hill Divide	Earth science museum has minerals and fossils
Kennedy Wheels	*See Jackson Wheels*	

continued ☞

What	Where	What's There
Kentucky Mine Park and Museum	Sierra City 1 mile northeast via State Highway 49	Site of lode gold mine. Guided walking tours from mine through 10-stamp mill; tools, mineral samples; photographs, memorabilia showing life in the mines
Kern County Museum and Pioneer Village	Bakersfield 3801 Chester Ave.	Life in the 19th and early 20th centuries; mineral collection
Klamath National Forest Interpretive Museum	Yreka 1312 Fairlane Rd.	Exhibits on geology, mining
Knight Foundry	Sutter Creek 81 Eureka St.	Producer of much mining equipment in early days, especially water wheels; visitors can see foundrymen using traditional methods
Knott's Berry Farm	Buena Park 8039 Beach Blvd.	Commercial establishment; visitors can pan for gold
Lake County Historical Museum	Lakeport 255 Main St.	Gem and mineral collection
Lake Oroville Visitor Center	Oroville 7 miles northeast of State Highway 162 to Kelly Ridge, then 1.5 miles north	Displays of gold rush era
Living Desert Reserve	Palm Desert 47900 Portola Ave., south of State Highway 111	Natural history museum has exhibit on geology of Coachella Valley
Los Angeles County Museum of Natural History	*See Natural History Museum of Los Angeles County*	
Los Gatos Museum	Los Gatos 4 Tait Ave.	Features the New Almaden mine, which furnished mercury for the gold mines
Malakoff Diggins State Historic Park	Nevada City 23579 North Bloomfield-Graniteville Rd.	Overview of hydraulic mine area; 7,000-foot tunnel drained water; exhibits on hydraulic mining and miners' way of life; restored buildings; film
Mariposa County Museum and History Center	Mariposa 12th and Jessie Sts.	Mining relics, miner's cabin, 5-stamp mill
Marshall Gold Discovery State Historic Park and Museum	Coloma On State Highway 49	Statue of Marshall, Marshall's cabin, working replica of Sutter's mill, ore cars, stamp mills, arrastras, museum with gold relics; restored Chinese apothecary shop

continued ☞

What	Where	What's There
Mary Aaron Museum	Marysville 704 D St.	Gold-mining equipment
Maturango Museum of the Indian Wells Valley	Ridgecrest	Kerr-McGee mining specimens; natural and cultural history
McLaughlin mine	Corporate office, San Francisco: Homestake Mining Company, 650-T California St. Mine: located near Knoxville	Active mine; tours available on request
Mesquite mine	Yuma, Ariz. 45 miles northwest (in California)	Active mine; Mesquite Overlook Trail (self-guiding) shows how mining is done
Mission San Jose Chapel and Museum	Fremont 43300 Mission Blvd.	Site of early gold milling and smelting
Monterey State Historic Park	Monterey 20 Custom House Plaza	Remains of old Monterey, headquarters of government when the gold rush started
Mount Ophir Mint	Mariposa	Site marked as "Mount Ophir Mint" may be erroneous
Museum of the City of San Francisco	The Cannery, near Fishermen's Wharf	Exhibits, photographs, documents
Natural History Museum of Los Angeles County	Los Angeles 900 Exposition Blvd. Exposition Park	Gold in crystals, nuggets, leaves, wires; gold rush artifacts and tools; gem and mineral exhibits; displays of life in California 1540–1940
Natural History Museum of Los Angeles County	Burbank 3d and Cypress	Branch of Natural History Museum of Los Angeles County
Nevada City	Nevada City, Nevada County	Early mining town; historical museum
Nevada State Museum	Carson City, Nevada 600 N. Carson St.	Minerals and ores, coins and mint mark collection, ghost town replica, reproduction of underground mine visitors can walk through
North San Juan	North of Nevada City, along State Highway 49	View east of hydraulic mining pits
North Star (Pelton Wheel) Mining Museum	Grass Valley Allison Ranch Rd. at end of Mill St.	Pelton wheel, early mining equipment, operable Cornish pump; working stamp mill model, diamond drill machines, gold melting crucibles, ore samples
Oakland Museum of California	Oakland 10th and Oak Sts.	Displays on history of gold rush times

continued ☞

What	Where	What's There
Old Las Vegas Mormon Fort State Historic Park	Las Vegas, Nev. Washington Ave. and Las Vegas Blvd.	Built to succor gold seekers on their way to the California goldfields
Old Sacramento	*See Sacramento*	
Oroville	Oroville	Historic gold town, worked initially by Cherokee Indians from Georgia; Chinese temple erected by Chinese miners
Pacific Grove Museum of Natural History	Pacific Grove 165 Forest Ave.	Mineral collection
Palm Springs Desert Museum	Palm Springs 101 Museum Dr.	Natural history of southwestern deserts, especially Coachella Valley and Colorado Desert
Pelton Wheel Mining Museum	*See North Star Mining Museum*	
Placerita Canyon Nature Center	Newhall 19152 Placerita Canyon Rd.	Artifacts from Don Francisco López's 1842 gold discovery
Placerville	Placerville	Historic gold town, formerly known as Old Dry Diggin's and Hangtown
Placerville gold mine	*See Gold Bug Mine*	
Plumas County Museum	Quincy 500 Jackson St.	Photographs and relics of mining days
Plumas-Eureka State Park and Museum	Johnsville 310 Johnsonville Rd. 4 miles west on County Road A-13	Mining photographs, tools, memorabilia from hard rock mines; partially restored stamp mill
Railtown 1897 State Historic Park	Jamestown	Displays memorabilia of Sierra Railway company that served the gold country; rides available
Randall Junior Museum	San Francisco 199 Museum Way off Roosevelt Way	Mineral, fossil displays
Randsburg Desert Museum	Randsburg 161 Butte Avenue	History of gold, silver, tungsten production; mine locomotive; stone mill for ore
Redwood National Park	Crescent City 1111 2d St. (superintendent's office)	113,200 acres on Pacific Coast from Crescent City to Orick. Gold Bluffs accessible by an unimproved road

continued ☞

What	Where	What's There
Sacramento	Sacramento; *see also Crocker Art Museum*	State capital. Capitol building has gold dome. Old Sacramento, a 4-block area, was the commercial district in the gold rush, now renovated buildings, museums
Sacramento History Center	Sacramento 101 I St. (Old Sacramento)	Million-dollar Mother Lode gold collection
Sacramento Room	Central Library, Sacramento	California books, maps, photographs
Sacramento Science Center and Junior Museum	Sacramento 3615 Auburn Blvd.	Rock and mineral displays
San Andreas	San Andreas, Calaveras County	Gold rush town; courthouse, museum
San Bernardino County Museum	Redlands 2024 Orange Tree Lane	Mineral, geology exhibit, mining history
San Diego Natural History Museum	San Diego Balboa Park	Displays on geology of American Southwest
San Francisco	San Francisco	Center of gold rush activity. Many museums and displays
San Francisco	*See also California Academy of Sciences California Historical Society Chinese Historical Society of America Museum of the City of San Francisco Randall Junior Museum Wells Fargo History Museum*	
San Francisco Maritime National Historical Park	San Francisco West end of Fisherman's Wharf	Includes maritime museum and library with displays on vessels of gold rush times
San Francisco Public Library	Civic Center	History and Archives Room
Santa Barbara Museum of Natural History	Santa Barbara 2559 Puesta del Sol Rd.	Contains mineral, geology exhibits
Sequoia–Kings Canyon National Parks	Three Rivers (superintendent's office)	Encompasses much of Sierran high country, including many old mining sites
Shasta State Historic Park	Redding 6 miles west on State Highway 299	Gold rush town; museum is in old courthouse
Sierra County Historical Park	*See Kentucky Mine Park*	
Sierra Museum	Downieville Main Street	Miniature operating stamp mill

continued ☞

What	Where	What's There
Siskiyou County Museum	Yreka 910 S. Main St.	Exhibits on geology; outdoor exhibits of mining equipment and restored buildings
Sonoma	Sonoma	Headquarters of short-lived (3-week) Bear Flag Republic
Sutter's Fort State Historic Park	Sacramento 27th and L Sts.	Restored fort has relics of life in the 1840s and gold rush days
Tahoe National Forest	Nevada City 631 Coyote St. (forest supervisor)	Forest encompasses much of Yuba River drainage, where large hydraulic, lode, and placer mines operated
Tropico Mine	Rosamond	Mine tours, museum
Tuolumne County Museum	Sonora 158 W. Bradford Ave.	Gold rush era artifacts; pioneer trails exhibit
Twentynine Palms Historical Society Museum	Twentynine Palms 6136 Adobe Road	Mining memorabilia
University of California Earth Sciences Building	Berkeley	Rock and mineral specimens, photographs, maps
Volcano	Volcano, Amador County (northeast of Jackson)	Gold rush town, remnants of limestone buildings
Wells Fargo Bank History Museum	Sacramento 400 Capitol Mall	History of Wells Fargo's part in the days of gold
Wells Fargo History Museum	Los Angeles 333 S. Grand Ave.	Many items of early days, 2-pound gold nugget, photographs, 19th-century stagecoach
Wells Fargo History Museum	San Francisco 420 Montgomery St.	Stagecoach, gold era memorabilia, gold nuggets
Yosemite National Park	Yosemite	Park encompasses former gold-mining sites

Sources of Quotations

Page 7   Sir Francis Drake, *The World Encompassed* (London: Nicholas Bourne, 1628), 80. Published in facsimile by University Microfilms, Ann Arbor, Mich., 1966.

11–12   *Acontecimientos en California de que hace memoria Don José de Jesus Pico, Capitan que fué de milicias auxiliaries, dictatos á Thomas Savage en San Luis Obispo, 1878.* Trans. Geraldine Martino. Manuscript in Bancroft Library. In Elisabeth L. Egenhoff, *The Elephant as They Saw It* (San Francisco: California Division of Mines, 1949), 13.

12   Emil T. H. Bunje and James C. Kean, *Pre-Marshall Gold in California* (1938; reprint, with notes, Sacramento: Historic California Press [Hammon's Archives and Artifacts], 1983), 25–27. Originally published as a Works Progress Administration contribution.

13   Bidwell quotations are also in John Bidwell, *Echoes of the Past about California* (1890; reprint, Chicago: R. R. Donnelley, 1928), 96–97. Originally serialized in *Century Magazine.*

16   Bunje and Kean, *Pre-Marshall Gold in California,* 9.

18   William Heath Davis, *Sixty Years in California* (San Francisco: A. J. Leary, 1889).

27   Rev. Walter Colton, "The News Comes to Monterey," chapter 6 of *The Land of Gold: Three Years in California, 1846–1849.* Cited in Milo Milton Quaife, *Pictures of Gold Rush California* (Chicago: Lakeside Press, 1949).

28   Quotations are available in many sources, including Egenhoff, *The Elephant as They Saw It,* 50–57.

30   *Literary American,* December 30, 1848.

40   Oscar Lewis, *Sea Routes to the Gold Fields* [1949] (New York: Ballantine Books, 1971), 19–20.

41   "Oh, California!" was published in *Out West,* 1904. Words by J. Nichols, music by Stephen Foster.

51   "Sweet Betsy from Pike" is from John A. Stone, *Put's Golden Songster* (San Francisco: Appleton, 1858). Words by John A. Stone (Ol' Put).

55   Palmer, "Pioneer Days in San Francisco," 544.

56   Palmer, "Pioneer Days in San Francisco."

58   From *Put's Original California Songster* (San Francisco: Appleton, 1855). Words by John A. Stone (Ol' Put).

64   Quotation from "Dame Shirley" is from Louise Amelia Clappe Knapp [Dame Shirley], *The Shirley Letters,* introd. and notes Carl I. Wheat (New York: Alfred A. Knopf, 1949), 30–31. [Written in 1851–1852; first published in *Pioneer Magazine* in 1854–1855.]

66–69   "Diving for Gold in '49" is from *Overland Monthly,* 1874. Republished in *Mineral Information Service,* April, May, June 1964, 60–61, 78–79, 92–95.

71   Jack Forbes, *Native Americans of California and Nevada: A Handbook* (Berkeley, Calif.: n.p., 1968), n.p. Originally published in William Ralganal Benson, "The Stone and Kelsey 'Massacre' on the Shores of Clear Lake in 1849," *California Historical Society Quarterly* (September 1932): 266–273.

73   Paul quotation is from Rodman W. Paul, *California Gold* (Lincoln: University of Nebraska Press, 1947), 127.

74   Borthwick quotation is from J. D. Borthwick, *Three Years in California* (Edinburgh: William Blackford & Sons, 1857).

75   Quotation about the *Phenix* is from J. Wesley Jones, "Pantoscope of California: A 'Lecture' Together with Pencil Sketches Depicting the Journey Across the Plains to California," *California Historical Society Quarterly* 6 (1927).

80   From *Put's Golden Songster.* (San Francisco: Appleton, 1858). Words by John A. Stone (Ol' Put).

83   From *Put's Golden Songster.*

88   From *Put's Golden Songster.*

101–102   D. A. Pretorius, "The Depositional Environment of the Witwatersrand Goldfields: A Chronological Review of the Speculations and Observations," *Council for Mineral Technology: Minerals Sci. Eng.* 1, no. 1 (1975): 18–47. Reprinted in Robert W. Boyle, *Gold: History and Genesis of Deposits* (New York: Van Nostrand Reinhold for the Society of Economic Geologists and Society of Economic Geologists Foundation, 1987), quote on 417.

115   John S. Hittell, *Mining in the Pacific States* (San Francisco: H. H. Bancroft, 1861), 358.

115–116   Brewer quotation is from William H. Brewer, *Up and Down California in 1860–1864: The Journal of William H. Brewer,* ed. Francis P. Farquhar (Berkeley: University of California Press, 1974), 326–327.

128–129   Judge Sawyer quotation is given in Robert L. Kelley, *Gold vs. Grain: The Hydraulic Mining Controversy in California's Sacramento Valley. A Chapter in the Decline of the Concept of Laissez Faire* (Glendale, Calif.: Arthur H. Clark, 1959), 233–234. Kelley is quoting the Sacramento *Record Union* for April 10, 1883.

128   Marysville *Appeal,* September 11, 1883. Cited in Kelley, *Gold vs. Grain,* 240.

138–139   Quotation on Allison Ranch mine is from "Mining for Gold in California," *Hutchings' California Magazine* 2, no. 1 (July 1857); 2, no. 3 (September 1857); 2, no. 4 (October 1857).

140–141   Louis Simonin, *Underground Life; or, Mines and Miners,* trans. and ed. H. W. Bristow (New York: Appleton, 1869).

197   "Loss of the 'Central America'" is from Stone, *Put's Golden Songster.* Words by J. A. Stone (Ol' Put), music by Stephen Foster.

199   Thompson is quoted in Tim Noonan, "The Greatest Treasure Ever Found: GOLD," *Life* 15, no. 3 (March 1992): 32–42.

207   Browne quotation is from J. Ross Browne, *Washoe Revisited* (New York: Harper & Brothers, 1869), 512–513.

228   Raymond E. Krauss, "Environmental Management at Homestake's McLaughlin Mine," *Gold '90. Proceedings of the Gold '90 Symposium, Salt Lake City, Utah, February 26 to March 1, 1990* (Littleton, Colo.: Society for Mining, Metallurgy, and Exploration, 1990), 509–519.

230–231   John L. Burnett, "The McLaughlin Mine," *California Geology* 39, no. 1 (January 1986): 15–16.

233   Philip quotation is from T. P. Philip, "Changing Trends in the Exploration, Mining and Metallurgy for Gold in the 1990's," *Gold '90,* 5.

242   Bachicha quote is a personal communication, oral and in writing.

247   John Williamson Palmer, "Pioneer Days in San Francisco," *Century Magazine,* 43 (1892): 544.

Sources of Illustrations

CHAPTER ONE

Map 1. Drawn by Doris Marsh.

CHAPTER TWO

Figure 1. Drawing by Theodor de Bry, Frankfurt, 1589. Courtesy The Bancroft Library.

Figure 2. From Elisabeth L. Egenhoff, *The Elephant as They Saw It* (San Francisco: California Division of Mines, 1949), 44.

Figures 3, 4. Drawing by G. M. Waseurtz of Sandels, redrawn by Elinor Rhodes.

Map 2. From *California Geology,* January/February 1996, 14.

Map 3. Drawn by Bill Nelson.

CHAPTER THREE

Figure 5. Courtesy the California History Room, California State Library, Sacramento.

Figure 6. From Thomas W. Knox, *Underground* (Hartford, Conn.: J. B. Burr and Hyde, 1873), 791.

Figure 7. Courtesy Wells Fargo Bank.

After the Rush

Pages 31, 32, 34. California State Library negs. 2759, 4691a, 4041. Courtesy the California History Room, California State Library, Sacramento.

Page 33. Courtesy California Historical Society, de Young Collection, FN-04418.

CHAPTER FOUR

Figure 8. From a print published by A. Donnelly, 1849.

Figure 9. Joseph P. Smith, "Steamer Hartford," 1849, Museum of the City of New York, Bequest of Mrs. J. Insley Blair in Memory of Mr. and Mrs. J. Insley Blair, 52.100.3.

Map 4. Courtesy San Francisco Maritime NHP, HDC 29, photo no. P89-061. Inset map drawn by Bill Nelson.

Figures 10, 11. Drawings by Frank Maryatt, in his *Mountains and Molehills* (1855; facsimile ed., Stanford: Stanford University Press, 1952), 359, 19. Courtesy Stanford University Press.

Map 5. Drawn by Bill Nelson.

Figure 12. From John Grafton, *The American West in the Nineteenth Century* (New York: Dover, 1992), 54. Courtesy Dover Publications.

Figure 13. From Thomas W. Knox, *Underground* (Hartford, Conn.: J. B. Burr and Hyde, 1873), 795.

Life in San Francisco

Pages 54, 55. From Bayard Taylor, *Eldorado; or, Adventures in the Path of Empire* (1850; facsimile ed., Glorieta, New Mex.: Rio Grande Press, 1967), frontispieces to vols. 1 and 2.

Pages 56, 58, 60 (bottom). From William Taylor, *California Life Illustrated* (New York: Published by author, 1861), 166, 202, 551, 554.

Pages 57, 59. From John Williamson Palmer, "Pioneer Days in San Francisco," *Century Magazine* 43 (1892): 154.

Pages 60 (top), 61. Drawings by Frank Maryatt, in his *Mountains and Molehills* (1855; facsimile ed., Stanford: Stanford University Press, 1952), 150. Courtesy Stanford University Press.

CHAPTER FIVE

Figure 14. Courtesy California Division of Mines and Geology.

Page 71. From J. Ross Browne, *Crusoe's Island* (New York: Harper & Brothers, 1864), 305. (Probably drawn by Browne himself.)

Figures 15–18. Courtesy Charles Romanowitz.

Life in the Mines

Page 79 (*top*). Drawing by Charles Nahl. Courtesy The Huntington Library, San Marino, California.

Page 79 (*bottom*). From Thomas W. Knox, *Underground* (Hartford, Conn.: J. B. Burr and Hyde, 1873), 805.

Pages 81, 82 (*bottom*), 85. By J. D. Borthwick, in John Grafton, *The American West in the Nineteenth Century* (New York: Dover, 1992), 18, 19. Courtesy Dover Publications.

Page 82 (*top*). From Grafton, *The American West*, 21. Courtesy Dover Publications.

Page 84. By Henry Bacon, in Grafton, *The American West*, 20. Courtesy Dover Publications.

How They Mined the Gold

Page 86 (*top*). From John Grafton, *The American West in the Nineteenth Century* (New York: Dover, 1992), 16. Courtesy Dover Publications.

Pages 86 (*bottom*), 87 (*bottom*), 89 (*bottom*), 90, 91. From Elisabeth L. Egenhoff, *The Elephant as They Saw It* (San Francisco: California Division of Mines, 1949), 76, 69, 102, 62, 100.

Pages 87 (*top*), 89 (*top*). From Thomas W. Knox, *Underground* (Hartford, Conn.: J. B. Burr and Hyde, 1873), 795, 815.

Page 92–93. By J. D. Borthwick, from Grafton, *The American West,* 17. Courtesy Dover Publications.

CHAPTER SIX

Figures 19–22. From Olaf P. Jenkins, "New Technique Applicable to the Study of Placers," *California Division of Mines Bulletin* 135 (1946): 162, 176, 177, 155.

Mining the Dead Rivers

Page 107. Drawn by Bill Nelson.

Pages 108–109, 111. Drawings by Alex Eng, from Hill, *Geology of the Sierra Nevada,* 92–93, 106–107. Copyright © 1975 The Regents of the University of California.

Page 110. Diagram from John D. Chakarun, "Tertiary Gold-Bearing Gravels, Northern Sierra Nevada," *California Geology* (June 1987): 123.

Pages 112–113. From J. D. Whitney, *The Auriferous Gravels of the Sierra Nevada of California.* Contributions to American Geology, 1:152. Memoirs of the Museum of Comparative Zoology. Cambridge, Mass.: [Harvard] University Press.

CHAPTER SEVEN

Figure 23. From *Hutchings' California Magazine* 2 (July 1857): 12.

Figure 24. From L. Simonin, *Mines and Miners* (London: William MacKenzie, n.d.).

Figure 25. From *U.S. Pacific Railroad Reports* 5 (1858): 265. From a daguerreotype by W. P. Blake. N. Orr, delineator.

Figure 26. From Ninth Report of the [California] State Mineralogist, 1890, opposite p. 130.

Figure 27. Lithograph by Edward Lewis and G. Bohm, from Ernest Seyd, *California and Its Resources* (London: Trubner, 1858).

Page 123. From Ninth Report of the [California] State Mineralogist, 1890, 136.

Figure 28. Photo by C. E. Watkins.

Figure 29. Photo by the author.

CHAPTER EIGHT

Figure 30. Britton & Rey Lithograph. J. E. Ogilby, delineator. Courtesy California Division of Mines and Geology.

Map 6. Modified from William B. Clark, "Gold Mines of Grass Valley," *California Geology* (March 1984): 46.

Figure 31. Courtesy California Division of Mines and Geology.

Figure 32. Courtesy California Division of Mines and Geology.

Figure 33. Drawing by Alex Eng, from Mary Hill, *Geology of the Sierra Nevada* (Berkeley: University of California Press, 1975), 86. Copyright © 1975 The Regents of the University of California.

All Dressed Up

Pages 145, 146. Drawing by Charles Nahl, from *Hutchings' California Magazine,* 1857.

Pages 147 (*top*), 148. From *Hutchings' California Magazine,* 1857.

Page 147 (*bottom*). Drawing by Doris Marsh, from an original by Don Garlick.

Figure 34. Drawing by Doris Marsh.
Figure 35. Photo by Randolph A. Koski. Courtesy U.S. Geological Survey.
Figure 36. Photo by William R. Normark. Courtesy U.S. Geological Survey.

The Moving Earth

Pages 159, 160, 161, 162, 163, 165. Drawings by Jane Russell, from Jacquelyne W. Kious and
Robert I. Tilling, *This Dynamic Earth* (Washington, D.C.: U.S. Geological Survey), 4,
2, 15, 30, 43, 54.
Page 163. Photo by Robert E. Wallace. Courtesy U.S. Geological Survey.
Page 164. Drawing by Doris Marsh, modified from a drawing in John M. Edmond and Karen
Von Damm, "Hot Springs on the Ocean Floor," *Scientific American* (April 1983): 86.

CHAPTER TEN

Map 7. Drawn by Doris Marsh, modified from *California Geology*, September 1984, 186.

California through the Ages

Page 174. Modified from Cordell Durrell, *Geologic History of the Feather River Country*
(Berkeley: University of California Press, 1987), 58.
Page 175. From drawing by Paul Bateman for Genny Smith, ed., *Sierra East: Edge of the
Great Basin* (Berkeley: University of California Press, 1999). Courtesy Paul Bateman.
Pages 176, 178. Drawings by Jane Russell, from Jacquelyne W. Kious and Robert I. Tilling,
This Dynamic Earth (Washington, D.C.: U.S. Geological Survey), 7, 56.
Page 177. From drawing by Paul Bateman for Jeff Putman and Genny Smith, eds., *Deepest
Valley: A Guide to Owens Valley, Its Roadsides and Mountain Trails,* 2d ed. (Mammoth
Lakes, Calif.: Genny Smith Books, 1995), 444. Courtesy Genny Smith Books.

CHAPTER ELEVEN

Figures 37–39. From Yellow Bird [John Rollin Ridge], *The Life and Adventures of Joaquin
Murieta, the Celebrated California Bandit* (1854; reprint, Norman: University of Okla-
homa Press, 1955), 86, xxxiv, 6.
Figures 40, 41, 43. Courtesy Wells Fargo Bank.
Figure 42. Drawing by Doris Marsh.
Figure 44. Courtesy Calaveras County Historical Society.
Figure 45. From *The Wasp.* Lithograph by Schmidt Label and Lithograph Company. Cour-
tesy Wells Fargo Bank.
Figure 46. Britton & Rey lithograph, 1854. "From a drawing made on the spot by one of the
passengers, A. T. Harrison." Courtesy The Bancroft Library.

Good-bye to the *Central America*

Page 200 (*top*). Courtesy The Mariners' Museum, Newport News, Virginia.
Page 200 (*bottom*). Drawing by Bill Nelson.
Pages 201, 202, 203, 204. Drawings by Frederick Anderson, from *Frank Leslie's Illustrated
Newspaper* 4, no. 96 (October 3, 1857): 281 (CSL neg. 25079), 281 (CSL neg. 25083), 273

(CSL neg. 25078); no. 97 (October 10, 1857): 289 (CSL neg. 25080); no. 98 (October 17, 1857): 312 (CSL neg. 25082), 305 (CSL neg. 25081). Courtesy the California History Room, California State Library, Sacramento.

CHAPTER TWELVE

Figure 47. From *Hutchings' California Magazine,* no. 52 (October 1860). Steel engraving based on a photo (probably a daguerreotype) by Robert H. Vance. Courtesy The Bancroft Library.

Map 8. Drawn by Doris Marsh.

CHAPTER THIRTEEN

Figure 48. Courtesy California Division of Mines and Geology.

Figure 49. From *California Geology* (November 1980): 245.

Figure 50. Courtesy White's Electronics, Sweet Home, Oregon.

CHAPTER FOURTEEN

Figures 51, 52. Courtesy Homestake Mining Company.

Figure 53. From *California Geology* (September 1983): 187.

Page 235. Drawing by Doris Marsh.

CHAPTER FIFTEEN

Figure 54. From *Gleason's Pictorial Drawing Room Companion* 1, no. 12 (July 19, 1851): 188.

Figure 55. Courtesy National Aeronautics and Space Administration.

Figure 56. Photo by James E. Stoots, Jr. Courtesy Lawrence Livermore National Laboratory.

Figure 57. Photo courtesy Mirage Hotel.

COLOR PLATES

Plate 1. Photo by Dane Penland, no. 81-7858. Courtesy Smithsonian Institution.

Plate 2. Photo by Chip Clark. Courtesy Smithsonian Institution.

Plate 3. Courtesy Wells Fargo Bank.

Plates 4, 5. Courtesy Homestake Mining Company.

Plates 6, 7. Courtesy U.S. Bureau of the Mint.

Suggestions for Further Reading

Thousands of books and articles have been written on California and its gold. This list is intended to serve as a beginning for those who hunger for more information. I hope most readers do, as this book is only a brief taste.

THE GOLD RUSH AND BEFORE

Coronado

Bolton, Herbert E. 1949. *Coronado: Knight of Pueblos and Plains*. New York: McGraw-Hill; Albuquerque: University of New Mexico Press. 491 pp.

Winship, George Parker, ed. 1904, 1922. *The Journey of Coronado, 1540–1542 from the City of Mexico to the Grand Canyon of the Colorado and the Buffalo Plains of Texas, Kansas and Nebraska, as told by himself and his followers*. New York: Allerton. 251 pp.

Drake

Drake, Sir Francis. 1628. *The World Encompassed*. London: Nicholas Bourne. Published in facsimile by University Microfilms, Ann Arbor, Mich., 1966. 108 pp.

Hakluyt, Richard. [1598–1600] 1907. *The Principal Navigations, Voyages, Traffiques and Discoveries of the English Nation*. New York: E. P. Dutton. Everyman's Library, 8 vols.

Wilson, Derek. 1977. *The World Encompassed*. New York: Harper & Row. 240 pp.

Pre-Marshall Discoveries

Bidwell, John. 1890. *Echoes of the Past about California*. Serialized in *Century Magazine*, 1890. Republished in 1928 by R. R. Donnelley, Chicago. Bidwell, 1–111.

Bunje, Emil T. H., and James C. Kean. 1983. *Pre-Marshall Gold in California*. Sacramento: Historic California Press [Hammon's Archives and Artifacts]. 70 pp.

Clark, William B. 1970. *Gold Districts of California*. Sacramento: California Division of Mines and Geology Bulletin 193. 186 pp.

Egenhoff, Elisabeth L. 1949. *The Elephant as They Saw It*. San Francisco: California Division of Mines. 128 pp. First issued as Centennial Supplement to *California Journal of Mines and Geology*, October 1949.

American Friends Service Committee. 1957. *Indians of California: Past and Present.* San Francisco: American Friends Service Committee. 38 pp.

Audubon, John Woodhouse. 1984. *Audubon's Western Journal, 1849–1850.* With a biographical memoir by his daughter, Maria R. Audubon, and an introduction by Frank Heywood Hodder. Tucson: University of Arizona Press. Taken from 1906 edition published by Arthur H. Clark, Cleveland, Ohio. 249 pp.

Brewer, William H. 1974. *Up and Down California in 1860–1864: The Journal of William H. Brewer.* Edited by Francis P. Farquhar. Berkeley: University of California Press. 583 pp.

Bruff, J. Goldsborough. 1949. *The Journals, Drawings and Other Papers of J. Goldsborough Bruff, Captain, Washington City and California Mining Association, April 2, 1849–July 20, 1851.* New York: Columbia University Press. 794 pp.

Clappe, Louise Amelia Knapp. 1949. *The Shirley Letters.* New York: Alfred A. Knopf. Introduction and notes by Carl I. Wheat. 216 pp. Written in 1851–1852; first published in *Pioneer Magazine* in 1854–1855.

Egenhoff, Elisabeth L. 1964. "Diving for Gold in '49." *Mineral Information Service* 17, pt. 1, no. 4 (April): 60–61; pt. 2, no. 5 (May): 78–79; pt. 3, no. 6 (June): 92–95.

Gudde, Erwin G. 1975. *California Gold Camps.* Edited by Elisabeth K. Gudde. Berkeley: University of California Press. 467 pp.

Holliday, J. S. 1981. *The World Rushed In.* New York: Simon and Schuster. 559 pp.

Jackson, Donald Dale. 1980. *Gold Dust.* New York: Alfred A. Knopf. 361 pp.

Jenkins, Olaf P. 1948. *Geologic Guidebook along Highway 49—Sierran Gold Belt.* San Francisco: California Division of Mines. 164 pp.

Lewis, Oscar. 1971. *Sea Routes to the Gold Fields.* New York: Ballantine Books. Originally published by Alfred A. Knopf, New York, 1949. 244 pp.

Marryat, Frank. 1855. *Mountains and Molehills.* New York: Harper and Brothers. Reprinted in facsimile by Stanford University Press, Stanford, Calif. 393 pp., plus notes.

Owens, Kenneth N., ed. 1994. *John Sutter and a Wider West.* Lincoln: University of Nebraska Press. 138 pp.

Paul, Rodman W. 1947. *California Gold.* Lincoln: University of Nebraska Press. 380 pp.

Quaife, Milo Milton, ed. 1949. *Pictures of Gold Rush California.* Chicago: Lakeside Press. 282 pp.

Stellman, Louis J. 1953. *Sam Brannan: Builder of San Francisco.* New York: Exposition Press. 254 pp.

Stone, J. A. 1855. *Put's California Songster.* San Francisco: Appleton.

Taylor, Bayard. 1950. *Eldorado or Adventures in the Path of Empire.* 2 vols. Republished in facsimile by Rio Grande Press, Glorieta, N. Mex., 1967. Vol. 1, 251 pp.; vol. 2, 253 pp. Index.

THE NATURAL HISTORY OF GOLD

Averill, Charles Volney. 1946. *Placer Mining for Gold in California.* San Francisco: California Division of Mines Bulletin 135. 357 pp.

Boyle, R. W. 1979. *The Geochemistry of Gold and Its Deposits (Together with a Chapter on Geochemical Prospecting for the Element).* Ottawa: Geological Survey of Canada. 584 pp.

Hill, Mary. 1972. Hunting Diamonds in California. Healdsburg, Calif.: Naturegraph. 80 pp. Originally published as *Diamonds in California.* Sausalito, Calif.: Pages of History, 1959. 80 pp.

———. 1975. *Geology of the Sierra Nevada.* Berkeley: University of California Press. 232 pp.

MINING FOR GOLD

Hydraulic Mining

Gilbert, Grove Karl. 1917. *Hydraulic Mining Debris in the Sierra Nevada.* U.S. Geological Survey Professional Paper 105. 154 pp.

Kelley, Robert L. 1959. *Gold vs. Grain: The Hydraulic Mining Controversy in California's Sacramento Valley. A Chapter in the Decline of the Concept of Laissez Faire.* Glendale, Calif.: Arthur H. Clark. 327 pp.

Lindgren, Waldemar. 1911. *The Tertiary Gravels of the Sierra Nevada of California.* U.S. Geological Survey Professional Paper 73. Reprinted by American Trading Company, Bellevue, Wash., 1977. 226 pp.

Whitney, J. D. 1880. *The Auriferous Gravels of the Sierra Nevada of California.* Contributions to American Geology. Vol. 1. Memoirs of the Museum of Comparative Zoology. Cambridge, Mass.: [Harvard] University Press. 569 pp.

Underground Mining

Clark, William B. 1984. "Gold Mines of Grass Valley, Nevada County, California." *California Geology* 31, no. 3 (March): 43–53.

Egenhoff, Elisabeth L. 1967. "The Cornish Pump." *Mineral Information Service* 20, pt. 1, no. 6 (June): 59–71; pt. 2, no. 8 (August): 91–97.

Wagner, Jack R. 1970. *Gold Mines of California.* Berkeley, Calif.: Howell-North Books. 259 pp.

PLATE TECTONICS AND THE BIRTH OF CALIFORNIA

Cone, Joseph. 1991. *Fire Under the Sea.* New York: William Morrow. 287 pp.

Corliss, John B., John A. Baross, and Sarah E. Hoffman. 1980. *A Probable Site for the Origin of Life.* Corvallis: Oregon State University School of Oceanography Special Publication.

Dickinson, W. R. 1981. "Plate Tectonics and the Continental Margin of California." In *The Geotectonic Development of California.* Englewood Cliffs, N.J.: Prentice Hall.

Edmond, John M., and Karen Von Damm. 1983. "Hot Springs on the Ocean Floor." *Scientific American,* April, 78–93.

Ernst, W. G. 1979. "California and Plate Tectonics." *California Geology* 32, no. 9 (September): 187–196.

Hammond, Allen L. 1975. "Minerals and Plate Tectonics: A Conceptual Revolution." *Science* 189 (September 5): 779–781.

———. 1975. "Minerals and Plate Tectonics (II): Seawater and Ore Formation." *Science* 189 (September 12): 868–869, 915–917.

Hart, Stephen. 1997. "Life's Scalding Origins." *Earth* 6 (3): 53.

McPhee, John. 1992. "Assembling California." *New Yorker,* pt. 1, September 7, 36–68; pt. 2, September 14, 44–84; pt. 3, September 21, 39–98. Also New York: Farrar, Straus and Giroux, 1993. 304 pp.

Moores, Eldridge. 1996. "Crust: The Story of Earth." *Earth* 5 (6): 30–33.

Rona, Peter. 1973. "Plate Tectonics and Mineral Resources." *Scientific American,* July, 86–95.

Smith, Roscoe M. 1981. "Source of Mother Lode Gold." *California Geology* 34, no. 6 (May): 99–103.

Bandits and Sunken Ships

Dillon, Richard. 1969. *Wells Fargo Detective: A Biography of James B. Hume.* New York: Coward-McCann. 320 pp.

Jackson, Joseph Henry. 1939, 1949. *Bad Company.* New York: Harcourt, Brace. 346 pp. Black Bart, 119–126.

Klare, Normand E. 1992. *The Final Voyage of the* Central America, *1857.* Spokane: Arthur H. Clark. 278 pp.

Marshall, Don B. 1978. *California Shipwrecks: Footsteps in the Sea.* Seattle: Superior. 175 pp.

Stone, J. A. 1858. "Loss of the *Central America.*" In *Put's Golden Songster.* San Francisco: Appleton.

Yellow Bird [John Rollin Ridge]. [1854] 1955. *The Life and Adventures of Joaquin Murieta, the Celebrated California Bandit.* Norman: University of Oklahoma Press. 159 pp.

Lost Mines

Bailey, Philip A. 1941. *Golden Mirages.* New York: Macmillan. 353 pp. PegLeg Smith, 23–117.

Conrotto, Eugene L. 1963. *Lost Desert Bonanzas.* Palm Desert, Calif.: Desert Southwest Publishers. 278 pp.

Dobie, J. Frank. 1930, 1978. *Coronado's Children.* Austin: University of Texas Press. 329 pp. Breyfogle, 184–190.

Drago, Harry Sinclair. 1966. *Lost Bonanzas.* New York: Dodd, Mead. 276 pp. Breyfogle, 81–103; PegLeg Smith, 47–56.

Lovelace, Leland. 1956. *Lost Mines and Hidden Treasure.* San Antonio, Tex.: Naylor. 252 pp. Breyfogle, 20–34; PegLeg Smith, 35–47, 192–198.

Mitchell, John D. 1940. "Lost Breyfogle Mine." *Desert Magazine* 3, no. 11 (September): 13–14.

Argall, George O., Jr. 1987. "The New California Gold Rush." *Engineering and Mining Journal* (December): 30–45.

Burnett, John L. 1986. "The McLaughlin Mine." *California Geology* 39, no. 1 (January): 15–16.

Clark, William B. 1972. "Diving for Gold in California." *California Geology* 25, no. 6 (June): 123–130.

———. 1978. "Gold Rush of the 1970s." *California Geology* 31, no. 9 (September): 199–205.

———. 1980. "Diving for Gold in California." *California Geology* 33, no. 11 (November): 243–249.

Daly, Les. 1980. "A New Gold Rush Draws Prospectors to Mother Lode." *Smithsonian* 10, no. 11 (February): 104–114.

Hill, Mary. 1974. *Diving and Digging for Gold.* Happy Camp, Calif.: Naturegraph. 47 pp.

Ricketts, A. H. 1943. *American Mining Law.* San Francisco: California Division of Mines Bulletin 123. 1,018 pp.

Silva, Michael A. 1988. "Cyanide Heap Leaching in California." *California Geology* 41, no. 7 (July): 147–156.

U.S. Forest Service. 1975. "Questions and Answers about the 1872 Act Use Regulations Affecting Prospecting and Mining in National Forests." *California Geology* 28, no. 7 (July): 159–163.

USES

Cohen, Daniel. 1976. *Gold: The Fascinating Story of the Noble Metal through the Ages.* New York: M. Evans. 186 pp.

Kagin, Donald H. 1981. *Private Gold Coins and Patterns of the United States.* New York: Arco. 406 pp.

Marks, Geoffrey, and William K. Beatty. 1975. *The Precious Metals of Medicine.* New York: Charles Scribner's Sons. 294 pp.

Marx, Jenifer. 1978. *The Magic of Gold.* Garden City, N.Y.: Doubleday. 470 pp.

Sutherland, C. H. V. 1960. *Gold: Its Beauty, Power and Allure.* London: Thames and Hudson. 196 pp.

Vicker, Ray. 1975. *The Realms of Gold.* New York: Charles Scribner's Sons. 244 pp.

Index

Designer:	BookMatters
Compositor:	BookMatters
Text:	11/15 Bulmer
Display:	Bulmer